THEORETICAL AND CRITICAL PERSPECTIVES ON TEACHER CHANGE

edited by

Phyllis Kahaney
Linda A. M. Perry
and
Joseph Janangelo

Ablex Publishing Corporation
Norwood, New Jersey

Cover designed by Matt Stevens.

Printed in the United States of America

Library of Congress Cataloging-in-Publication Data

Theoretical and critical perspectives on teacher change / [edited by]
  Phyllis Kahaney, Linda A. M. Perry, Joseph Janangelo.
      p.   cm.
    Includes bibliographical references (p.   ) and index.
    ISBN 0-89391-976-4 (cloth). — ISBN 1-56750-059-5 (pbk.)
      1. Teachers—Attitudes. 2. Teachers—Psychology. 3. Teaching.
  4. Learning. 5. Educational change. 6. Education—Philosophy.
  I. Kahaney, Phyllis. II. Perry, Linda A. M., 1947–
  III. Janangelo, Joseph.
  LB1775.T43   1993
  371.1—dc20   93-22589
                                                              CIP

Ablex Publishing Corporation
355 Chestnut Street
Norwood, NJ 07648

Table of Contents

Contributors

Lil Brannon is an Associate Professor of English and Director of the Writing Center at the University at Albany, SUNY. She is co-author with Cy Knoblauch of *Critical Teaching and the Idea of Literacy* (Boynton/Cook, 1993) and *Rhetorical Traditions and the Teaching of Writing*. Her work has appeared in numerous professional journals including *College English, College Composition and Communication,* and *Journal of Basic Writing.*

James Britton is an Emeritus Professor of Education and a previous Head of the English Department, Institute of Education, University of London. Britton is a former English teacher in British secondary schools and Educational Editor to John Murray Publishers. From 1966-72, he was Director of the Schools Council Writing Research Unit. He was awarded an honorary doctorate in 1977 by the University of Calgary and the David Russell Award for Distinguished Research on the Teaching of English by the National Council of Teachers of English. Publication credits include *Language and Learning: The Development of Writing Abilities, 11–18; Prospect and Retrospect;* and *English Teaching: An International Exchange.*

C.T.P. Diamond is a Professor in the Joint Centre for Teacher Development (OISE/Faculty of Education, University of Toronto). His 1991 book, *Teacher Education as Transformation: A Psychological Perspective* (Open University Press), explores the reconstruction of teachers' meanings. Diamond helps to coordinate the Among Teachers Community (ACT).

Carol Gilligan is a Professor in the Human Development and Psychology Program at Harvard University, Graduate School of Education, and a founding member of the Harvard Project on Women's Psychology and Girls' Development. She is author of *In a Different Voice: Psychological Theory and Women's Development* (Harvard University Press, 1982) and, most recently, *Meeting at the Crossroads: Women's Psychology and Girls' Development* (with Lyn Mikel Brown) (Harvard University Press, 1992). Her recent articles include: "Joining the Resistance: Psychology, Politics, Girls and Women," *Michigan Quarterly Review,* 1990.

Gary Graves has taught English Language Arts and Science for twenty-four years. He is now a full-time education consultant in "curriculum, computers, and change." Graves lives in Missoula, MT.

Gail E. Hawisher is an Associate Professor of English and Director of the Center for Writing Studies at the University of Illinois, Urbana-Champaign. Her most recently published work includes *Evolving Perspectives on Computers and Composition Studies: Questions for the 1990s*; and *Re-Imagining Computers and Composition: Teaching and Research in the Virtual Age.* She also coedits *Computers and Composition* (with Cynthia L. Selfe), and the *CCCC Bibliography on Composition and Rhetoric.*

Joseph Janangelo is an Assistant Professor of English at Loyola University of Chicago. His most recent publications have appeared in *Computers and Composition, The Iowa English Bulletin,* and *WPA: Writing Program Administration.*

Phyllis Kahaney is an Assistant Professor of English and Director of Writing at the University of Hawaii at Hilo. Her most recent research focuses on adult writing in the workplace (in *Interdisciplinary Handbook of Adult Lifespan Learning*) and on the roles of truth and candor in legal writing.

Cheris Kramarae is a Professor of Speech Communication; Sociology; and Women's Studies at the University of Illinois at Urbana-Champaign. Besides feminist scholarship, she has authored, edited or coedited nine books on women and language. These publications include *Language, Gender and Society; Technology and Women's Voices; A Feminist Dictionary; Radical Women's Press of the 1850's; The Revolution in Words;* and *The Knowledge Explosion: Generations of Feminist Scholarship.* She is currently coediting, with Dale Spender, *The International Encyclopedia of Women's Studies.*

Diane M. Lee is an Associate Professor at the University of Maryland, Baltimore County, where she teaches courses in Human Learning and Cognition and the Study of Teaching. Her current research interests include everyday problem-solving and the role of wisdom in teaching.

Laura M. W. Martin, Vice President of Production Research at the Children's Television Workshop, has an M.S. in Early Childhood Education and a Ph.D. in Experimental Psychology. She was previously a teacher and administrator; her research focuses on learning and technology.

Denis Newman currently is a division scientist at Bolt Beranek and Newman Inc., a Cambridge, MA based research and development firm, where he conducts research on the social organization of learning and the use of computers in schools. He has a Ph.D. from City University of New York in Developmental Psychology.

Linda A. M. Perry is a Professor and Chair of Communication Studies and Co-Director of the Gender Studies Program at the University of San Diego. She is a member of the Editorial Board for *Women and Language*. Among her recent publications is *Constructing and Reconstructing Gender: The Links Among Communication, Language and Gender* (Coedited with Lynn Turner and Helen Sterk) (SUNY Press). She is currently editing a volume entitled *Women's Words/Women's Worlds*.

Gordon M. Pradl is a Professor of English Education at New York University. He is co-author of *Learning to Write/Writing to Learn*, has edited *Prospect and Retrospect: Selected Essays of James Britton*, and is completing a book entitled *Literature for Democracy*. He also serves as coeditor of the journal *English Education*.

Cynthia L. Selfe is a Professor of Composition and Communication and Head of the Humanities Department of Michigan Technological University. Selfe is the current Chair of the NCTE College Section and the coeditor of both *Computers and Composition* and the *CCCC Bibliography on Composition and Rhetoric* (with Gail E. Hawisher).

Jan D. Sinnott is a Professor of Psychology at Towson State University, Baltimore, Maryland. Her recent books include *Interdisciplinary Handbook of Adult Lifespan Learning*; *Bridging Paradigms: Positive Development in Adulthood and Cognitive Aging* (with John Cavanaugh); and *Everyday Memory and Aging* (with Robin West).

Joan N. Steiner has taught high school English since 1972. She has a Ph.D. in English Education from New York University and is Chair

of the Teachers of English Committee on Tracking and Grouping
Practices, K-12.

Mark B. Tappan is an Assistant Professor and Co-Chair of the Program
in Education and Human Development at Colby College, Waterville,
ME. His research and teaching interests focus on moral development
and education, adolescent development, educational theory, and
interpretive research methods. He is coeditor (with Martin Packer) of
*Narrative and Storytelling: Implications for Understanding Moral
Development* (Jossey-Bass, 1991).

Margaret E. Vaughan is an Associate Professor at Salem State College,
Salem, MA where she teaches courses in psychology. She was
awarded a post-doctoral fellow at Harvard University from 1981-
1983, where she worked with Dr. B. F. Skinner.

Preface

Theoretical and Critical Perspectives on Teacher Change seeks to establish a dialogue between the theoretical and practical components of teaching, between the barriers that inhibit change and the factors that help overcome those barriers. This volume does not actively lobby for a particular new course of action, but presents theories that are already at the heart of modern educational practice and shows how these theories have been used by teachers and educators of teachers.

The dialogue in this book takes place within and is informed by a multitude of disciplines including psychology, communication studies, gender studies, technology, composition, rhetoric, and education. Authors of the main chapters address pedagogical issues from their chosen theoretical perspective. Each chapter is followed by a brief response that draws on the experiences and expertise of classroom teachers and other theoreticians. As such, a dialogue between the theory and practice of change is established between the chapter authors and respondents.

When conceiving of this collection of essays, we particularly wanted to achieve a balance in the educational contexts of the authors. Therefore, we invited authors who are high school teachers, teacher educators, academic researchers, college professors, and other professionals. We have attempted to balance differences in the career spans of the authors from novices of few years' experience to those entering their fifth decade of teaching or researching in their areas of expertise. In fact, some of the authors have themselves gone through changes in relationship to each other throughout their careers. For example, some of the authors in this volume were originally related as teacher and student, mentor and apprentice, expert and novice. The changes in these relationships, like the changes suggested throughout this book, took place through interaction.

As with all major projects, there are many unmentioned people whose encouragement and skills help bring a project to fruition. We thank our friends and families for their steadfast support while accomplishing this volume. We also thank Barbara Bernstein, our initial contact at Ablex, for guiding us through the beginning stages of production, The University of San Diego for providing indexing and release-time funding, and Monica Wagner for typing the final drafts and cross-checking references.

It is our hope that this volume will inspire additional dialogues between teachers and researchers; that teachers, students, and others invested in the processes of teaching and learning who read this will have new tools and skills with which to grow; and that each of us will acquire a tolerance for the differences in our unique processes of teaching and learning.

Introduction

Gordon M. Pradl
New York University

Recently at a teachers' conference in England, I attended a "great debate" about the low morale of teachers and the general mess education is in throughout the country. In these conservative times, amid the West's declining economic power, I expected the businessman on the panel to lecture the audience on standards and the need for more assessment—why were teachers mucking about and not getting students down to the basics? Instead, when his turn came to speak, he focused on two qualities that he hoped teachers in the future would take as their paramount educational goals for children: *confidence* and *flexibility*. He wasn't concerned with employees failing to follow orders or speaking incorrectly; rather, he wanted to know where their initiative was? How were they going to adapt to ever-changing conditions in the workplace if they didn't know how to work together, how to solve problems creatively in a social setting? And what surprised me the most was his plea for drama activities and role playing in the curriculum. Through this kind of "play," he argued, students come to understand other points of view. In doing so, they end up less rigid about their own perspectives on the world and more open to negotiation and compromise, more open to change.

What this businessman was describing captures in many respects the concerns of the various educators in this volume. As they reflect on teacher change, they come face to face with a number of inherent contradictions regarding change. Such contradictions appear because the way we interpret and relate to change, both individually and collectively, depends ultimately on our social construction of it.

Change, in other words, is not some material object or process out there waiting to be discovered. Instead, *change* remains what *we* make of it for our own purposes. Thus any discussion of change requires that we locate ourselves accurately within an arena of conflicting agendas before we are able to make useful proposals within the field of education.

The most striking conflict exists between economics and politics. One side wants change taken seriously because change is the key characteristic of contemporary economic life. On the other side are those who are interested in change because they wish to push some ideological program, one intended to distribute more equitably the potential benefits of freedom and democracy. In the first case, we're facing brute material facts—technologies being displaced, markets disrupted, and demographic and cultural patterns dislocated. As Benjamin Disraeli remarked in 1867 about the imperative of contemporary industrial society, "Change is inevitable. In a progressive country change is constant." In the second case, we are contesting different social visions—how should we relate to each other, what principles and values should we hold? In either case, the hardest response to face is often our own *resistance*.

Most of us, it seems, would simply prefer things to remain the same—the *status quo* looks more appealing, especially when we think that somehow we are benefiting. Accordingly, incumbency with all its faults is generally more reassuring than a future that risks being in doubt, risks placing us in some positions we are unsure of. Voters, for instance, never tire of complaining about politicians in general, but they seem particularly reluctant to challenge their own immediate representatives. Yet from any perspective it is clear that we are living in a period of rapid change and during such periods we seem especially prone to nostalgia, that frame of mind which sees change as leading us in a downward direction. Conjuring up "the good old days" remains a convenient way for us to cling to some fantasy of order and control.

The question we need to consider is what actually happens to us when we are in the process of becoming *different*. First and foremost this means we must give up for a time the certainty of control. To be out of control is to be thrust into a world in which we begin to doubt our present knowledge. Yet "not knowing" feels uncomfortable, so we try to avoid ambiguity and indeterminancy, try to see the world in black and white terms. As the psychologist Geroge Kelly explains, we enter events always in anticipation of them, so it is perfectly natural to shy away from those occasions and situations where we are not prepared with a social script to meet the faces that we will meet. For instance, a teacher whose classes center on his own talk is going to find it very hard to make room for student talk, and then to hear that talk if and when it occurs. Whether we are trying to adjust to altered conditions in our environment or actually trying to alter who we are and how we interact with those around us, change will not be easy.

In education, contrasting intentions further intensify feelings of resistance. On the one hand, are we being pragmatic and simply preparing students for life in a complex and unpredictable world of constant change? Or, on the other hand, do we have a larger mission in mind as we seek to prepare students to actually change social relationships and institutions in that world? In both instances many problems need to be addressed. Yet, regardless of what position or faith we subscribe to, teachers themselves need to be at the center of changing attitudes and approaches.

Central to any shift in how we view teaching and learning is the issue of authority and control. For instance, to consider using more student-centered approaches to instruction in an classroom that previously had been teacher dominated immediately exposes the teacher to the stress of having to readjust her role relationships with students. It is precisely this readjustment of role relationships that serves to pinpoint the dilemma we face in trying to bring about any kind of educational change. When teacher educators urge teachers to see beyond their traditional ways of being with students in the classroom, this is not just a matter of adding to the teachers' knowledge base. Instead, teachers are being pushed to transform themselves. This means they must have enough *confidence* to be *flexible* in living with indeterminancy: not always knowing where their control is in the classroom, not always knowing what the learning outcomes will be. If students are allowed to participate in the negotiations that determine what is to be studied and how their learning is to proceed, the teacher will have to relinquish to the students a significant amount of responsibility for initiation.

But our capacity as teachers to adapt to these new relationships is hardly unrestricted. We would certainly never claim to be educating students for obsolescence; however, we often end up doing exactly that because we have difficulty seeing the connection between learning and self-determination. Ironically, that is also the larger problem or contradiction we face in our society and the reason we keep losing our grip on how to bring about teacher change. The social message remains mixed. While we want to be ready for change, we don't readily want to give up our little stake of privilege that helps keep change at bay. These are the distribution and cost questions that all readers of this book will have to ask of themselves: Who initially will lose what? What will be the attendant compensations? What are the true implications of creating a *confident* and *flexible* citizenry? Who will remain to be exploited?

What the various critiques of teacher change offered in this book have in common is an ecological perspective. This means that each author views teacher transformation in terms of competing social and institutional contexts. The distinct advantage of such a position is that it avoids blaming isolated teachers for resisting change and instead encourages us to examine the entire system within which a teacher is acting as a professional. Further, in every instance it allows us to see that the kind of *confidence* necessary to begin the journey toward change requires a supportive social network. In concert with others, teachers need the opportunity to construe and actively test their own understanding of where they are and of the "difference" gap that marks where they might want to be.

In working with teachers, it is necessary to keep clarifying how *they* are reading the change situations they are struggling with. Mark Tappan's essay and Carol Gilligan's response provide us with a useful dialogue of competing interpretations of one teacher's change of mind about what to do with a "disruptive" child in her class. Initially, Chris commits herself to working with the child to overcome his problems, but after five months of struggle, she decides to have him removed from the classroom. In doing so, however, Chris acknowledges her conflicting feelings about wanting to get rid of Clarence: "I do and I don't." Tappan uses this conflict to summarize two major moral orientations that have been identified in our culture: *justice*, which emphasizes "an absence of oppression or an ideal of equality, reciprocity, and fairness between persons," and *care*, which emphasizes "safeguards against disconnection or an ideal of responsive relationship, loving and being loved, listening and being listened to, and responding and being responded to." Part of the struggle faced by this teacher is determined by these competing "voices," for, as Tappan suggests, borrowing an idea from Bakhtin, persons are "polyphonic"—they are able to speak the languages of both *justice* and *care*.

By raising a number of questions about how schools pressure teachers to adopt one kind of discourse over another, Tappan helps us to see how change is always framed within competing sets of moral explanations. What complicates the circumstances of school life is how the voice of *justice* has come to dominate, a voice generally associated with male methods of control. Thus many dilemmas experienced by female teachers as they try to sort through conflicting educational decisions might be better illuminated if we attempted to understand how women feel and what they are thinking from the perspective of *care*.

Gilligan, however, wants to take our reading of this teacher's struggle a step further and see it as a "question of how or whether she can stay with Clarence and also be with the other children in her class." By shifting our frame of the situation, Gilligan is able to understand Chris' change of mind as a story about a female teacher breaking free of conventionalized images of women and self-sacrifice. In deciding to remove Clarence, Chris shifts from "trying to become the angel in the house" and so becomes more responsible for acting on her feelings in the situation. By including more of a sense of her own self in the conflict, Chris comes closer to realizing "what good teaching means: a willingness to listen more fully to her own voice in relationships and also a deepening appreciation of the relational conflicts which are an inescapable part of teaching." In emphasizing the web of relationships that surrounds teaching decisions and change, Gilligan is able to conclude: "Within a relational framework and within a culture which both idealizes and devalues women, Chris's act is an act of resistance and courage rather than an act of capitulation."

In her essay on gender stereotyping, Linda Perry continues this focus on how the perspective of *care* is so often ignored in education. Her illustrations of the numerous ways teachers limit the educational opportunities of female students in the classroom offers a strong indictment of a system in need of change. On college campuses in almost every area, from admissions and financial aid to campus employment and health care, a systematic pattern of discrimination works against women. Further, research has demonstrated "that when women and men engage in identical behavior, the behavior is devalued for women." We sex-segregate women by thinking of them as the "quiet and nonassertive" students in class and we also exclude them by sex-typing courses such as computer science versus business education. In sum, the picture is not a pretty one from either a *justice* or a *care* point of view, but it *is* successful in keeping women "in their place," in keeping their voices silenced.

Unfortunately, simply identifying an injustice does not lead to a quick remedy; otherwise the "problem" of gender discrimination would now be a thing of the past. And so Perry probes deeper to find reasons why institutional and teacher change in this area is so difficult. One explanation she pursues comes from General Systems Theory: the school as a system is often more closed than open and flexible because too frequently it protects itself by domesticating new information rather than using new information as an occasion for change. The use of "rules" helps keep old conceptions and convictions in line because they often operate at an unspoken level and so remain unexamined— we "naturally" reinforce the rough and tumble of boys on the playground, but are startled when we see any girls exhibiting such behavior. Thus the rules for female behavior, while predominantly social in origin, become confused with iron-clad laws of nature. Although "biologically based behaviors do not include determination to succeed, nurturance, intelligence, kindness, seriousness, or any other behaviors that affect learning and education," educational institutions continue their deep-seated prejudices against women.

Change in this crucial area can only come about when the various parts of the system are considered as a whole. Thus Perry, and Cheris Kramarae who responds to her essay, see the importance of flooding the entire educational enterprise with alternative options for countering gender prejudice. Again, an ecological perspective allows us to acknowledge that the context of each learning event experienced by a woman suggests yet a larger context. Until all these various contexts are in alignment, it is easy for students to retreat into preexisting stereotypes. For instance, the materials of any course offer opportunities for engaging women's perspectives and accomplishments, but the teacher simultaneously needs to be sensitive to nonsexist language use and aware of gender issues in the conduct of classroom activities. Further, there should be an awareness of how the classroom climate also helps to contribute to the larger school or campus climate. Each and every day-to-day behavior in all these spheres is not only mutually supporting, but provides the social basis for encouraging individual teacher change. If we fail to see these connections, we'll lose the opportunity to move toward a society in which, as Perry puts it, "educational and life experiences are based on abilities and aptitudes rather than on biological sex."

Pat Diamond's essay continues a concern for honoring the perspective of the teacher who desires or is in the midst of change. "The challenge for in-service teacher educators," Diamond suggests, "is to help teachers see themselves as capable of imagining and trying alternatives—and eventually are self-directing and self-determining." He is very aware of their resistances; nevertheless, he believes teachers can be "given opportunities to experience themselves as self-fashioning people who can make themselves into what they want to be." The social arrangements and conventional wisdom in schools, however, seldom permit opportunities for self-reflection and growth. Because teachers frequently conceive of control as operating externally to them, the excuse "They won't let me!" can serve as a powerful rationale even when, as Diamond's research has shown, there is no basis for such a conclusion. The task, then, is to create conditions that support teachers in articulating and testing their educational beliefs and theories in action. *Confidence,* or how teachers feel about themselves, is again a crucial change factor as Diamond seeks to help teachers get in touch with their own agency.

By using the idea of a "fixed-role," an approach from Personal Construct psychology pioneered by George Kelly, Diamond shows how playing with a teacher's script and self-image might allow these teachers to distance themselves from their routines and begin experimenting with their own teaching practices. The two case studies he presents reveal no magical results, but they do encourage us to see change as a multidimensional partnership. In a "what if?" mode, teachers begin to experience how alternatives in vantage point can get them closer to the consequences of their behavior. Such a trying of alternative roles needs a protected interpersonal space, one which offers options, not judgments. Teacher educators might help teachers move beyond feeling stuck or ineffective through taking seriously each teacher's vital contribution to the process of reflecting on existing educational practices. Change, Diamond reminds us, is empowerment, not imposition: "Construed as it is from a given perspective, any teaching can always be varied, while ever higher levels of self-consciousness can be attained. . . . By first knowing their own frames of reference and then by struggling to look at things in other ways, teachers can change." And as James Britton underscores in his response to Diamond's essay, we are very much back to matters of drama when we take George Kelly's ideas to heart, for "what is involved is 'make-believe'—a role familiar from most people's childhood."

Laura Martin's essay extends our inquiry into the reasons why professional relationships that facilitate rather than direct are so important for teachers attempting to take on new roles in the classroom: "The situational constraints and historical work patterns in schools mean that teachers' daily practices actually may work against taking a scientific approach" of "reflection and analysis." Arguing against teacher isolation, Martin borrows the ideas of Vygotsky, who emphasized how it is the *inter*psychological connections between two or more persons that determines the *intra*psychological learning within the individual. In other words, what new information we take in and how we shift our perspective is deeply dependent upon the social web of meanings that we share and articulate with those with whom we are learning.

Describing three teacher in-service projects, Martin concludes that change depends very much on teachers learning "new communication strategies and new ways to organize information environments." But such learning only happens when the teacher is experimenting with new practices within her own socially constituted "zone of proximal development." In his response to her essay, Denis Newman builds on this idea by calling for further inquiry into how teachers, within their own supportive professional communities, come to build the confidence that undergirds change. In attempting to understand from a Vygotskian perspective the resistance of teachers to new ideas and practices, both Martin and Newman confirm how much more we need to study the actual social processes involved when teachers collaboratively construe and try new teaching behaviors as part of their own commitment to learning.

Jan Sinnott invites us to see teacher change in terms of the "dialogue quality of reality." By examining the "new" sciences—from quantum mechanics and chaos theory to cooperative evolution and cognitive theory—she challenges us to join their innovative reconceptualizations of knowledge and knowing. Knowledge in this world of science is characterized by open and relational social systems rather than closed and isolated individual systems. Drawing on the nature of inquiry and theory building in current science, Sinnott constructs a model of the teaching process that would be compatible with these changing realities, but she also makes note of those factors, such as the bureaucratic and authoritarian structures of schools, that serve as "roadblocks to change in the classroom."

Sinnott's useful presentation provides more than enough reach to take seriously the fact that all teachers already act in complex ways. We need, however, to investigate further how they are denied realization of their own processes of genuine learning. How might such teachers come to acknowledge that their personal "knowing" is relational and probablistic, not unitary and absolute? The flexibility required to flourish in schools marked by these new conditions arises in those teachers who are supported in their creative disorder, so once again the challenge is social and institutional and not a matter of blaming individual teacher victims.

In her response to Sinnott's essay, Diane Lee further elaborates on activities that would be consistent with this vision of dialogue: more room for the personal and the affective dimensions of our lives, more story telling and reflective writing, more student choice, more interrelating of the subject matter areas—all things that would usefully disrupt the flow of any conventional teacher-centered classroom. In short, the accommodating teacher in this instance would have to surrender a certain amount of control and simultaneously risk being more vulnerable, and so teacher educators will need to pay careful attention to the psychological costs involved.

Margaret Vaughan's essay reports her own growing awareness of the importance of carrying on dialogue with teachers. Because there are few structural or administrative incentives for teachers to alter what

they are currently doing with students, business remains pretty much
as usual. But, as Vaughan struggled with the recalcitrant, she realized
that "focusing on the resistance of teachers implies that the fault lies
with them, just as teachers ultimately blame their students . . . the
most fruitful approach is to assume the problem lies within us. It is our
job to ensure change, not our students'." Telling teachers something
new only worked when they were already positioned to understand its
benefits. In most other instances, Vaughan as teacher consultant finally
had to work in "concert" with others—"when trying to change the
behavior of someone else, more often than not, my behavior had to
change first."

This lesson effectively counters any notion that change can come
about from some top-down, formulaic directive. Teachers have theories and intentions that must be considered and like most persons, they
are resentful of advice that hasn't been asked for. As Joan Steiner
argues in her response, assisting teachers in exploring the origins of
their practice invites a dialogue between teachers and teacher educators. Describing her positive experience with mainstreaming, Steiner
shows how a policy of heterogeneity encourages teachers to be more
permeable to change. Exchanging stories becomes a way for teachers to
learn from each other.

The rhetoric of teacher empowerment and change often does not
come from those who are listening closely to teachers themselves.
Joseph Janangelo seeks to expose certain misleading tropes used by
various educational critics to characterize a teacher's role in a liberatory pedagogy. Identifying "muses," "performers," "prophets," and
"martyrs" as enforcing reactionary and romantic stereotypes of teaching, Janangelo argues that such images "delude teachers about their
personal and professional responsibilities, disempower them from
making significant changes in their working conditions, and discourages them from seeing themselves as worthy of better treatment by the
academy." At the heart of his critique is a concern that those who cry
out most militantly for teacher change are frequently stuck in their own
rigid agenda, having lost the ability to be "polyphonic." Teacher
bashing, in the name of whatever honorable cause, only perpetuates
divisions and further resistance within the profession. Teachers grow
in confidence and become more flexible when they concentrate on
what they *can* accomplish rather than dwelling on feeling guilty for all
the things they will never get done. Without a realistic and sympathetic picture of the conditions of teaching, much radical discourse
ends up dissuading rather than persuading.

In her response, Lil Brannon takes exception to Janangelo's con-
flating of "images of critical teaching with liberal romantic images that

have captured the popular imagination." She too rejects these images, but on gender grounds. Painting the teacher as a self-effacing, solitary servant plays into the patriarchal system of domination and thereby misrepresents how the "critical teacher" depends upon social alliances, which in turn sustain the moral orientation of *care*. Brannon also champions narratives of teaching when she points to "the power of discourses outside those 'typical' of educational inquiry—the stories of teachers—that pose problems about the role educational research plays in the daily life of the classroom." Such discourses, however, are "often dismissed as merely anecdotal and certainly unscholarly." Brannon wants to stop the objectification of "teacher" that constitutes so much of educational criticism. "Instead of constructing alliances with teachers," she points out, "the educational research enterprise is dependent on finding fault with what teachers do." Taken together, Janangelo and Brannon provide compelling arguments for putting teachers, rather than "experts," at the center of our efforts to bring about educational change.

Gail Hawisher and Cynthia Selfe further extend our understanding of the relationship between change and cultural values by offering a sweeping critique of how the strategic employment of technology is fundamentally shaped by existing social patterns and beliefs, especially in education. They argue that although more student-centered approaches to learning are evident in schools today, introducing the computer into teaching environments does not guarantee the triumph of this trend. As long as teacher-centered practices predominate, the computer as a tool for learning actually reinforces hierarchical teacher control and continues to marginalize already underrepresented student groups in our society. Because of this, Hawisher and Selfe emphasize, "reform efforts, especially when they are computer-supported, must proceed simultaneously on at least two levels if we hope for success: in local arenas—in the minds of individual teachers and students and within computer-supported learning spaces—and in the broader political arenas where social and political policy is made."

Use of the computer in schools has frequently disappointed the expectations of those educators who saw it as a powerful force to help democratize classrooms. Hawisher and Selfe trace the history of this disappointment, especially in the area of computer-supported writing, but they note two powerful applications—computer-based conferences and hypertext—both of which could augment educational change by encouraging students to gain significant control over their own language activities. Gary Graves' response to the Hawisher and Selfe essay shows equally the power and the optimism of their analysis. When we ignore the larger contexts and belief systems that constrain what is possible in individual classrooms, we frustrate the change process. Telling the story of these larger cultural imperatives helps us to set a broader base for collaborative change among teachers at all levels.

The concluding essay by Phyllis Kahaney helps us to comprehend how our view of knowledge is an important prerequisite to change. The teacher's perspective on knowledge and how she "knows" that knowledge serve to position the teacher's social relationships within the educational system. It is more helpful to see change, Kahaney emphasizes, as part of "an ongoing process called 'learning,' instead of as a product or a 'thing.' " To illustrate this, she features an instructive anecdote about two teachers struggling to change. One senior professor, who initially appeared resistant to the ideas Kahaney was presenting in a Writing Across the Curriculum seminar, ends up excited about trying out new interactive methods in his classroom. In contrast, a junior faculty member, who at first presented herself as looking for new teaching approaches, shut down in the process of the seminar and retreated back to the safety of her lectures.

This surprising reversal in response to the kinds of open changes being encouraged by Kahaney brings us back to the relationship between *confidence* and *flexibility*. The younger teacher unfortunately was under great threat to prove herself, which weakened her sense of confidence and gave her a greater need to control her classes. This caused her to lose the kind of openness and flexibility required for an attempt at student-centered approaches. But even more important, her view that *she* was in control of knowledge prevented her from taking seriously the role of students in the making of meaning. In contrast, the senior professor was at a stage in his career where he had little to lose and so could be more "playful" with the ideas that Kahaney was urging on him. Once again, holding different intentions and understandings of how meaning is made leads to quite variant results in the classroom. Therefore, unless teachers are able to voice publicly their own concerns and understandings regarding knowledge and control, it is difficult to know where the change process is to begin.

As an ensemble, these nine essays lead us inexorably to conclude that, despite the urgency of educational change, *the teacher who is changing is clearly at risk.* However, a community of teachers working together, telling their stories, and experimenting with alternatives can provide a significant compensation for those who initially experience themselves losing power and control over their students. Once we understand that change involves the long and difficult process of teachers gaining their own agency and altering their perspective on knowledge and relationships, we will be well-advised to foster those democratic conditions which best encourage *confidence* and *flexibility* within teachers themselves.

Educators at any level who are committed to changing school practices must understand that such change depends upon a prior political commitment. Democratic beliefs and attitudes must come to characterize all the various networks of social relationships that mark the teaching/learning enterprise: teacher and student, teacher and teacher, teacher and administrator, school and university. One symptom of the status and hierarchical pattern that undermines teacher change resides in the presumably innocent but degrading term, "training." This concept from the heyday of "behaviorism" implicitly encourages us to see change as coming from without, as something that is done *to* us. The use of such terminology exposes the fact that teachers finally are looked down upon, as rats running through someone else's maze. Truly respecting each teacher's capacities and perspectives, and accepting their key role as reflective professionals in instituting change, would suggest replacing "training" with the word that should bind us all together, "education."

In short, the real struggle here is to take teachers seriously, to understand what *they* are saying. Teacher educators must join as partners with teachers in the hard work and play required to shift perspectives and try alternatives. Without such joint effort and mutual respect, teachers' voices will remain silent and their energies will go elsewhere. Yet, with such an effort, change can become central to learning itself and thus part of the ongoing human endeavor.

Relational Voices and Moral Development: Reflections on Change*

Mark B. Tappan
Colby College

One of the central events in Tracy Kidder's (1989) book *Among Schoolchildren*, which chronicles a year in the life of a teacher, Chris Zajac, and her fifth-grade class in Holyoke, MA, is the decision Chris makes to remove Clarence, a difficult and troubled child, from her class and send him to a special Alpha class. From the first week of school in September Chris recognized Clarence as a child with problems—he was defiant, he hit and kicked other children, and, most of all, "he paid almost no attention to her lessons and his work. It seemed as if every time that she glanced at Clarence he wasn't working" (p. 8). Yet, in spite of these difficulties, Chris was committed to keeping Clarence in her classroom, and to working with him to help him overcome his problems. "All right, buster," she thought to herself, "what you need is what I've got" (p. 19).

Over the course of the next five months, however, Chris gradually, and with a great deal of soul-searching, changed her mind about Clarence. His continuing difficulties, problems, outbursts, fights, and refusal to work finally necessitated a psychological evaluation to determine whether or not he should be moved to a special class for troubled students—the Alpha class. The decision was made, and Clarence was sent away, yet Chris still struggled with the moral implications of her decision:

*The preparation of this chapter was supported, in part, by the Lilly Endowment. Thanks to Lyn Mikel Brown, Carol Gilligan, and the editors of this volume for helpful comments on various versions of the manuscript.

As she thought of it later on—and it was a long time before she could stop thinking about it—the situation was impossible. Nobody had told her ahead of time that Clarence might be sent to an Alpha class this year. She hadn't had time to find a settled attitude. But even after the decision was made and she had all too much time to think, she still didn't know how to feel.

Chris worried about Clarence. She had reason. To send him away was to tell him the same old news: he was a problem; he had failed. And to help Clarence by placing him in a special class among a number of other notoriously unruly children—might as well say his behavior would improve if he was made to join a street gang. She couldn't argue for doing that to him.

And yet at the same time, removing Clarence from the class seemed like a solution. He had not committed any act of extreme violence; he hadn't thrown chairs at other children or come to school with weapons. But he did beat up and intimidate other kids. More and more since Christmas, he had begun to seem like a wrecker in the room. Was it fair to let one child's problems interfere with the education of nineteen other children, many of them just as needy as Clarence? When she looked back and imagined herself saying "No! I don't want him taken away," she imagined herself feeling just as guilty as she would have if she'd said, "Yes, by all means, Alpha." In retrospect, sending Clarence to Alpha seemed like a decision to accomplish something that was probably right by doing something that was probably wrong.

She had one, awful, sinking fear. Had she wanted, deep down, to get rid of Clarence? She hadn't acted on that desire, but had she felt it? "I don't want to get rid of him. I don't!" she told Paul, the sympathetic vice principal, later. "I mean"—she looked up at Paul—"I do and I don't." (pp. 166–167)

I am interested in how and why teachers—like Chris Zajac—*change* in the ways in which they think about, feel about, and respond to moral conflicts and dilemmas in their lives—like the one Chris faced in her relationship with Clarence. My aim in this chapter is to present recent work in the psychology of moral development, and to reflect on the implications of this work for understanding why teachers change in their moral thinking, feeling, and acting.

Key to my discussion is the idea of *difference*; change always goes hand-in-hand with difference—difference between one way of thinking, feeling, or acting and another. Hence, I would argue, a perspective on difference is prerequisite to understanding processes of change. It is also important to acknowledge that issues of *value* are central to any exploration of change—particularly change considered in relation to human development and education. Both developmental psychology and education are fundamentally value-laden enterprises, dedicated not just to facilitating and encouraging change, in general, but to facilitating and encouraging a specific kind of change—change directed toward a goal, end-point, or *telos* that had been imbued with value (see Kaplan, 1983, 1986; White, 1983). Thus, I would also argue, any discussion of teachers and change must include a consideration of the values, assumptions, and biases that determine which changes are seen as *positive* (i.e., as "educational," "developmental," or "healthy") and which changes are seen as *negative* (i.e., as "regressive," "harmful," or "unhealthy"). In other words, without a careful analysis of its *moral* dimensions, an exploration of change as it relates to teachers, education, and development can be nothing more than an incomplete and, ultimately, relativistic examination of difference *qua* difference.

I begin with a brief overview of the work of Carol Gilligan and her colleagues on two different "relational voices" (or "moral orientations")—*justice* and *care*. In particular, I review recent theoretical and empirical work that provides evidence to suggest that significant differences in moral perspective (particularly gender differences) can be reliably identified in the narratives that individuals tell about conflict and choice in their lives. I then turn to a consideration of the ways in which such a two-voice framework might inform our understanding of how and why teachers change—on both the individual and the institutional levels. Finally, I return to Chris Zajac, to offer some concluding thoughts about her experience in light of my reflections on moral development and change.

TWO DIFFERENT VOICES: JUSTICE AND CARE

The recent work of Carol Gilligan and her colleagues focuses directly on the issue of difference in moral development via the distinction between the relational voices of justice and care. This distinction arose initially from observations made in the course of Gilligan's research on the relationship between moral judgment and real-life action. Studies of college students describing experiences of moral conflict and choice and pregnant women who were considerable abortion shifted the focus of moral development research from people's thinking about hypothetical dilemmas (see Kohlberg, 1981, 1984) to their construction of actual life choices they faced and decisions they made (see Gilligan, 1977, 1982, 1987a; Gilligan & Belenky, 1980; Gilligan & Murphy, 1979; Murphy & Gilligan, 1980).

In this context, Gilligan and her colleagues observed that some men who scored at the highest levels of Lawrence Kohlberg's (1981, 1984) scale of moral development defined moral conflicts in their lives as problems of justice, but found principles of justice and fairness to dictate solutions that they considered in some sense to be morally problematic (see Gilligan & Murphy, 1979). For example, Gilligan and Murphy (1979) quote one young man who says, "The justice approach was really blinding me to a lot of issues . . . in a sense I was trying to make it a justice issue, and it really blinded me to a lot of the realities of the situation" (p. 96). Furthermore, Gilligan also noted that the some women, especially when describing their own experiences of moral conflict and choice, defined and resolved moral problems in ways that differed from those described in theories of moral development and in the measures traditionally used for its assessment (Gilligan, 1977, 1982). For example, one young woman says, "In my life situation I relate morality with interpersonal relationships that have to do with respect for the other person and myself . . . because they have . . . feelings that can be hurt, an awareness that can be hurt" (Gilligan, 1977, p. 485).

Previous interpretations of observed gender differences in moral reasoning (as well as individual and cultural differences) have been constrained by the assumption that there is a single moral perspective—that is, the male-defined "justice" perspective (see Freud, 1925/1963; Kohlberg, 1981, 1984; Piaget, 1932/1965). Gilligan's analysis of women's voices, however, clarified an alternative approach to moral decision making—the "care" perspective (see Gilligan, 1977, 1982). The identification of these two voices, orientations, or perspectives points to a more complex conception of moral thinking, feeling, and acting, and provides a new framework for thinking about differences—and change—in moral experience (see also Tappan, 1990).

The distinction between the justice and care voices reflects different dimensions of human relationships that give rise to moral concern. As such, these two voices are generated by concerns for specific visions of a safe or ideal human relationship: the justice voice reflects an absence of oppression or an ideal of equality, reciprocity, and fairness between persons; the care voice reflects safeguards against disconnection or an ideal of a responsive relationship, of loving and being loved, listening and being listened to, and responding and being responded to. These ideal visions are experienced as being undercut, in the case of justice, by oppression, domination, inequality, and/or unfairness of treatment; in the case of care, by detachment, abandonment, inattentiveness, and/or lack of responsiveness. Insofar as one takes as "blameworthy" such things as oppression, domination, and unequal treatment, or carelessness, abandonment, and inattentiveness, by one person with respect to another, one can speak of justice and care as both *relational voices* and *moral orientations*. In other words, people characteristically express these actual or potential experiences of vulnerability in relationships in these different moral terms (Brown, 1989; and Gilligan, 1982, 1987a, 1987b).

From a developmental standpoint, both inequality and responsiveness in relationships are universal human experiences; all children are born into a situation of inequality vis-à-vis their parents as caregivers, and yet no child survives in the absence of some kind of adult response or concern. Since everyone has been vulnerable, therefore, to both oppression and abandonment, two relational voices—one of justice and one of care—and two moral injunctions—not to treat others unfairly and not to turn away from someone in need—recur in human experience (Gilligan, 1987a, 1987b; Gilligan & Wiggins, 1987). Thus, in other words, Gilligan's conception of the voices of justice and care refers to the dimensions of fairness and responsiveness in *all* relationships, and considers moral development both in terms of changes in the understanding of what justice means and in terms of changes in the understanding of what constitutes care.

Research by Gilligan and her colleagues on relational voice as a dimension of moral thinking, feeling, and acting initially addressed three questions: 1) Do people articulate concerns about justice and concerns about care in discussing conflicts they face or choices they make?; 2) Do people tend to focus their attention primarily on one voice and minimally represent the other?; and 3) Is there an association between voice and gender? Evidence from a series of studies that included a common set of questions about actual experiences of conflict and matched samples of males and females provides affirmative answers to all three questions (Gilligan, 1987a).

Gilligan and Attanucci (1988) report that when asked to describe a conflict they had faced, 55 out of 80 (69%) educationally advantaged American adolescents and adults voiced concerns about *both* justice and care in their narratives of real-life experiences of conflict and choice. This suggests that individuals are *polyphonic*—that is, they can speak in the language of both justice and care, and thus are not limited to a monotonic voice or a single orientation in dealing with their conflicts and attempts at resolution.

Despite this plurality of voices exhibited by individual subjects, however, Gilligan and Attanucci (1988) also note that for almost two thirds of the subjects in the studies they reviewed (51 out of 80), one voice clearly *dominated* over the other voice. Thus, for example, an individual who presented two care considerations while discussing a moral conflict was more likely to give a third and fourth than to balance care and justice concerns—a finding consonant with the assumption that justice and care constitute organizing frameworks for moral decision making. The men and women involved in these studies (high school students, college students, medical students, and adult professionals) were equally likely to demonstrate this *dominant focus* phenomenon. In other words, two thirds of both males and females fell into one of the dominant focus categories (justice or care), while the remaining one third showed no dominant focus, but rather a mixture of justice and care. These findings suggest that individuals tend to "prefer" one or the other voice, even though they are capable of using both.

Finally, Gilligan and Attanucci observe that the *dominant focus* for males and females was strikingly different. Although not all women with a dominant focus showed a preference for the care voice, where the care voice was dominant, it was manifested almost exclusively by females in these samples. Thus, more than half of the women who showed a dominant focus preferred the *care* voice (12 out of 22); in contrast, of the 31 men who manifested a dominant focus, 30 showed a preference for the *justice* voice.

How can these findings be interpreted? They clearly indicate that neither voice (justice or care) is *gender-specific*. They do, however, suggest that the two voices tend to be *gender-related*: males are oriented toward justice more frequently than females, while females are oriented toward care more frequently than males (see also Gilligan & Wiggins, 1987; Lyons, 1983; Rogers, 1988).[1]

Additional research has not only supported this finding, but has also generated new insights about the interplay of the voices of justice and care. Kay Johnston (1985, 1988) has explored the relationship between voice and problem-solving strategies by creating a standard method for identifying justice and care in response to two of Aesop's fables. In particular, she was interested in the voice spontaneously used to frame the solution to the fable, whether individuals could switch voice, and what voice individuals would use to frame the "best" solution to the problem posed by the fable.

Johnston asked 60 11- and 15-year-old boys and girls to state and solve the problem posed by the fables, and then she asked, "Is there another way to solve this problem?" The majority of her subjects initially framed the problem in the fable in terms of either justice or

---

[1]It is important to stress, however, that these findings are based, by and large, on samples of educationally and economically privileged, predominantly white, Americans. Further research on diverse cultures and subcultures will thus be necessary to determine whether this dominant focus phenomenon is truly gender related, or whether it is a result of some kind of gender/class/education interaction.

care—that is, either they assumed a detached position and appealed to a rule or principle for resolving the competing claims in the fable, or they took personal interest in the situation in an effort to discover or create a way of taking care of all the characters in the story, in an attempt to respond to all of their needs. Furthermore, roughly one half of her subjects spontaneously switched voice when asked if there was another way to solve the problem; the rest did so when the interviewer provided cues to the form such a switch might take. Finally, Johnston asked her subjects which of the situations they described was the best solution, and most answered in terms of one voice or the other.

Johnston (1985, 1988) found gender differences with respect to relational voice/moral orientation to be similar to those reported by Gilligan and Attanucci (1988). Boys more often spontaneously used and preferred justice solutions to the fables she posed, while girls more often spontaneously used and preferred care solutions. More important, however, is the fact that children and adolescents can shift perspectives and speak in both voices when invited to do so, which raises a number of very interesting and provocative questions relevant to understanding how and why individuals change in the ways in which they morally think, feel, and act:

> The demonstration that children know both [voices] and can frame and solve moral problems in at least two different ways means that the choice of moral standpoint is an element of moral decision. The role of the self in moral judgment thus includes the choice of moral standpoint, and this decision, whether implicit or explicit, may become linked with self-respect and self-definition. Especially in adolescence, when choice becomes more self-conscious and self-reflective, moral standpoint may become entwined with identity and self-esteem. [The] finding that spontaneous moral [voice] and preferred [voice] are not always the same raises a number of questions as to why and under what conditions a person may adopt a problem-solving strategy that he or she sees as not the best way to solve the problem. (Gilligan, 1987a, p. 27)

Thus, although the gender relatedness of these two voices is important to stress, particularly in light of Gilligan and her colleagues' ongoing work on female development and the development of a care voice (see Brown, 1989; Gilligan, 1990; Gilligan, Brown, & Rogers, 1990), the significance of the fact that a majority of Gilligan and Attanucci's (1988) and Johnston's (1985, 1988) subjects manifested a plurality of relational voices should by no means be overlooked. This research demonstrates that human beings not only speak in multiple voices, but they can and frequently do oscillate from one voice to another in their transactions with others. Indeed, as the Russian literary critic Mikhail Bakhtin (1981) has argued, as human beings we not only have the capacity to switch from one voice to another over time, but we are also polyphonic or multivocal in our utterances at any one time (Clark & Holquist, 1984; Emerson & Morson, 1987; Tappan, 1991, 1992). Therefore, insofar as any conception of the moral development of "individuals" is dependent, at least in part, on a specific conception of the person, a reconception of human beings as fundamentally polyphonic must lead to a significant reconsideration of both our conception of what constitutes moral development and our understanding of change.

RELATIONAL VOICES, TEACHERS, AND CHANGE

If teachers, like other human beings, are fundamentally polyphonic, and thus can not only speak in, but also understand, multiple voices—specifically, the voices of justice and care—how does this influence our thinking about the ways in which they can change? My preliminary answer to this question will involve reflection on the interaction between individual teachers and the cultural, historical, and institutional context in which they live and work.

Gilligan and her colleagues have conceptualized the voices of justice and care as phenomena primarily associated with an individual's psyche—that is, as Bakhtin might say, as manifestations of the "speaking personality, the speaking consciousness" (Holquist & Emerson, 1981, p. 434). Thus, as Johnston's (1985, 1988) research suggests, a change or switch in moral voice can occur if and when an individual is asked to think about or respond to a moral problem in a different way. The metaphor, in fact, that Gilligan (1987a) uses to describe this process is fundamentally psychological—the Gestalt experiments on perceptual organization using ambiguous figures (like the rabbit–duck figure) that can be seen in two different ways, but not at the same time:

> The fact that children, at least by the age of eleven, are able to shift moral orientation and can explain the logic of two moral perspectives, each associated with a different problem-solving strategy, heightens the analogy to ambiguous figure perception and further supports the conceptions of justice and care as organizing frameworks for moral decision. (p. 27)

Yet, while the voices of justice and care clearly manifest themselves in the context of an individual's psychological functioning, they are also cultural, historical, and institutional phenomena. In fact, they could also be called "social languages" (Bakhtin, 1981; Wertsch, 1991)—ways of speaking and communicating (i.e., types of discourse) associated with specific sociocultural groups, organizations, or institutions. Justice and care, on this view, can be seen as two generic languages or modes of discourse, operating in this culture at this time, that represent different moral considerations and ethical injunctions regarding how individuals should treat one another. These two languages, furthermore, can be seen not only as arising out of different types of social relationships in childhood (i.e., experiences of inequality and attachment), but also as sustained and supported by different social and institutional arrangements in the culture in which we live (see Tappan, 1992). In particular, it is clear that, in our culture, at this time, the justice voice is predominant and privileged, while the care voice is subordinate and devalued—in part because of the androcentric, patriarchal, male-dominated and controlled nature of our society, and in part because of the strong tradition of individualism in our national and cultural history (see Bellah, Madsen, Sullivan, Swindler, & Tipton, 1985; Brown, 1989; Gilligan, 1982; Miller, 1976).

Such a view of these two voices as social languages suggest that *changes* in the voice(s) in which an individual speaks, or in the voice(s) she can understand, will be influenced neither solely by her own psychological makeup, nor by the cultural, historical, and institutional context in which she lives and works, but by an interaction between these two sets of factors. Thus, for example, on the simplest level we might expect that a young man, living in this culture at this time, may find it quite difficult to change from a predominant justice focus to a predominant care focus in response to moral conflicts and dilemmas, not only because of his own socialization as a male, but also because the sociocultural context in which he lives does not encourage or support men speaking in the care voice—at least publicly. Similarly, we might expect that a young woman attending law school in this culture at this time may find it quite difficult *not* to change from a predominant care focus to a predominant justice focus, again because of the pressure from the sociocultural context of the law school and the legal system to think about moral and legal problems solely from the standpoint of the justice perspective. In fact, Lyn Brown (1989, 1991) has recently documented a struggle against losing the care voice in a study of the development of girls aged 7 to 16. As girls reach adolescence, and as they are taught to speak and understand the predominant social language of our culture, they appear to lose, or at least experience societal pressure not to speak about, some of the knowledge about care and the power of relationships they knew, and expressed, as young children.

But what about teachers? From the standpoint of this analysis, teachers are like everybody else—that is, the ways in which their relational voices/moral orientations change, or do not change, are influenced both by their individual psychological makeup and by the cultural, historical, and institutional contexts in which they live and work. We can also assume that certain teachers living and working in certain contexts will find it much easier to change than other teachers living and working in other contexts. For example, teachers working in a context in which open dialogue between teachers themselves (and with others outside the school) is encouraged and facilitated, and where opportunities to come into contact with new and different ideas, ideologies, and practices are readily available, might be more likely to change than teachers working in a context that discourages open dialogue and, instead, seeks to maintain a rigid conformity to a certain set of ideas, ideologies, and practices. Needless to say, the complexities of such interactions are so varied and variable that it is impossible to generalize beyond certain banalities. Nevertheless, I would argue that all teachers occupy a crucial position in our society, standing between the social, cultural, and historical tradition on the one hand, and the students to whom they are supposed to impart knowledge of and about the tradition on the other. Does occupying such a position make teachers more or less susceptible to change than members of other professions?

Paradoxically, perhaps, I suspect that the answer is "Yes" on both counts. Teachers are *more* susceptible to change because they witness daily the effects of what they teach, and they must constantly reflect on their practice in order to adjust to the changing dynamics of the classroom—both interpersonal and educational. Teachers are responsible, fundamentally, for facilitating "positive" change in their students; hence, because they are in the business of change, there is always some pressure for them to change as well. Yet, I would argue, teachers are also *less* susceptible to change because their role is to impart a social, cultural, and historical tradition that is extremely static and slow to change. There are institutional pressures to "cover" a certain amount of material, defined by a curriculum that is often as much a result of social and political considerations as it is of educational and developmental considerations. These are pressures, therefore, to remain unreflective and unchanged, to make sure that students learn what they are "supposed" to learn, and to insure that teachers keep their jobs. Moreover, these conflicting pressures—to change and not to change—often lead to moral conflicts and dilemmas that are difficult to resolve.

CONCLUSION

In conclusion, I return to Chris Zajac, the fifth-grade teacher who changed her mind, however reluctantly, about her difficult student, Clarence. Do the above reflections offer any insight that might help us to understand Chris's changing response to her moral dilemma?

One way to interpret her change, using the two-voice framework outlined above, is to suggest that Chris, in her response to the dilemma posed by Clarence, has changed from a predominant care perspective—focused on maintaining her relationship with Clarence and responding to his unique individual needs—to a predominant justice perspective—focused on concerns about the unfairness and injustice of her attention to Clarence and his disruptions concerning the other students in her class. The decision to send Clarence away was clearly not an easy one, and Chris wavered in her thinking—listening, as it were, to the two voices dialogue back and forth in her mind. Many of the most difficult moral decisions in our culture, marked by irreducible ambiguity and irresolvable tension, occur when the moral voices of justice and care conflict (see Gilligan & Wiggins, 1987). This is clearly the situation in which Chris found herself, and the observation that, "in retrospect, sending Clarence to Alpha seemed like a decision to accomplish something that was probably right by doing something that was probably wrong" simply acknowledges a timeless truth—that such dilemmas do not have simple, straightforward solutions.

Why did Chris change her mind about Clarence? While the specific details of this situation are obviously too complex, and the interaction between Chris's psychological functioning and the sociocultural environment in which she lives and works is too complicated to warrant a quick and easy explanation, let me nevertheless point to one set of issues that, I would argue, must be considered in any interpretation of her change. This is the way in which the cultural, historical, and institutional context of the school, and the language of justice and fairness privileged in that context, exerts subtle and sustained pressure to overcome the language of care and response spoken not only by Chris Zajac, but also by the scores of former and current elementary school teachers—the vast majority of whom have been, and continue to be, women. Such pressure, I would argue, influenced Chris to change her mind about Clarence, as she began to think less and less about her own concerns to take care of and help Clarence, and more and more about the institutional demands for a "just" resolution of this problem—that is, for a psychological evaluation and potential reassignment of a difficult student. I do not mean to suggest that Chris simply did what the school "told" her to do—she clearly had her own very strong opinions about what to do about Clarence, and about what her professional responsibilities were in this situation. I do want to suggest, however, that to assume that Chris's change of mind resulted simply from a change in her own personal beliefs and attitudes is to misunderstand the interaction between the individual and her sociocultural, historical, and institutional context that is ultimately responsible for all moral change and, hence, all moral development (see Tappan, 1992).

In conclusion, then, I have suggested that teachers, like Chris Zajac, change in the ways they think, feel, and act in response to moral conflicts and dilemmas, at least in part, when they change the relational voice(s) and, hence, the moral language(s) that they speak, hear, and understand. I have also pointed to some issues to consider in thinking about why such change occurs—the most important of which is the interaction between the teacher and the cultural, historical, and institutional context in which she lives and works. In the final analysis, however, the question of change—like the question of difference—is one that is always fraught with moral tensions and ambiguities. For, as Chris Zajac confesses, "I don't want to get rid of him. I don't! . . . I mean . . . I do and I don't."

REFERENCES

Bakhtin, M. (1981). *The dialogic imagination.* (M. Holquist, ed., C. Emerson & M. Holquist, trans.). Austin, TX: University of Texas Press.

Bellah, R., Madsen, R., Sullivan, W., Swindler, A., & Tipton, S. (1985). *Habits of the heart: Individualism and commitment in American life.* Berkeley, CA: University of California Press.

Brown, L. (1989). *Narratives of relationship: The development of a care voice in girls ages 7 to 16.* Unpublished doctoral dissertation, Harvard University, Cambridge, MA.

Brown, L. (1991). A problem of vision: The development of voice and relational knowledge in girls ages 7 to 16. *Women's Studies Quarterly, 19* (1–2), 52–71.

Clark, K., & Holquist, M. (1984). *Mikhail Bakhtin.* Cambridge, MA: Harvard University Press.

Emerson, C., & Morson, G. (1987). Penultimate words. In C. Koelb & V. Lokke (Eds.), *The current in criticism.* West Lafayette, IN: Purdue University Press.

Freud, S. (1963). Some psychological consequences of the anatomical distinction between the sexes. In P. Rieff (Ed.), *Sigmund Freud: Sexuality and the psychology of love.* New York: Collier Books. (Original work published 1925.)

Gilligan, C. (1977). In a different voice: Women's conceptions of self and morality. *Harvard Educational Review, 47,* 481–517.

Gilligan, C. (1982). *In a different voice: Psychological theory and women's development.* Cambridge, MA: Harvard University Press.

Gilligan, C. (1987a). Moral orientation and moral development. In E. Kittay & D. Meyers (Eds.), *Women and moral theory.* Totowa, NJ: Rowan & Littlefield.

Gilligan, C. (1987b). Remapping the moral domain: New images of the self in relationship. In T. Heller, M. Sosna, & D. Wellber (Eds.), *Reconstructing individualism: Autonomy, individuality, and the self in Western thought.* Stanford, CA: Stanford University Press.

Gilligan, C. (1990). teaching Shakespeare's sister. In C. Gilligan, N. Lyons, & T. Hanmer (Eds.), *Making connections: The relational worlds of adolescent girls.* Cambridge, MA: Harvard University Press.

Gilligan, C., & Attanucci, J. (1988). Two moral orientations: Gender differences and similarities. *Merrill-Palmer Quarterly, 34,* 223–237.

Gilligan, C., & Belenky, M. (1980). A naturalistic study of abortion decisions. In R. Selman & R. Yando (Eds.), *Clinical-developmental psychology* (New directions for child development, No. 7). San Francisco: Jossey-Bass.

Gilligan, C., Brown, L., & Rogers, A. (1990). Psyche embedded: A place for body, relationships, and culture in personality theory. In A. Rabin, R. Zucker, R. Emmons, & S. Frank (Eds.), *Studying persons and lives.* New York: Springer.

Gilligan, C., & Murphy, J. M. (1979). Development from adolescence to adulthood: The philosopher and the dilemma of the fact. In D. Kuhn (Ed.), *Intellectual development beyond childhood* (New directions for child development, No. 5). San Francisco: Jossey-Bass.

Gilligan, C., & Wiggins, G. (1987). The origins of morality in early childhood relationships. In J. Kagan & S. Lamb (Eds.), *The emergence of morality in young children.* Chicago, IL: The University of Chicago Press.

Holquist, M., & Emerson, C. (1981). Glossary. In M. Bakhtin, *The dialogic imagination.* Austin, TX: University of Texas Press.

Johnston, D. K. (1985). *Two moral orientations—Two problem-solving strategies: Adolescents' solutions to dilemmas in fables.* Unpublished doctoral dissertation, Harvard University, Cambridge, MA.

Johnston, D. K. (1988). Adolescents' solutions to dilemmas in fables: Two moral orientations—Two problem-solving strategies. In C. Gilligan, J. Ward, & J. Taylor (Eds.), *Mapping the moral domain.* Cambridge, MA: Harvard University Press.

Kaplan, B. (1983). A trio of trails. In R. Lerner (Ed.), *Developmental psychology: Historical and philosophical perspectives.* Hillsdale, NJ: Lawrence Erlbaum.

Kaplan, B. (1986). Value presuppositions in theories of human development. In L. Cirillo & S. Wapner (Eds.), *Value presuppositions in theories of human development.* Hillsdale, NJ: Lawrence Erlbaum.

Kidder, T. (1989). *Among schoolchildren.* Boston, MA: Houghton Mifflin.

Kohlberg, L. (1981). *Essays on moral development, Volume I: The philosophy of moral development.* San Francisco, CA: Harper & Row.

Kohlberg, L. (1984). *Essays on moral development, Volume II: The psychology of moral development.* San Francisco, CA: Harper & Row.

Lyons, N. (1983). Two perspectives: On self, relationship, and morality. *Harvard Educational Review, 53,* 125–145.

Miller, J. (1976). *Toward a new psychology of women.* Boston, MA: Beacon Press.

Murphy, J. M., & Gilligan, C. (1980). Moral development in late adolescence and adulthood: A critique and reconstruction of Kohlberg's theory. *Human Development, 23,* 77–104.

Piaget, J. (1965). *The moral judgment of the child.* New York: The Free Press. (Original work published 1932.)

Rogers, A. (1988). *The question of gender differences: A validity study of two moral orientations.* Unpublished manuscript, Harvard University, Cambridge, MA.

Tappan, M. (1990). Hermeneutics and moral development: Interpreting narrative representations of moral experience. *Developmental Review, 10,* 239–265.

Tappan, M. (1991). Narrative, authorship, and the development of moral authority. In M. Tappan & M. Packer (Eds.), *Narrative and storytelling: Implications for understanding moral development* (New directions for child development, No. 54). San Francisco, CA: Jossey-Bass.

Tappan, M. (1992). Texts and contexts: Language, culture, and the development of moral functioning. In L. T. Winegar & J. Valsiner (Eds.), *Children's development within social contexts: Metatheoretical, theoretical, and methodological issues.* Hillsdale, NJ: Lawrence Erlbaum.

Wertsch, J. (1991). *Voices of the mind: A sociocultural approach to mediated action.* Cambridge, MA: Harvard University Press.

White, S. (1983). The idea of development in developmental psychology. In R. Lerner (Ed.), *Developmental psychology: Historical and philosophical perspectives.* Hillsdale, NJ: Lawrence Erlbaum.

Response to Tappan: "Relational Voices and Moral Development: Reflections on Change"

Carol Gilligan
Harvard University

My brief response to Mark Tappan's interesting and provocative chapter on relational voices, human development, and teacher change picks up two interrelated issues: the concept of moral orientation as a way of understanding Chris's decision to send Clarence to the Alpha class, and the fact that Chris is a woman.

My research began with an interest in the sense of self and the ways people respond to conflicts in their lives. My approach was that of a naturalist—to listen to people's voices—and in listening, I heard a difference between the ways women speak of "self" and of living in relationship with others and the ways psychologists in the past have spoken about the self and about psychological development. Women's voices brought a different voice into psychological theories, changing the conception of self and also reopening the question of what it is to be human. Against the backdrop of a psychology that had stressed separation and individuation, autonomy and independence, women's voices spoke of the relational nature of human living—that we live and grow in connection with others, that we are interdependent. Moral problems for women typically arise in situations where it seems impossible to act without breaking connections; in the face of relational conflicts, women frequently seek ways of maintaining and strengthening connection—in part because the experience of connection is so fundamental to women's sense of self. To change relationships is to change the experience of self, and conversely, psychological development or a change in the experience of oneself changes relationships or one's way of living with other people. Self and relationship are, in this sense, fundamentally and paradoxically interwoven.

I say this as an introduction to responding more specifically to Mark Tappan's way of understanding Chris Zajac's actions and his bringing of the concept of moral orientation to the interpretation of the change in her response to Clarence. To speak of moral orientation or the framework Chris uses in approaching the question of how she should live and act is to talk about Chris's worldview, and Tappan implies that she changes her view of the world from a care orientation to a justice approach—that she moves from acting in relation to Clarence to separating herself from him. This interpretation implies a division between self and relationship, which I would like to question in offering a different way—that is, a relational approach—of under- standing and speaking about Chris Zajac.

What seems most important to Chris Zajac in thinking about what to do in her relationship with Clarence is not the distinction between justice and care, but rather the question of how or whether she can stay with Clarence and also be with the other children in her class. Chris's change of mind and heart occurs in the context of this web of relationships. And it is in this context that she acts both in wanting Clarence to stay in her class and in deciding that he should leave. It is Chris's changing experience of herself in relationship that leads her to change her mind about Clarence and come to a different understanding of how she can best care in this difficult situation.

Chris's responses to the conflict she faces resonate strongly with the responses of other women to similar relational problems. The change in Chris corresponds to a major shift in the lives of many women. She moves from an understanding of relationship, confused by the conven- tions of female virtue that equate goodness with self-abnegation or self-sacrifice, to a clarification of relationship as connection between self and other. Key to this process is the realization at some level that silencing oneself breaks rather than makes connection between oneself and others. Since the psyche or self grows in authentic relationship, Chris's bringing herself into relationship with Clarence and the problem he poses in her class sets into motion a process of growth that challenges her experience of herself as a teacher. Can she want Clarence to leave her class and continue to think of herself as a good teacher, or does being a good teacher mean sacrificing her voice in relationships?

Chris begins her relationship with her class in September by trying to become the angel in the house—the person who is always there for other people. She listens empathetically to all of her students and tries to be as careful and loving as she can in responding to them. In doing so, however, she shows a readiness and also a willingness to silence herself and turn a deaf ear to the voice that tells her that what she is trying to do is impossible. She wants to be a good teacher to Clarence and help him develop in the face of serious problems; she also wants to be a good teacher and encourage the development of her other students.

Over time, this desire to be responsive or empathic with the needs of all of her students brings Chris to the point of exhaustion, and in response to her sense that what she is attempting is not working, she begins to change. Aware of feelings and thoughts that are at odds with her sense of herself as a good teacher, she questions what being a good teacher means. This struggle is articulated in the final paragraph of the passage that Mark quotes at the beginning of his chapter:

> She had one aweful, sinking fear. Had she wanted, deep down, to get rid of Clarence? She hadn't acted on that desire, but had she felt it? ''I don't want to get rid of him. I don't!'' she told Paul, the sympathetic vice principal, later. ''I mean''—she looked up at Paul—''I do and I don't.'' (Kidder, 1989, p. 167).

When a woman can feel and respond to her own feelings and thoughts and also stay in connection with others, she is in authentic relationship—in touch with herself and also with others. To act from this position of truth, however, means to forego idealized images of relationships and of women—images of relationships as involving self-sacrifice rather than self-development and images of women as selfless, as without voice or agency in their care. For Chris to act in the way that she does is to risk her sense of herself as a good woman and a good teacher. At the same time, it also suggests a change in her sense of self and in her understanding of what good teaching means: a willingness to listen more fully to her own voice in relationships and also a deepening appreciation of the relational conflicts that are an inescapable part of teaching.

My response to Chris Zajac's actions thus differs from the interpretation offered by Mark Tappan. Mark suggests that Chris' change of mind and heart occurs as she gives up the moral language of care (which, in this reading, is a language of selflessness in relationship) and takes up the dominant social and moral language of justice, thus justifying the exclusion of Clarence. In my reading, Chris is coming to a more authentic understanding of relationship and rejecting conventions of relationship that have impeded her ability to speak in relationship and to be a good teacher. Rather than seeing Chris as capitulating to a rights or justice orientation and giving up her caring voice, I see her concerns with justice as a way of correcting an understanding of care that excluded, rather than included, herself. To include herself and also her students in the compass of her empathy and care means to know what she knows and also to face the difficult choices that are inherent in her situation, given the presence of Clarence in her class and the absence of other resources. Within a relational framework and within a culture that both idealizes women and devalues women, Chris's act is an act of resistance and courage rather than an act of capitulation (see Brown & Gilligan, 1992; Gilligan, 1990; Rogers, 1990).

In his chapter, Mark Tappan integrates my previous work and that of my colleagues on the relational voices of justice and care with his recent work on language and culture. His perspective on teacher change leads in a positive direction away from the overly individualistic focus on the teacher as an isolated individual to a view of the teacher as embedded in a web of relationships—not only in the classroom but also in the world at large. To replace a view of the self as living and growing in separation with a representation of the self as developing in and through connection leads us to consider more fully the relational worlds in which Chris Zajac is living and functioning as a teacher. The act of teaching is an act with profound moral and political, as well as personal, consequences. Teachers are inescapably involved with questions that are central to the development of societies and cultures: What is worth learning and knowing; what is worth changing or preserving?

For women who are teachers, it is both essential and ultimately risky to maintain their voices in relationship and thus to be in authentic connection with themselves, their students and their work. Chris Zajac, in facing honestly a difficult relational problem in her classroom, moves to a deeper understanding of the psychological conflicts and the real choices involved in good teaching.

REFERENCES

Brown, L., & Gilligan, C. (1992). *Meeting at the crossroads: Women's psychology and girls' development.* Cambridge, MA: Harvard University Press.

Gilligan, C. (1990). Joining the resistance: Psychology, politics, girls and women. *Michigan Quarterly Review, 29,* 501–536.

Kidder, T. (1989). *Among schoolchildren.* Boston, MA: Houghton Mifflin.

Rogers, A. (1990). *The development of courage in girls and women.* Unpublished manuscript, Harvard University, Project on the Psychology of Women and the Development of Girls, Cambridge, MA.

2

Sex Stereotypes, Social Rules, and Education: Changing Teachers and Teaching Change*

Linda A. M. Perry
The University of San Diego

On the first day of class in my Gender studies course, most students tell me that inequality based on sex differences is long past, that they all have equal opportunities for educational success, and that each can have a career and a family because both spouses will equally contribute at home. I hate to be the bearer of bad news, but it just isn't so. Our behavioral choices continue to be limited by sex stereotypes—how males and females are "supposed" to be and behave. Expectations, based on those stereotypes, consist of behaviors, attitudes, and beliefs one is expected to hold and exhibit *because* he is male, or *because* she is female.

Sex stereotypes limit equal educational opportunities for females and males. Teachers and educational institutions have an opportunity to participate in changing these stereotypes and the resultant expectations. Change, however, is difficult because we, as teachers, often don't recognize that we behave in ways that do not foster equal educational opportunities for females and males.

Sadker and Sadker (1985) note, "When we told teachers about our findings [that males and females do not receive equal opportunities in the classroom], they would often dismiss them by saying, 'Maybe other teachers do that—but I don't. I'm fair to all my students' " (p. 30). Only when the teachers were shown videotapes of themselves teaching were

_____

The author thanks the following people for reading earlier drafts of this essay and providing invaluable feedback: Cynthia Caywood, Matthew Parrish, and Heather Nichols.

they able to recognize that their treatment of male and female students was inequitable. Before teachers can change, they must be aware of their inadvertent discriminatory behaviors.

In order to aid in that awareness, sex stereotype problems in two areas are delineated in the first section of this chapter: in the educational climate and in educational content. Next, to demonstrate the complexity of altering sex stereotypes, tenets of General Systems Theory are used to explain how change circulates between educational institutions and the cultures in which they reside. Finally, suggestions for bringing about change on campus and in the classroom are presented. These suggestions include day-to-day changes teachers can make to help create sex-equitable educational environments.

THE EDUCATIONAL CLIMATE

No person in the United States shall, on the basis of sex, be excluded from participation in, be denied the benefits of, or be subjected to discrimination under any education program or activity receiving federal financial assistance. (Title IX of the 1972 Education Amendments)

The educational climate can be described as "the social/ psychological context within which the teacher and student interact and form their relationship" (Rosenfeld & Jarrard, 1985, p. 205). The educational climate, however, does not appear to be the same for females and males.

Although the rationale for the education of women has changed since the 1950s when women were educated in order to be better wives and mothers (Hill, 1986), some underlying attitudes remain. Brown (1990) explains that although many people believe that males and females receive an equal education, this is not so. It is still a "chilly" educational climate for females on campuses and in classrooms (Hall & Sandler, 1982, 1984; Sandler, 1991).

Campus Climate

Hall and Sandler (1984) researched student experience on college campuses. They found that in most areas of education, males made out better than females. These areas include: admissions and financial aid (males were admitted more often and received better financial aid); academic advising and career counseling (males received more and better advice and counseling); projects with other students and faculty (males were selected more than females); lab and field work (males received more opportunities); work study and campus employment (males received more desirable jobs); internships (males were preferred over females); health care (males received better health care); campus safety (male complaints were taken more seriously); residential, social, and cultural life (males had more freedom and more choices); athletics (males received more scholarships and recognition); and student government (males were seen as better leaders and so received more opportunities).

Females and males do not have the same educational experiences even when they attend the same schools. Hall and Sandler (1984) explain that, "Indeed, though faculty, staff and students of both sexes want to be fair, and believe they are, sex-based expectations, roles and "rules" often determine how students are actually treated" (p. 2). Besides campus climate problems, classroom climate limitations also affect students' educational experiences.

Classroom Climate

Discrimination against females occurs at all levels of education. Spender (1981) highlights the problem by noting that "Educational theories from student dissatisfaction to curriculum innovation usually render women invisible . . . [and] educational practices from the organisation [sic] of institutions, to classroom interaction usually help to exclude women" (p. 157). Hall and Sandler (1982) found that females in grade schools, as compared to males, are talked to less by their teachers, not asked "higher order" questions, shown rather than instructed on how to accomplish a task, spoken to only when in close proximity of the teacher (boys' locations do not affect the amount of attention they receive), and praised for the form and neatness of their work more than for its intellectual quality.

Brown (1990), who studied sex stereotypes in high schools, explains that a fear was created in the early part of this century that a liberal arts education for females would cause males to lose respect for education and/or cause females to become masculine. This fear set the foundation for the education of women throughout the century at all levels of education. Contemporary high schools still do not offer balanced opportunities for females and males. Much of the discrimination that occurs is through misdirection of classroom activities and misappropriation of classroom materials, both of which will be discussed later in this chapter.

Hall and Sandler (1982) provide a list of ways in which female students are treated differentially (in a particular way *because* they are female) in college classrooms. Female students are treated by male professors as sexual beings less capable and less serious than men, discouraged from classroom participation, counseled away from math and science courses and majors, subjected to their work being devalued when it equals their male counterparts' work, called "gals" or "girls" while the males are called "men", given less eye contact than males, given less positive nonverbal feedback than men, and called by their names less often than men. Most problematic, Dziech and Weiner (1984) found that 30% of female students were sexually harassed—that is, expected to tolerate sexual advances by professors.

All of the above examples suggest that female students are not expected to achieve as well as male students do. The problem, however, is not isolated to female students; female faculty also encounter more negative classroom experiences than do their male counterparts.

In her article, "Women Faculty at Work in the Classroom, or, Why It Still Hurts to Be a Woman in Labor," Sandler (1991) highlights the ways in which female faculty are treated differentially by students. Sandler notes that female faculty are expected to be more personal and supportive, evaluated as less available even when they spend more time with students than male faculty, asked more questions about their credentials, scrutinized more, rated more harshly, interrupted by male students more than are male faculty, recipients of more negative nonverbal feedback (scowls and frowns), and evaluated on personality factors more than are men. They are considered successful because of luck or affirmative action rather than talent, intelligence, or hard work; more likely to be called "Miss," "Ms.," or "Mrs." rather than "Professor"; evaluated by their clothing or physical appearance; and treated as sex objects by their male students.

Females experience greater sex stereotype and expectation problems than do males. However, males' classroom experiences are also limited. Males are steered away from humanistic studies in favor of math and science, expected to achieve sometimes beyond their abilities, limited in their perception of females based on their observations of females' experience (that is, they treat females in sexist ways because that is the way they see females being treated), provided role models that facilitate external (career) success but do not facilitate internal (emotional) success, held more responsible for the state of the political and environmental world, and are caught under the pressure always to preserve their masculinity (Hall & Sandler, 1982; Sadker & Sadker, 1985; Pearson, Turner, & Todd-Mancillas, 1991).

Changes in the campus and classroom climates are needed to provide equal educational opportunities for females and males. As teachers begin to treat male and female students equitably, students will more likely have educations based on their abilities and not on sex stereotypes and expectations. If students have equal opportunities to learn they will, hopefully, also have equal opportunities to succeed. For such opportunities to occur, problems in educational content also must be addressed.

EDUCATIONAL CONTENT

Educational content, including classroom activities and materials, influences students both explicitly and implicitly. Students receive explicit messages in which they are told to behave in prescribed ways that differentiate them from those of the opposite sex. Students also receive implicit messages that determine their place in school and society. Pearson and West (1991) state that "Students may learn more about power relationships than subject matter in their interactions with teachers in the classroom. . . . Countless studies show that when women and men engage in identical behavior, the behavior is devalued for women" (p. 24). The following look at classroom activities and materials will provide a better understanding of the ways in which teachers send explicit and implicit messages that prescribe sex-based behaviors for students.

Classroom Activities

Two primary areas of classroom activities are included here to expose the ways in which males and females are treated differently in the classroom. These are (1) sex-segregating students and (2) sex-typing courses. Sex-segregating students means separating males from females in activities. Sex-typing courses means perceiving certain academic subjects as more appropriate for one sex than for the other sex.

Sex-segregating female from male students sends implicit messages to students about where they "fit" in the educational process, that is, what the students are allowed to do and be, based on their biological sex. Pearson (1985) provides an excellent example:

> When my 13-year-old daughter was in first grade, she and her classmates were asked to line up for lunch. The teacher commanded, "Boys on this side and girls on the other side." Because Kate had grown up in a home where boys and girls were not separated on the basis of their genitalia, she was surprised. Because she had grown up in a home where people were verbal, she asked the teacher, "Why not blacks and whites? Why not fats and thins? Why not short people and tall people?" To the first grade

teacher who had always divided her children up on the basis of their biological sex, her practice seemed innocuous. To a six-year-old who had some awareness of sexism, the requirement was obnoxious. (p. 3)

Sadker and Sadker (1985) did a three-year study of over 100 elementary classrooms. One outcome of sex-segregation they found was "that teachers would be drawn to the more assertive boys' sections of the classroom where they would get involved in extended interaction. The girls' section was 'invisible' and ignored" (p. 31). Hall and Sandler (1982) generalize that the outcome of the separation is that females receive less attention and males become more competitive. In the process, added attention to boys results in better opportunities for them to learn—opportunities girls do not receive. Thus, sex stereotypes become implicitly endorsed: boys will be boys, girls will be quiet. Compounding that endorsement is the sex-typing of courses.

Sex-typing courses perpetuates sex stereotypes. In this case, some academic subjects are thought to be most appropriate for females and other subjects most appropriate for males. Interest and ability in diverse subjects do not become the property of one sex over the other until children become socialized to move toward or away from academic areas based on their sex. Sadker and Sadker (1985) note the following effects of sex-typing courses:

- Although girls start out with an educational advantage, their scores on achievement tests decline as they "progress" through school. In contrast, boys' scores rise and eventually surpass those of girls, particularly in the areas of math, science, and technology.
- There are twice as many boys as girls in computer science courses, which lead to careers in programming and systems analysis. However, in business education courses, where computer training in word processing and data processing is designed to train students for lower paying clerical and secretarial positions, there are twice as many girls.

Belenky, Clinchy, Goldberger, and Tarule (1986) explain that the problem of sex-typing courses is greatest in science. While females are pushed away from math and science and toward social sciences and humanities, the opposite is true for males (Klein, 1985; Einerson, 1989). Everybody loses when decisions about course selection are based on sex stereotypes rather than personal interest and/or abilities. Further complicating this problem is the selection of classroom materials.

Classroom Materials

Two choices made by teachers create additional barriers to equal education for females and males: (1) textbooks and other classroom materials, and (2) language use. These choices indicate teachers' sex-based expectations.

Textbooks and other classroom materials send implicit messages to students about their roles in the classroom and in society. For example, Scott and Schau (1985, p. 218) explain that there needs to be a great concern about selection of classroom materials because classroom materials "have tremendous potential to influence children. And they do." What are some characteristics of classroom materials that are not sex equitable?

Whether we look at pictorial representations of females and males (more males pictured than are females; males portrayed as active, females as passive or as observers; males portrayed engaged in professional roles, females in domestic roles), or at the discussions about male and female activity (males are discussed more positively and more often but are seldom portrayed as sensitive to others), we recognize that neither sex is provided well-rounded representations of what it means to be male or female (Pearson, 1985; Stewart, Stewart, Friedley, & Cooper, 1990). It appears that the majority of textbooks reflect sex biases. Sometimes, females are hardly represented at all (do women have a history?) or are misrepresented (are there no kind, loving stepmothers?) (Sitt, 1988). Males, on the other hand, are not represented in a variety of roles, either. For example, males are seldom pictured as caretakers, affectionate parents, or in nontraditional roles such as secretaries and nurses.

An equitable representation of females and males would go a long way toward creating positive role models for boys and girls, and would allow students to make choices based on their skills and aptitudes rather than their biological sex. The outcome could resonate throughout the educational system and the culture at large. Besides offering more equitable representations of females and males in textbooks, nonsexist language choices need to be adopted by teachers.

Sexist language use excludes females in many ways. Webb (1986) defines sexist language as "gender-specific terms that may be interpreted as either generic or gender specific and language forms that convey derogatory or stereotyped images of males or females" (p. 22). Sexist language includes using generic pronouns ("he," "him," "his") in reference to members of a group that includes males and females, and using "man" independently or as a suffix or prefix as applicable to both sexes.

Language shapes our reality (Whorf, 1956). Among other problems, sexist language distorts perceptions of reality, produces images and knowledge that are masculine, and excludes female experience (Scott and Schau, 1985; Kramarae, 1980, 1981). Because men have been the primary shapers of language in Western society, women's experiences are not represented. If females are not included in the language, they become "invisible" and muted (Kramarae, 1981). Women are silenced when they attempt to describe their lives in a language that does not represent their life experiences.

When the generic "he" is used, most readers perceive a male actor rather than a female one (Cole, Hill, & Dayley, 1983). Miller and Swift (1988) explain that during language evolution, the truly generic term "man" (referring to females and males) came to refer specifically to males. Once that happened, "man" should no longer have continued to be considered generic.

Frank and Anshen (1983) contend that sexist language and generic language affect the ways females and males perceive themselves and their roles. Describing what most often takes place in the classroom, Stewart, et al. (1990) put it very well:

> Teachers may inadvertently communicate sex-role stereotypes by their use of sexist language. For example, when a teacher asks, "Why were the fathers of our country so concerned about religious freedom?" or "If a lawyer knows his client is guilty, what should he do?", the teacher may communicate that males have been more important throughout history or that all lawyers are male. Teacher expectations can be a powerful force in the classroom because they can affect a student's sense of intellectual and personal worth. (p. 158)

Because they are creators and teachers of cultural norms such as sex stereotypes, classroom educators would do well to select classroom materials and language choices that equally represent males and females. Change, however, is often difficult and slow. And, because cultural change is dynamic rather than linear, examination of it is arduous. General Systems Theory, however, provides a format that might be helpful for examining the dynamic nature of educational and cultural change.

GENERAL SYSTEMS THEORY

Bertalanfy (1968) defines General Systems Theory (GST) as "models, principles, and laws that apply to generalized systems or their subclasses, irrespective of their particular kind, the nature of their component elements, and the relations or 'forces' between them'' (p. 32). In this section, I use some basic tenets of GST to examine the creation, recreation, and maintenance of sex stereotypes within culture, and within educational institutions.[1]

Systems and Subsystems

Theorists describe two types of systems—open and closed (Watzlawick, Bavalas & Jackson, 1967). Open systems exchange information with the environment; closed systems do not. In "classical" systems theory, this description is useful. Ludwig von Bertalanfy (1968) and other pioneers of systems theory were primarily concerned with making distinctions between systems that reached entropy (closed systems) and those that maintained a steady state (open systems). Human interactional systems, such as educational institutions, are not so easily defined.

Interactional systems exist somewhere on a continuum between open and closed. The less information there is, and the more difficulty with which information is exchanged between the systems and the environment, the more closed is the system. The more an otherwise open system becomes closed, the more likely it is to become dysfunctional, and the more it becomes dysfunctional, the more it becomes closed.

Educational institutions are regarded as open systems because they exchange information with the environment. As with systems in general, as educational institutions become more closed, they become more dysfunctional. Let me provide an example.[2] A particular grade school teacher was sexually abusing female students. He was in a position of power and used that position to prevent information about his activities to be known outside his classroom. The students did not readily report his behavior because they were afraid. They feared they would not be believed; they feared the teacher would retaliate; some even feared the loss of special attention of an authority figure. Because the exchange of information was limited between the classroom and its environment, the classroom situation became more closed and more dysfunctional.

Each person learns sex-based expectations within a particular culture. Cultural systems consist of subsystems such as families, religious

---

[1]The following does not overview General Systems Theory (GST) in great detail. Rather, GST is used as a tool for teasing out some of the ways change circulates throughout systems and subsystems. I am presenting GST from a social scientific perspective which further limits its application.

[2]This example is based on a recent true-life incident. I am not citing sources in order to limit any further trauma to those involved.

groups, political groups, and educational institutions. A subsystem is a division, or internal unit, that could itself be considered a system. For example, classrooms are independent systems at one level and subsystems of encompassing school systems at another level. Schools, too, are both independent systems and subsystems of encompassing school district systems, and so forth.

Systems and subsystems are symbiotic (Capra, 1982); that is, a system and its subsystems are interdependent. Thus, a change in one part of an open system reverberates throughout the system (Bertalanfy, 1968; Capra, 1982). What happens to and within a particular system (e.g., culture) is reflected in its subsystems (e.g., educational institutions) and vice versa.

The abusive teacher describe above is a good example of how symbiosis works. The classroom situation created change in the students' behaviors and, therefore, affected other classrooms and the students' home lives. Eventually, the teacher's behaviors became public information. The consequences of his behavior created change throughout the system and subsystems: the classroom, the school, and the community in which this school resides. For example, the teacher was fired, prosecuted, and sent to prison; workshops were held for all children attending this school; the abused students received counseling; parents began to visit classrooms unannounced; discussions were held about problems of child abuse; and so forth. Changes in the subsystem (classroom) reverberated throughout the system (school) which, as a subsystem, reverberated throughout the superordinate system (community).

Sex stereotypes are constructed and reconstructed in the reflexive process between culture and its encompassed subsystems. Because schools and the cultures in which they exist are symbiotic, changes in day-to-day behaviors and responses enacted by teachers can filter through the subsystem (school) and system (culture) to create change in sex stereotypes and the resultant expectations.

Rules and Meta-rules[3]

Change requires flexibility (Capra, 1982). Unfortunately, most educational institutions are not very flexible. Rules are needed in schools to

---

[3]Rules and meta-rules are not included in GST per se. GST does look at patterns of behavior and relationship rules, however. Patterns of behavior are those behaviors repeated over time. Any pattern repeated over time can develop into a normative rule. Relationship rules define what is acceptable and unacceptable behavior within a relationship. Cultural patterns of behavior and those relationships (both professional and personal) that develop in cultural systems are bound by certain expectations, or rules.

control behavior and provide guidelines. Teachers and students are expected to follow behavioral rules in order for teachers to teach and students to learn. Some of these rules include behavioral expectations based on the biological sex of teachers and students. Usually, neither teachers nor students realize they are following sex stereotype rules. Instead, they believe they are behaving according to innately determined behaviors for females and males. Social rules are confused with laws of nature. To clarify, let's look at how rules work.

There are three basic types: spoken objective rules, unspoken rules, and meta-rules (rules about rules) (Laing, 1972; Stair, 1972). Spoken objective rules are those that are explicitly stated. For example, a classroom rule might be "Do not call out answers without raising your hand." An unspoken rule might be as mundane as "Everyone will come to school with clothes on." Meta-rules are rules that instruct us about the rules. One meta-rule is "Don't recognize that a rule exists." An example of a meta-rule follows:

A little boy who has fallen and skinned his knee receives the spoken rule, "Don't cry, act like a man." The rule about the rule (meta-rule) is, "Don't question the spoken rule because it is based on laws of nature—it's the way males are." The problem is that the meta-rule is not based on nature but on nurture—it is a rule based on the male sex stereotype.

Sex stereotype behaviors are the outcome of biological *and* sociological processes. Studies show, however, that socialization plays a greater role in forming these stereotypes than does biology (Maccoby & Jacklin, 1974; Klein, 1985; Schau & Tittle, 1985). Socialization means that people learn to behave a certain way (according to sex stereotypes, for example) and to expect certain behaviors (sex-based expectations, for example). Sex stereotypes generate rules and meta-rules for behavior based on one's biological sex. These rules and meta-rules then create sex-based expectations. Unfortunately, social rules become obscured as biological mandates.

In reality, however, male and female behaviors are not so different. When "male" and "female" behaviors are mapped out on overlapping spheres, most behaviors overlap (See Figure 2.1). Distinctly female or male behaviors are biologically based functions such as lactation and sperm production. Most other behaviors appear to be culturally determined. In fact, there is more behavior variance within sex groups (females *or* males) than there is across sex groups (males *and* females) (Brown, 1989).

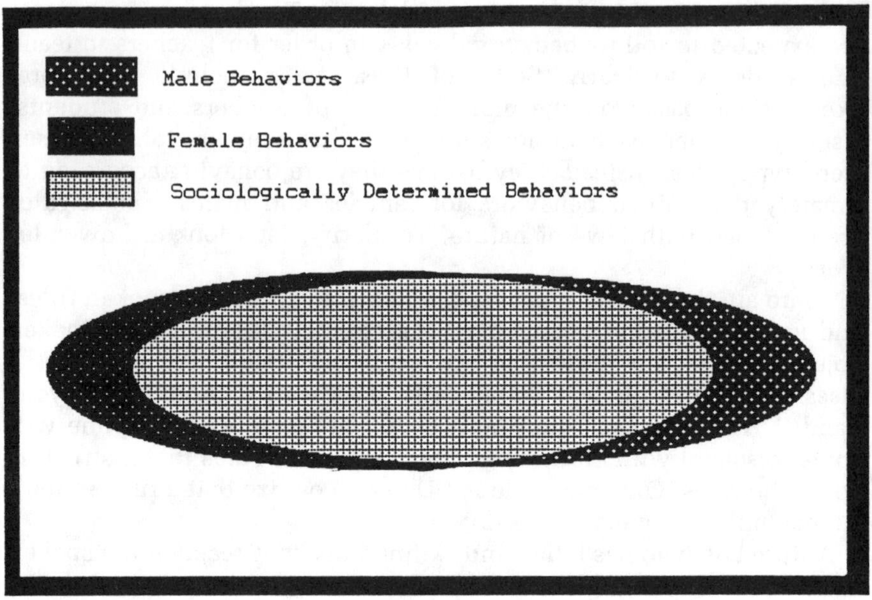

Figure 2.1.

Biologically based behaviors do not include determination to succeed, nurturance, intelligence, kindness, seriousness, or any other behaviors that affect learning and education. Nonetheless, females and males are treated differently in our educational systems and in the culture at large. So,

> regardless of the best intentions and well-stated philosophies of education, behaviors are based on deep-rooted assumptions that differentiate between the appropriate behaviors, roles, and jobs for women and men. These assumptions may not even be conscious but they result in subtle differences in the way we treat people—what we expect from them, how we think they should act, what we think they should look like, and how we think they should respond to us. (Sitt, 1988, p. xiv)

Because behavioral repertoires of females and males are created sociologically more than biologically, there is a greater chance that sex stereotypes can be changed. However, changing behaviors is difficult because first we have to recognize that rules and meta-rules exist, and then we have to realize that changing the rules might create instability. This raises the question, "What is the relationship between stability and change?"

Stability and Change

In the midst of needed change there is a mutual need for stability. Open systems seek stability for survival (Bertalanfy, 1968). Stability, however, is not static. That is, the general definition of a system may remain stable while internal changes occur. A biological example provided by Capra (1982) will clarify this point. Every seven years or so, every cell in our bodies is replaced. We have no problems, however, in still recognizing each other. Although we may show signs of aging (change) our appearance is similar to what it was seven years earlier (stability). Stability is achieved *through* fluctuations (changes) in the system and not through static adherence to its initial state (Bateson, 1972). Educational institutions (open systems) can remain stable even as the needed changes occur.

There is a sensitive balance between the mutual needs for stability and change. Too little change creates rigidity; too much change creates chaos. Overreliance on sex stereotypes limits an individual's opportunities, but overturning them might create too much instability for that person. To the extent that sex stereotypes limit the individual's choices, they need to be changed; to the extent they give the individual stability, they need to remain the same.

Change is needed in educational institutions to overcome limitations created by sex stereotypes. Such limitations can be overcome because educational institutions are open systems and open systems are capable of transcendence, or "the ability to reach out creatively beyond physical and mental boundaries in the process of learning, development, and evolution" (Capra, 1982, p. 269). When discussing the needed changes in sex stereotypes, Sadker and Sadker (1982) emphasize that

> change seldom comes easy or fast. There are few quick and dirty tricks that will break down the barriers that have existed for centuries. Identifying the problem is only the first step. In many ways, it is the easiest step to take. The real opportunity belongs to the teachers. (p. 5)

While it is suggested that teachers have an opportunity to bring about change in sex-based expectations, it is recognized that they are not the sole holders of this responsibility. However, teachers play a major role as change agents because they are members of educational institutions and the culture at large; they control classroom activities and select classroom materials; and they decide whether or not to use sexist language. To help teachers make changes in day-to-day behaviors, the following section offers suggestions for everyday change in educational climate and content.

SUGGESTIONS FOR EDUCATIONAL CLIMATE CHANGE[4]

The educational climate includes campus and classroom problems. By making the following changes, these climates can be improved.

Changes in Campus Climate

- Provide academic and career counseling that inspires students to select nontraditional paths.
- Organize a committee to address issues of sex stereotypes and expectations. Have them investigate the extent of the problem on your campus.
- Provide sex sensitivity courses and programs for faculty, teaching assistants, administrators, and staff.
- Develop strategies to enlighten faculty, teaching assistants, administrators and staff about their own sex stereotypes.
- Seek funds that will help support campus changes.
- Present programs to teach students, faculty, teaching assistants, administration and staff methods for broadening sex stereotypes and expectations.
- Create an ongoing review of school policies and activities to insure sex fairness.
- Include knowledge about sex stereotypes and expectations criteria for hiring at all levels including administration, staff, and faculty.
- Encourage journalist and broadcast media to provide equal coverage of female and male campus events.
- Use campus newspapers and other media to create awareness.
- Issue a conflict of interest statement against sexual relationships between faculty and students.
- Include policies on sex stereotyping and expectations in school bulletins, faculty handbooks, and student materials.

---

[4]Some of these suggestions can be found in a number of sources, others in only one source, and still others come from my own experiences. For that reason, I list all sources here rather than cite them in the text. Those readers who would like more extended information on what can be done to bring about changes in sex-based educational limitations, please refer to the following references: Borisoff & Merrill, 1985; Bowker & Dunkin, 1992; Chickering & Gamson, 1987; DeFrancisco, 1990; Dumond, 1990; Frank & Anshen, 1983; Gilligan, 1982; Lockheed & Klein, 1985; Pearson, 1985; Peterson, 1991; Rosenfeld, 1983; Sadker & Sadker, 1985; Sandler & Hall, 1982; Sandler & Hall, 1985; Sitt, 1988; Stewart et al., 1990; Webb, 1986; and Wood & Lenze, 1991.

Many of the above sources were gathered with the help of an annotated bibliography created by Anita Taylor (1991). I thank her for permission to use that list. I also thank Jill Nakamura and Anastasia Hyll, both of whom helped gather these and additional sources.

- Create a clear sexual harassment policy that is distributed to all members of the educational institution.
- Support exhibits that deal with sex stereotyping.
- Distribute flyers that help campus members become more aware of their language and behavior.
- Fund speakers and programs dealing with problems resulting from sex-based expectations.
- Invite speakers who represent nontraditional career and personal choices.
- Evaluate residential facilities and policies to ensure they are equal for females and males.
- Evaluate on-campus groups such as clubs, fraternities, and sororities for sex stereotyping.
- Create and/or support a Gender Studies, Women Studies, and/or Men Studies program.
- Provide training programs to help females take more leadership roles on campus.
- Provide encouragement for the hiring of males in support services such as nurses and secretaries.
- Participate in research on sex stereotypes and roles.
- Evaluate course curricula across campus to ensure a balanced representation of male and female issues.

The campus and the classrooms it contains are interconnected as system and subsystems. Changes to the campus will, therefore, trickle into classrooms. Changes in classrooms will help speed up the process while filtering other changes back onto the campus. Suggestions for changes in the classroom climate follow.

Changes in Classroom Climate

- Encourage equal participation by all students.
- Assign classroom tasks nontraditionally (males asked to be class secretaries, females asked to move furniture).
- Invite speakers to your classroom who represent groups concerned with sex-bias issues.
- Invite both males and females to participate as research, teaching and/or lab assistants.
- Recognize that the teacher is a role model and should behave accordingly.
- Show flexibility about sex-based expectations.
- Provide guidelines against sex stereotyping on the first day of class or in the syllabus.

- Offer in-class observations of teachers to provide feedback about their sensitivity to sex stereotypes.
- Invite a colleague to attend your class to evaluate your sensitivity to sex stereotype issues.
- Offer students opportunities to give feedback about your role as a facilitator for change.
- Include items about sex fairness on your teaching evaluation if such items are not already included.
- Create role-playing activities that allow sex stereotypes to be discussed.
- Develop strategies to recruit and retain underrepresented groups in sex-typed majors.
- Include an introductory course that teaches about sex stereotyping and expectations.

Changes in campus and classroom climates will promote changes in sex stereotypes and expectations. Additional changes need to be made in educational content to facilitate reaching that goal.

SUGGESTIONS FOR EDUCATIONAL CONTENT CHANGE

Educational content solutions are delineated in two areas: classroom activities and classroom materials. Suggestions for changes in the sex-segregating of students, sex-typing of courses, selection of classroom materials, and language choices are presented in the following sections.

Changes in Classroom Activities

Suggestions for eliminating *sex-segregating:*

- Encourage female students to take leadership roles in classrooms.
- Encourage male students to take supportive roles in classrooms.
- Reinforce nontraditional play.
- Offer opportunities for open discussion of sex stereotyping and expectation issues.
- Discontinue sex-segregating of students.
- Develop strategies for dismissing myths about sex-typed activities.
- Assign seating so that students do not sex-segregate themselves.

Suggestions for altering *sex-typing of courses:*

- Encourage female students in math and science areas.
- Ask female students questions that require critical thinking as well as factual information.
- Allow female students opportunities to improve answers.
- Become familiar with literature on sex stereotypes and expectations so you can include these issues in other topics.
- Discover the contributions of minority members to the topic under discussion. (Include women in history and science, for example.)
- Instruct rather than assist female students in completing tasks.
- Encourage nontraditional career choices.

Changes in Classroom Materials

Suggestions for improving *textbooks and classroom materials:*

- Screen all written materials for sexist language.
- Select textbooks and other classroom materials that portray people in nontraditional roles.
- Select textbooks and other classroom materials that use non-sexist language.
- When textbooks and materials are used that contain sexist portrayals or language, point it out and discuss the inherent problems.
- Use classroom textbooks and materials written and/or created by females.
- Critique student writing regarding sex stereotypes.

Suggestions for ending *sexist language use:*

- Avoid special categories for females and males in nontraditional careers (avoid "female" doctor, "male" nurse) when teaching.
- Intervene when students rely on sex stereotypes or use sexist language.
- Minimize clichés such as "boys will be boys," and "act like a lady."
- Provide equal nonverbal attention to males and females (equal eye-contact, facial expressions, etc.)
- Use the same vocal tone with females and males.

- Vary use between female and male pronouns when teaching or use plural pronouns.
- Use equivalent terms for males and females. Use "boys and girls," "gals and guys," "men and women"; do not use "men and girls," "men and ladies," or "men and gals."
- Use examples in your teaching that include equal numbers of males and females.
- Use language that does not categorize all people as men. Replace words ending with "man" with words ending with "person"; replace the use of "man" with a word such as "people." Use "police officer" rather than "policeman," "fire fighter" rather than "fireman," etc.
- Refer to women as "Ms." instead of "Miss" or "Mrs."
- Refer to women professionals by their title such as "Dr." or "Professor" rather than "Mrs. so and so" or "Janie," especially if these titles are juxtaposed to referring to men as "Dr." or "Professor."

Teachers and others involved in education can choose to make changes in campus and classroom climates, and in classroom activities and materials. By doing so, a change in sex stereotypes and the resulting expectations might occur both within the educational systems and the culture at large—a change that could enhance the probability of equal educations for males and females.

CONCLUSION

Because sex stereotypes affect students' and teachers' experiences in classrooms, on campus, and in society, the need for change in those stereotypes is clear. In seeking change, it is useful to remember that sex stereotypes are sociologically created rather than biologically mandated. Biology does not have to be destiny because it is possible to alter sex stereotypes.

The symbiotic nature of systems (culture) and subsystems (educational institutions) indicates that teachers' choices and behaviors filter throughout the cultures and educational institutions in which they reside. Therefore, as teachers' choices and behaviors become more nonsexist, sex stereotypes and expectations will change.

Borisoff and Merrill (1985) note that because of changing social roles (women pursuing careers and men sharing more equally the responsibilities of the home), "both sexes are required to demonstrate communicative behavior that previously belonged to the opposite sex" (p. 1).

It is most important that the definition of sex stereotypes changes along with alterations in social role expectations.

It is hoped that teachers and others involved with education will become aware of the effects of sex stereotyping and incorporate the suggestions provided in the final section of this chapter to make changes in their educational behaviors and choices. Not only will these changes provide more equal educational opportunities for female students, male students, and faculty, but they will also affect the quality of life experiences in general. An equal chance to reach one's full potential is available when educational and life experiences are based on abilities and aptitudes rather than on biological sex.

REFERENCES

Bate, B. (1988). *Communication and the sexes.* New York: Harper and Row.

Bateson, G. (1972). *Steps to an ecology of mind.* New York: Ballantine.

Belenky, M. F., Clinchy, B. M., Goldberger, N. R., & Tarule, J. M. (1986). *Women's ways of knowing: The development of self, voice and mind.* New York: Basic Books.

Bertalanfy, L. von (1968). *General systems theory: Foundations, development, applications.* New York: George Braziller.

Borisoff, D., & Merrill, L. (1985). *The power to communicate: Gender differences as barriers.* Prospect Heights, IL: Waveland Press.

Bowker, J. K., & Dunkin, P. R. (1992). Enacting feminism in the teaching of communication. In L. A. M. Perry, L. H. Turner, & H. Sterk (Eds.), *Constructing and reconstructing gender: The links among communication, language, and gender* (pp. 261–268). Albany, NY: State University of New York Press.

Brown, V. B. (1989, October). *Patriarchy and the women's movement.* Guest Lecture, The University of San Diego, San Diego, CA.

Brown, V. B. (1990). The fear of feminization: Los Angeles high schools in the progressive era. *Feminist Studies, 16*(3), 493–526.

Capra, F. (1982). *The turning point: Science, society, and the rising culture.* Toronto: Bantam Books.

Chickering, A. W., & Gamson, Z. F. (1987). Seven principles for good practice in undergraduate education. *The Wingspread Journal/Special Section, 9*(2).

Cole, C., Hill, F., & Dayley, L. (1983). Do masculine pronouns used generically lead to thoughts of men? *Sex Roles, 9,* 737–750.

DeFrancisco, V. L. (1990, October). *Integrating gender issues in the intercultural communication classroom: Moving beyond the "variable" approach.* Paper presented at the Annual Meeting of the Organization for the Study of Communication, Language, and Gender, Reno, NV.

Dumond, V. (1990). *The elements of nonsexist language usage.* New York: Prentice-Hall.

Dziech, B., & Weiner, L. (1984). *The lecherous professor.* Boston, MA: Beacon Press.

Einerson, M. J. (1989, October). *Adapting Gagne's learning theory and expectancies to stereotyped gender differences in the learning process.* Paper presented at the Annual Meeting of the Organization for the Study of Communication, Language, and Gender, Cincinnati, OH.

Frank, F., & Anshen, F. (1983). *Language and the sexes.* Albany, NY: State University of New York Press.

Gilligan, C. (1982). *In a different voice.* Cambridge, MA: Harvard University Press.

Hall, R. M., & Sandler, B. R. (1982). *The classroom climate: A chilly one for women?* Washington, DC: The Project on the Status and Education of Women.

Hall, R. M., & Sandler, B. R. (1984). *Out of the classroom: A chilly campus climate for women?* Washington, DC: The Project on the Status and Education of Women.

Hill, A. O. (1986). *Mother tongue, father time.* Bloomington, IN: Indiana University Press.

Klein, S. S. (Ed.). (1985). *Handbook for achieving sex equity through education.* Baltimore, MD: Johns Hopkins University Press.

Kramarae, C. (1980). Proprietors of language. In S. McConnell-Ginet, R. Borker, & N. Furman (Eds.), *Women and language in literature and society* (pp. 58–68). New York: Praeger.

Kramarae, C. (1981). *Women and men speaking.* Rowley, MA: Newbury House.

Laing, R. D. (1972). *The politics of the family.* New York: Vintage Books.

Lockheed, M., & Klein, S. S. (1985). Sex equity in classroom organization and climate. In S. S. Klein (Ed.), *Handbook for achieving sex equity through education* (pp. 189–217). Baltimore, MD: Johns Hopkins University Press.

Maccoby, E., & Jacklin, C. (1974). *The psychology of sex differences.* Stanford, CA: The Stanford University Press.

Miller, C., & Swift, K. (1988). *The handbook of nonsexist writing: For writers, editors and speakers* (2nd ed.). New York: Harper & Row.

Pearson, J. C. (1985, November). *Gender and communication: Application in the communication classroom.* Paper presented at the Annual Meeting of the Speech Communication Association, Denver, CO.

Pearson, J. C., Turner, L. H., & Todd-Mancillas, W. (1991). *Gender and communication* (2nd ed.). Dubuque, IA: W. C. Brown.

Pearson, J. C., & West, R. (1991). An initial investigation of the effects of gender on student questions in the classroom: Developing a descriptive base. *Communication Education, 40*(1), 22–32.

Peterson, E. E. (1991). Moving toward a gender-balanced curriculum in basic speech communication courses. *Communication Education, 40*(1), 60–72.

Rosenfeld, L. B. (1983). Communication climate and coping mechanisms in the college classroom. *Communication Education, 32,* 167–174.

Rosenfeld, B., & Jarrard, M. W. (1985). The effects of perceived sexism in female and male college professors on students' descriptions of classroom climate. *Communication Education, 34,* 205–213.

Sadker, M. P., & Sadker, D. M. (1982). *Sex equity handbook for schools.* New York. Longman.

Sadker, M. P., & Sadker, D. M. (1985). Sexism in the classroom. *Vocational Education Journal, 60,* 30–33.

Sandler, B. R. (1991). Women faculty at work in the classroom, or, Why it still hurts to be a woman in labor. *Communication Education, 40*(1), 6–15.

Satir, V. (1972). *Peoplemaking.* Palo Alto, CA: Science and Behavior Books.

Schau, C. G., & Tittle, C. K. (1985). Educational equity and sex role development. In S. S. Klein (Ed.), *Handbook for achieving sex equity through education* (pp. 78–90). Baltimore, MD: The Johns Hopkins University Press.

Scott, K. P., & Schau, C. G. (1985). Sex equity and sex bias in instructional materials. In S. S. Klein (Ed.), *Handbook for achieving sex equity through education* (pp. 218–232). Baltimore, MD: The Johns Hopkins University Press.

Sitt, B. A. (1988). *Building gender fairness in schools.* Carbondale, IL: Southern Illinois University Press.

Spender, D. (Ed.). (1981). *Men's studies modified: The impact of feminism on the academic disciplines.* Oxford, UK: Pergamon Press.

Stewart, L. P., Stewart, A. D., Friedley, S. A., & Cooper, P. J. (1990). *Communication between the sexes* (2nd ed.). Scottsdale, AZ: Gorsuch Scarisbrick.

Taylor, A. (1991, October). *Selected, annotated bibliography on nonsexist communication.* Paper presented at the Annual Meeting of the Organization for the Study of Communication, Language, and Gender, Milwaukee, WI.

Title IX of the 1972 Education Amendments, 20, United States Code ß1681.

Watzlawick, P., Bavalas, J., & Jackson, D. (1967). *Pragmatics of human communication: A study of interactional patterns, pathologies, and paradoxes.* New York: W. W. Norton.

Webb, L. (1986, Spring). Eliminating sexist language in the classroom. *Women's Studies in Communication, 9,* 21–29.

Whorf, B. L. (1956). *Language, thought, and reality.* Cambridge, MA: The Massachusetts Institute of Technology Press.

Wood, J. T., & Lenze, L. F. (1991). Strategies to enhance greater sensitivity in communication education. *Communication Education, 40*(1), 16–21.

Response to Perry: "Sex Stereotypes, Social Rules and Education: Changing Teaching and Teaching Change"

Cheris Kramarae
Speech Communication
University of Illinois at Urbana–Champaign

A graduate student talks:

> Every morning I read my Tarot cards, take vitamins and drink herb tea, trying to prepare myself for another day on campus. For me, a Black woman, it's a very hostile place. I stay sane only because every other weekend, I meet with other university women to talk about what the university is trying to do to us, and about alternative ways of thinking and living.

The methods of staying sane may differ. One graduate student told me that she tries to imagine the professors as three-year-olds "when they were still basically good people, before they were 'educated.' " Another keeps track of all the sports and war metaphors she hears in lectures, saying, "It helps me understand why I feel that the campus seems a battleground."

The reasons they feel campuses are inhospitable are very clearly reviewed in Linda Perry's essay. Yet, as her essay states, many undergraduate women say that sexual inequality is a problem of the past. While Women's Studies courses at many universities are constantly oversubscribed (indicating that many students, particularly women, are conscious of problems and seeking information and solutions), many women and men appear to believe that while, once upon a time, life in the U.S. wasn't good for white women and certainly not for women of color, those problems have been worked out. If indeed that educational climate is as nasty as Perry's essay describes, why isn't every woman student observing the problems? To address that question, in this response I briefly consider the reasons some undergraduates believe that inequality based on sex differences is a thing of the past, some limitations of General Systems Theory for discussing classroom interaction, and some challenges addressed by ecofeminism.

DELAYED AWARENESS

I think about my own educating experiences in college. As an undergraduate I worked hard, followed assignments, and was rewarded with good grades. Since I had learned in high school I was not good at math, I did not feel "coerced" first into nursing training and later into journalism and communication (while my brothers, who learned that they were good at math, followed our father into electrical engineering courses and careers). It seemed clear to me, as an undergraduate, that traditional boundaries would not restrict me, or any other "good" student, in any basic ways. Then, the week of graduation, I had my first job interview. The department head had been asked by the publisher of a daily newspaper to send his best midyear graduate for an interview. A city editor had just been fired and the publisher didn't have time to do a lengthy search; they needed someone immediately. Since I had the best record of the few midyear graduates, I was advised by the department head to send off my vita, and then to appear a few days later for an interview. I told the receptionist my name. She went into the publisher's office and returned. I waited. And waited. When I was finally asked into the office, the editor and the publisher said that they might as well tell me why I had had to wait. They had no idea that a woman (well, the editor said "girl") would arrive for the interview. They had thought that my name was *Chris*. They wondered why I had applied, saying that they had never considered hiring a woman. I got the job (they needed someone immediately), but I also got the beginning of my important postcollege education as a woman. In the next years I learned that the idea of equality taught in my university courses contained a lot of pretense.

Many of today's female journalism students go through a similar process. While they comprise two-thirds of the graduates, earning higher grades and expressing more ambition than do the male students, these women are still having trouble getting equally good jobs. In the late 1980s, 76 percent of newspaper dailies had no female associate editors, executive editors, managing editors, editors, or editorial chiefs, and newsrooms were 65 percent male (Sklar, 1992).

It's not just journalism students who go through this process, of course. Many students in many fields have similar experiences, particularly girls and women who learn well the information offered in high school and college. While girls *know* about the seemingly petty harassment by boy peers (e.g., the snapping of bra straps, comments about breasts—too large, too small, etc.), girls are not encouraged to think of the sexual harassment and rapes, which all young women experience or learn about, as part of the educational experiences, built into or allowed as a part of the structure. If they work hard, they often receive good grades. In undergraduate classes, they are not alone; there are many white women in most of the college classes that women take. Anger about, or questioning of, the instructor's syllabus is not encouraged or rewarded. So there is little attention to anything other than "malestream" ideas and histories that give little attention to race and gender hierarchies. There is a lot of attention to wars of various kinds, and to victories and defeats. But seldom do schools lead discussions on sexual harassment, child abuse, violence against women, the growing economic plight of women and men of color, homophobia, or reproductive rights. (These omissions have been pointed out by "strong-minded women" for many years. For example, in 1856, Elizabeth Cady Stanton wrote about women being educated by the "little" thoughts of "dead men"—the philosopher, the poet, the saint—who have taught boys and girls that silence is most becoming in a women [*The Lily*, 8:4,31.] Further, while there is harassment from male peers, many heterosexual women also experience some courtship courtesies from the men, such as the opening of doors, and the giving of corsages—acts which seem to be signs of kindness, courtesy and cooperative living.

For many women, semblances of equality and cooperation change once they are out in the work world or into graduate school. Many women are either in sex-segregated work places, underpaid in relation to men, or in graduate school, underrepresented. In either place, they are considered less essential than are their male peers. Recently a physicist, a colleague on a committee evaluating candidates for a high administrative position, told me that while interest in recruiting and retention of women and men of color was a worthy concern, our primary concern *had* to be with "excellence." Equity, in his mind, was quite a separate concept from excellence. For many of us, it takes these kinds of experiences to realize that sexual inequalities live on.

GENERAL SYSTEMS THEORY

In her essay, Linda Perry talks about the importance of the context of the educational system in examining and understanding the creation, recreation and maintenance of sex stereotypes. She found General Systems Theory useful in thinking about the ways the behaviors in the classroom are interwoven with other "subsystems," and how changes in one system reverberate throughout the system. For example, school rules, explicit and implicit, are related to other rules in other institutions. Rules, such as no loud cursing of teachers in the hallways, but not ones against boys talking aloud in the hallways about the size of girls' breasts, are similar to rules in offices and factories.

The rules in most schools are based on white, middle-class values—because those are the rules the people with authority feel most comfortable with. The rules are not, for example, based on the core values of the African-American culture. The historic forces that determine what the rules are and what is considered good or bad curricula are closely related to the power forces of the school district, community, and nation. As Perry argues, teachers living in the educational institutions and in the surrounding culture do have opportunities to bring about some changes in the formal and informal rules about expectations for girls and boys, women and men. She provides many specific, clear, useful suggestions for teacher-initiated changes designed to change climate, content, materials, and language use. It is a list that should serve as a basis for many faculty discussions on school policy. The approach Perry uses stresses the interconnectedness of all people and problems, and provides a way of considering the types of gender hierarchies that operate in school systems.

BEYOND GENERAL SYSTEMS

While General Systems Theory is an expansive approach, much feminist theory is even more encompassing in what is included as the component elements and relationships. Explicitly or implicitly, most classroom theories are concerned primarily with the interests and institutions of men (and a few women, at times). Ecofeminists, however, expand the boundaries of systems to include much more than men and a few women. The general systems we've been taught in classrooms are not participatory systems (with changing, creative dynamics) as much as they are dualistic systems—with elite men opposed to, and trying to master, nature. The relation of men and other animals is presented as basically antagonistic or hierarchical with man as the natural recipient of other animals' works and lives. The rest of "nature" is also to be controlled. In contradiction and repair, ecofeminism is building upon the more inclusive worldviews and spirituality of cultures not given much credence in our textbooks.

Our present educational system gives us little help in thinking about what a new, global consciousness might be. We can, however, begin thinking about what our educational system does support. I think of the dynamics at our "highest" academic rituals, the annual conferences which in the U.S. are usually held in high-rise hotels with sealed air systems. No trees (but lots of paper). No old people. No children, except behind closed doors away from the meetings. No poor people. Speeches primarily by white males. There is, of course, no one experience of "the world." But are these presenters the ones who are most likely to know the larger reality? What kind of gestalt notions are encouraged by the speech making and the partying of these conferences? What does being enlightened mean? And why does it seem to have so little to do with the illumination of sunlight and knowledge of the earth? What concepts of diversity and interconnections are learned at these conferences and brought back to our classrooms?

Perry's suggestions for change can help us rethink what our educational system is and how broad our visions of what teaching and learning might be if we were wise enough to look for a panoramic view. If we become aware of the interdependency of *all* Earth's life-forms, we can move toward more comprehensive understanding and analysis. Connecting the personal and global diagnostically could bring immense therapeutic changes to our education system.

REFERENCES

Sklar, Holly (1992, March). Washington, D.C.: Divide and conquer. Z *Magazine*, 13–18.

3

In-Service Education as Something More: A Personal Construct Approach

C. T. P. Diamond

Joint Centre for Teacher Development
Ontario Institute for Studies in Education
Faculty of Education, University of Toronto

INTRODUCTION

From nearly 20 years of experience with teachers, I am convinced that they need opportunities to experience themselves as self-fashioning people who can make themselves into what they want to be. Accordingly, ways need to be found for in-service teacher education to help them learn to grow in these self-determined directions and to play better classroom parts. However, in-service or continuing teacher education is typically seen more modestly as consisting of any deliberate and formalized activity, whereby teachers working beyond their preservice years upgrade their professional understanding, skills, and attitudes (Diamond, 1991).

It was found that research into teacher development suggested that becoming and staying a teacher involves complex changes and development—not only in teaching behavior but also in cognition, affect, and personal knowledge—and that these changes occur within powerful contexts (Calderhead, 1988). Given this wide range of concerns, it was not surprising to find that conceptualizations in teacher education remained very fragmented. There seemed to be only disconnected bodies of research on a diverse array of topics, extending from teachers' belief systems, teacher thinking, and personal practical or narrative knowledge, through classroom interaction, socialization, and planning and problem solving, to the translation of subject matter into teaching practice. However, thanks to the pioneering work of Britton (1970) on language and learning, it was discovered that, in a two-volume work

devoted to *The Psychology of Personal Constructs,* Kelly (1955) provided a theoretical framework that could usefully incorporate all these
different aspects of teacher development. From this point of view, the
overall goal of in-service was seen as no less than the transformation of
perspective.

I eventually came to use Kelly's (1955) theoretical constructs in order
to design and implement individualized in-service programs. I took
several years to learn to provide teachers with Fixed Role Treatments or
with new ways of experimenting with and promoting their own
personal theories and classroom practices. In such interventions,
teachers are offered alternative teaching scenarios to enact. In a form of
role play, they are invited to explore new relationships and ways of
teaching. Fay Smith was taking a university course with me, and Ann
Jones was a colleague of hers. Both teachers were self-selected and,
more than a mere sample, they represented a rare opportunity for me.
My case studies of their trying to change their teaching are described
below. Their stories illustrate some of the varying degrees of change
that in-service might promote.

My earlier study of 15 other teachers and their plight (Diamond,
1979) had alerted me, as a teacher educator, to the need to explore a
more fundamental form of in-service. But what examples were at hand
for me to learn from? In Herman Hesse's (1963) novel, *Steppenwolf,* the
character of Pablo assumes the role of a chess player in order to offer
the other characters opportunities for the "buildup" or development of
so-called personality. This opportunity requires, however, that he be
lent the roles or aspects into which each of their personalities can be
broken. Pablo then magically transforms these elements into a variety
of possibilities and displays them in successive scenes where each
aspect is seen enacting its own world. He adds that this is the art of life:
"You may yourself as an artist develop the game of your life and lend
it animation. You may complicate and enrich it as you please. It lies in
your hands" (p. 215).

So, too, I thought, in teacher in-service education. Teachers could be
helped to explore the kinds of teachers they presently are and the kinds
of teachers they eventually want to become. The effort of the in-service
would not be to give teachers the "right" answer, nor to make their
construct systems conform to those of any consultant or teacher
educator. Instead, the teachers would be provided with occasions for
learning to test the adequacy or usefulness of their own constructs. To
facilitate this process of enrichment, I would use the role-playing
approaches, much as in the spirit of directing characters in a Pirandello
play who learn about themselves—at least in part through the experi-

ence of contrasting what they are with the new masks that they are asked to assume by way of experimentation.

Learning to teach in these terms would be portrayed as simply another aspect of life to be examined and then either confirmed or changed. All constructs are to be seen not only as representing our own private versions of the reality of teaching, but also as setting the limits beyond which we find it difficult to imagine teaching. Constructs thus act as both frames and cages, expanding and restricting our range of teaching actions. Accordingly, it can be claimed that, in any version of teaching as in any in-service, something more will always be wanting or lacking. Further teacher change or development is always still possible. But I realize that a number of obstacles would need to be overcome.

OBSTACLE I: "THEY WON'T LET ME!"

Many poignant portraits have been painted of teachers from all levels of education who have tried to influence the contexts in which they work. The strains and frustrations of feeling that no one is ever listening, for example, can foster burnout, and "an insidious charring [may] slowly eat away at [them]" (Shulman, 1983, p. 502) in the performance of their duties. Like their students, teachers often report feeling excluded, and that school offers them little scope for personal choice or individual initiative. Such a struggle for voice and representation makes it difficult for teachers to go beyond the limitations of present procedures and arrangements. Confronted with schooling structures and political pressures, they may learn to cope "by becoming merely efficient, by functioning compliantly—like Kafkaesque clerks" (Greene, 1978, p. 28). As I revisited former student teachers of mine in the schools over many years, I felt the urgency of the need to provide them with countering perspectives so that they could escape such confinement. The importance of a thwarted self and a threatened teacher identity kept recurring as themes in their reported experiences.

While some teachers may protect themselves by remaining relatively uninvolved and teach in a basic survival mode, others may become so bored and devoid of any hope of greater effectiveness that they no longer seem to care about teaching and learning. Lacking awareness of their own personal meanings and realities, they cease to relate to their students or themselves. They become unwitting accomplices in an inequitable system. Lacking a sense of self and possibility, they can sit back and claim that they are entirely constrained and defined by their decreed teaching roles. They can slip into the habit of becoming resisters, of blaming teaching ineffectiveness upon contrary circumstances and noncaring institutions. Anyone is blamed rather than oneself.

I had watched this kind of fate progressively overtaking my former student teachers. As I continued to meet with them as a supervisor of the practicum experiences of yet more beginning teachers, I realized the need to help change their experiences of teaching. As Nias (1991) also found, once students began teaching, many would telephone or write, "seeking reassurance, support and information from an interested, professionally knowledgeable colleague who did not have control over their careers which was now vested in their headteachers" (p. 147). These concerns prompted my year-long doctoral study of the construct systems and classroom practices of 97 teachers of tenth-grade English (Diamond, 1979). I narrowed down the second stage of the research to tracking the classroom experiences of 15 teachers who demonstrably represented a range of understandings of teaching written composition. Given that numerous gaps opened up between their intentions and classroom actions, I found that all the teachers were in need of support and welcomed the chance to discuss their teaching. They were just not able to implement their own teaching goals with much fidelity or congruence. While this finding may reflect the limitations of any attempt to subsume the understandings of others, the teachers themselves acknowledged the gaps. They also admitted that their school administrators rarely, if ever, intruded into the area of classroom instruction.

If the teachers could not reasonably blame "them," as generalized others, for the chains they seemed to wear, I wondered if the teachers in their pre-service programs had learned to imprison themselves. By not having been challenged to make important decisions about their teaching, they may have forgotten how to choose. If they had been treated for so long by us as voiceless technicians, they may have simply accepted silence as their fate. This explanation raised the uncomfortable possibility that teachers themselves might thereafter be determining their fate to be thought of as already determined. Teachers might be digging the very graves which they claim are threatening to swallow them up. But there may be even worse to come if they dare to step outside and go beyond the safe and familiar routines of teaching, as they are presently known.

I realized that, in venturing to find new avenues of freedom such as those offered by notions of mentorship or supervision, they found considerable distress. The teachers had not been prepared for teaching that involved them in risk taking. Rather than exploring teaching from the frontiers of their own personal experience, they sought refuge within the known conventions and contented themselves to serve as the self-martyring victims of the demands of others. As William James's story (1892) illustrates, many teacher education programs may not equip us as teachers to be able to break out afresh from our training: "In a railroad accident a menagerie-tiger, whose cage had broken open, is said to have emerged, but presently crept back again, as if too much bewildered by his new responsibilities, so that he was without difficulty secured" (p. 10).

In order to accept the invitation to assume personal responsibility for venturing beyond existing boundaries, I came to see that teachers may need to learn first to recognize threats to their power of choice and then to develop new ways of coping. When they experience a strong sense of "top down," or external demand, they can come to recognize that this may sometimes be illusory and may reflect only the projection of their own internal demands. Instead of reacting repeatedly with rigid patterns, teachers can learn to react more vividly to the actual, specific events in their classrooms. Their perceived lack of alternatives or the feeling of being "stuck" can be the psychological cost paid for having lost both the sense of personal search and the feel of the freshness of experience.

Kelly (1955) believed that "all of our present interpretations of the universe are subject to revision and replacement" (p. 15). This vision of progressive enlightenment or transformation of perspectives provides hope that all of us as teachers can change. However, we are more likely to give up a self-defeating viewpoint, even if it is one that is an integral part of ourselves, if we have first become personally aware of the meaningful implications of some alternative behavior. In this instance, such behavior would involve becoming more self-determining and effective. We all need help to forge personally effective, alternative approaches to teaching.

OBSTACLE II: SLOWNESS TO CHANGE

If many teachers have experienced only anxiety and threat in teacher education programs, little change is likely to eventuate as a result of more of the same in their in-service education. We all need to realize that change is possible only when there is some understanding of an alternative to present practices. Raphael (1976) is too logical when he insists that "one does not replace a lie, nor does one need to have a replacement in order to show that it is one. Nonsense is not replaced, it is simply eliminated" (p. 56).

In teaching, no one voluntarily risks conceptual confusion or the anguish of relinquishing life-long professional beliefs—even if it appears to have been recommended in a staff development day. Psychologically, no one takes the extra trouble. If change or movement is to occur, it is possible only when there is a framework or perspective within which it can take place. If a way of teaching has become meaningful and familiar, it is difficult for anyone to divert from this worn track to some as yet unmarked path.

Crockett and Meisel (1974) have shown that large-scale change is especially challenging when a person's central, highly implicatory constructs are involved. We are slow to change in any way that entails too many related changes. The prospect of massively linked change is too daunting. In addition, if a teacher's construct system is weakly disconfirmed, as in the failure of only a segment of an isolated lesson, little or no response may be made. On the other hand, if an inference on a central or superordinate construct can be directly and strongly refuted ("I just can't seem to function as an effective teacher anymore!"), substantial change may occur. In the case studies below, Fay shows that once change occurs in a tightly connected construct system—as with collapsing dominoes—change is greater among the interrelated constructs than among those that are independent and peripheral. Conversely, Ann shows that if constructs are segmented or only loosely connected, relatively fewer changes follow disconfirmation of even the most central beliefs.

OBSTACLE III: INEFFECTIVE PEDAGOGY

When I used their mean class scores as the criteria of growth, I did not find that any of the above group of 15 English teachers was able to promote significant overall gains in their students' achievement in, or in their attitudes towards, personal and public writing. To ensure member checking, and by way of validity-seeking corroboration, I subsequently reinterviewed the teachers about the disturbing findings. To my surprise, none of them disputed the lack of pupil progress. Instead, they stoically accepted that I had represented the way things are during the last year of compulsory schooling. One teacher readily agreed that "by the end of the second semester the students' work in English had fallen away." Another reported: "I discussed the decline with other teachers and they agreed that it appears in their classes, too." A third teacher also found that the lack of effectiveness accorded with her own experiences of the year: "I can say with my students that in the last half of the year I had a very negative effect on them because

I just lost it and I know the class did, too. There was nothing I could do." A fourth explained: "Often a lot of things you do don't have much impact, depending on the type of student you have. . . . Really, there's not much we can do. It all depends on the kind of home they come from." Confronted by such discouraging accounts, I began to wonder how teachers could keep running so fast with such little result. Given such disconfirmation of classroom practices, how can the teachers' construct systems continue to survive? The case studies of Fay and Ann were subsequently conducted to help answer such questions.

Three explanations seemed possible as to why teachers may be unable to test and elaborate their personal theories and philosophies of teaching more decisively:

1. Their construing may have become so circular that they endlessly test and retest the same hypotheses, for example, "teaching the skills in isolation" in the hope of improving students' writing. They remain unable to accept the disquieting implications of the data they collect.

2. The teachers may have moved into a kind of "wait and see" state where constructions are left so vague and loose, for example, "teaching for personal growth," that they cannot provide expectations that are clear enough to be tested. The result is that they simply mill around the same issues, projecting that dispirited feeling of "they won't let me!"

3. In contrast, the teachers may have moved in the opposite direction of constriction of understandings, believing that "nothing works." Events then seem to refuse to comply with the teachers' rigid predictions. When teachers enclose their meanings with such tightened construct systems, they do not have to deal with invalidating evidence.

There are grounds for accepting the second explanation, that is, that the teachers may have experienced invalidation of their teaching practices so frequently that they eventually begin to loosen the links between their constructs. They then no longer bother to generate specific and testable predictions. As one teacher explained:

> You just don't see growth with a lot of kids. They may try a bit harder or just become a lot happier in your room. But that doesn't mean that their writing improves. They're better as people, that's all.

The experience of finding one's ideas rendered invalid may be avoided, but at the cost of teaching almost entirely within a seemingly unpredictable and largely meaningless pedagogical world.

This loosening of meaning structures may help explain why teaching has often been depicted as a pretheoretical perspective, providing only a sensate, existential knowledge of a simply personal nature that eludes abstract, theoretical explanations. Jackson's (1968) other characterizations describe such teachers as "here-and-now" oriented, instinctive rather than reflective, people of action and feeling rather than of control and thought. Given the simultaneous nature of the demands made on them, teachers can become so hurried and harried that they come to have little time or inclination for reflection. As one of the 15 teachers commented: "I honestly don't think teachers go around in their heads and separate those ideas out. Your ordinary classroom teacher doesn't break it down."

Comments such as these do not provide warrant for in-service programs that reject the validity of teachers' personal practical knowledge; however, they may indicate that teachers who are faced with repeated invalidation of parts of their construct systems first of all resort to altering the pattern of relationships between their constructs. They may repeatedly change their pedagogic "theory" in an "eclectic" or oscillating fashion. Eventually, they may begin to loosen or unravel the relationships between their constructs and so abandon the theory-building business altogether. As I indicate in the scenarios provided below for Fay and Ann (see Appendix B), a central role for in-service teacher educators can be to let themselves be used as anchors or marker points by teachers so that the teachers can then learn to validate themselves against the understandings of trusted others. Given this degree of security, the teachers can form and reform their own pedagogical theories and relationships. The challenge for in-service teacher educators is to help teachers to see themselves as capable of imagining and trying alternatives—and eventually as self-directing and self-determining.

"GETTING UNSTUCK": SOME OPTIONS FOR IN-SERVICE EDUCATION

Distancing

Day (1984) found that in-service teacher educators can make significant contributions when they move away from seeing themselves as the prime designers and interpreters of teachers' thoughts and actions. Both groups need to adopt more interdependent roles in which collaboration, consultation, and negotiation serve as the first principles of the shared program. In Day's classroom-based model of in-service education, four teachers had sequences of their lessons filmed. The videos of their teaching practices were discussed at length in order to generate more personal, pedagogical theory after much reflection and deliberation. One teacher reported: "I came to trust my own ability." Another learned to evaluate and modify her own solutions to the teaching problems she encountered. In this way, Day functioned as a central member of the team of teachers rather than remaining apart from them. He showed that when teacher educators learn to become teachers among teachers, the teachers are able to distance themselves from the everyday world of the classroom and so open themselves to influence by others. While distancing may be an essential first step towards self-evaluation, both processes help to define perspective transformation as the goal of teacher education (Diamond, 1991).

To enable such cognitive change, teachers' stable and increasingly impermeable patterns of interpretation and action need to be reflected upon and even breached. In this way, they can reduce the immunity of their constructs to accustomed invalidation. Teachers can be helped to look at their existing practices and become accustomed to seeking alternative interpretations of the same classroom events. By becoming more aware of their routines, teachers can learn to devise fresher hypotheses and patterns. By gaining access to their own learning about teaching and by imagining alternative perspectives, teachers may seek the continued transformation of their meanings. Such expansion can also be promoted by sharing different perspectives with the teachers— those of their students, those of teacher educators, and even those of the teachers themselves at different stages in their careers. In these ways, the contrasts and all their different implications can be explored. In-service education can then help release teachers from the imprisonment of their contracted and seemingly impermeable perspectives.

Self-Characterization and Fixed-Role Treatment

Like all of us, teachers choose between the alternative roles that are defined for them by their own personal constructs. These constructs constitute an implicit network or perspective from which teachers structure their thinking in order to view their own behavior and that of others. We are paradoxically both controlled by and set free by our viewpoints, and, in order to choose which role we will play, we need to be more aware of possible alternatives. Fixed-Role Treatment is a technique that permits us to investigate teachers' personal constructs and to induce or assist change. However, very little research into this procedure has been documented.

Even in fields other than teaching, the research is limited. Karst and

Trexler (1970) treated anxiety associated with public speaking; Bonarius (1970) presented a case study showing the phases involved in the role change of a patient; and Radley (1974) proposed that role enactment might be a formalized reflection of the constructive processes by which people are able to make explicit their construct roles in order to choose between them. In the two case studies which follow below, I devised two programs of Fixed-Role Treatment in order to help change the construct systems underlying the classroom pedagogies of Fay and Ann (see Diamond, 1985).

Fay and Ann taught in the same large suburban high school. Fay was twenty-two years old, a four-year university-trained and degreed teacher of two years' experience; Ann was twenty years old, a three-year college-trained teacher with a diploma, and in her first year of teaching. Both had only very limited experience of teaching English, and only Ann had been trained specifically to teach it.

Since both felt very uneasy about teaching English, I thought it would be especially appropriate to explore the possibility with them that words can provide a useful means of sorting out and reorganizing their teaching worlds. Words can supply labels for their constructs and can help them gain some purchase on their own construction processes and on those of others. Fay approached me about her difficulties and those of Ann. Accordingly, I invited each of them to provide a 500-word professional self-description or characterization of how they perceived themselves as English teachers. The suggested format for this self-reflective composition was derived from Kelly's (1955) procedures:

> I want you to write a teaching sketch of Julie Brown, just as if she were the principal character in a play. Write it as it might be written by a friend and professional colleague who knows her INTIMATELY and very SYMPATHETICALLY, perhaps better than anyone could know her. Be sure to write it in the third person. For example, start out by saying:
> "As a teacher, Julie Brown is. . . ."

Each teacher substituted her own name for the mythical Julie. Kelly (1955) had chosen the words carefully so that "sketch" suggested that the general structure of present practices, rather than their elaborate detail, was to be described. This meant that only the teachers' central and interrelated constructs were of concern to us. The emphasis on the third person indicated that this was not to be a chronicle of faults or virtues, but rather a distanced and synoptic view of each as a whole teacher. The other phrases sought to reduce any threat and to encourage the production of speculation as well as fact. Both self-characterizations (see Appendix A) were shared with me for textual and diagnostic analysis.

Other Characterization (Alternative Scenario) and Fixed-Role Treatment

By way of an "other characterization" or restorying response, I devised a role character sketch for each of the teachers that centered on a less routinized and more proactive teaching style for them both (see Appendix B). These imagined protagonists were called Carole Spencer and Jill Hartley, respectively. The teaching scenarios were designed to be sympathetic to and to fit the classroom situations confronting each of the teachers. Both were encouraged to "become" the teachers outlined in the sketches in every way possible for five consecutive teaching days. They each then attempted to construe and teach as they believed these other imagined teachers would. Given the "busyness" of their teaching lives, I met only once with Fay, who also provided Ann with feedback during this time. Fay and Ann each observed the reactions of their own classes to any changes in their teaching.

In order to produce the initial self-characterizations, the two teachers had to organize their self-perceptions as teachers. They thus produced their own personal self-diagnoses, within the frameworks of their own construct systems. By examining these self-portraits I could sense, at least partially, how their construct systems could so threaten to constrain them that they might paint themselves into corners. They would then be virtually "stuck" with little hope of transcending their present teaching difficulties. I adapted the methods of analyzing such sketches as provided by Kelly (1955) and by Bannister and Fransella (1980).

As shown in Appendix A, Fay's opening sentence was: "Fay feels there are many areas of concern in her own teaching methods and content that need attention"; and her last sentence was: "Her lessons seem to be dull and uninteresting—and time consuming." Being a better, more efficient and interesting teacher seemed to be emphasized as her major teaching construct. Ann's first sentence was: "Ann is still 'finding her feet' "; and her last sentence was: "Most importantly she has to become determined to improve herself and to overcome these problems in order to help herself and, of course, her students." Ann's major construct seemed to relate to struggling to find out for herself rather than being told the right answers by others.

The most important requirement of each of the alternative role sketches was that the main perspective implied by the role would be usefully different from and contrast with that of the teacher. Fay's sketch (Carole) was written around the relatively simple theme of enjoying her own contributions and those of her students, rather than being policed by people in authority. Ann's sketch (Jill) encouraged her not to settle passively for the "right" answers as supplied by others, but rather to search for her own solutions through active collaboration with her students. The tone of each sketch was positive. For example, I wrote for Fay that "of course not everything works—just most of it!" This was offered as a counter-perspective to the generalized theme of "there was nothing I could do."

I sought to read and respond to each self-characterization in terms of its central motif and variety of subordinate themes. Each text was analyzed thematically by searching for key words and phrases, and then by assembling a combined index of their use. Fay and Ann seemed to share two recurring motifs in teaching: "Difficulty" and "How To." They thus had a common view of teaching as a problematic and pragmatic activity. While Fay repeated three other themes in her self-portrait: "Concern (areas of)," "Students," and "Time Wasting", Ann used another six themes to delineate her teaching self: "Interest," "Motivation," "Find Out," "Herself," "Problems," "and Suggestions." While Fay seemed to focus on her students, Ann, a teacher in her first year, concentrated more on herself. She was, however, also very concerned to interest and motivate her students.

This analysis confirmed that Fay's alternative sketch could usefully stress her enjoying being with students, rather than continuing to focus on her wasting time and worrying about efficiency. She was also encouraged to put activity before generalized anxiety. Similarly, Ann's sketch could helpfully stimulate her to form a community with her students, rather than seeking alternatively either to beguile them with interest or to discipline them with assessment. The sketches also included specific "How To" activities in order to meet both teachers' more practical and daily needs.

FAY AND ANN

Fay seemed to be more comfortable than Ann in assuming the role of her teaching character, and greater change became apparent in her personal constructs of teaching English. She felt she was no longer "stuck" without an alternative. While reported student reaction did not seem to favor either teacher dramatically, some promising responses came from two of Fay's classes. She reported an increased awareness of alternative teaching strategies, feelings of greater self-understanding and self-confidence, decreased tension, and a desire to continue to explore areas in teaching that she had previously considered unsafe. Fay wrote: "I am ready to try new things. I feel freer and less pressured." There was no more creeping back inside!

In contrast, Ann reported feelings of threat and anxiety when she faced the prospect of trying alternative methods. While she described the coping mechanisms that she had established at the beginning of the year as still working adequately enough, she did admit that her class of tenth-grade boys posed discipline problems for her. Although Ann became more aware of her own ability to change her personal constructs, she still expected some kind of external deliverance from that responsibility. While Ann felt that her alternative teaching role might possibly have been more successful with another of her classes, she also felt too constrained by the demands of the administration for these students' assessments just at that time. As a first-year teacher, she registered a strong sense of external demand.

Fay reported that her previous confusion, lack of knowledge, and overall pessimistic pattern were seemingly replaced by her becoming less worried and by her feeling "happier, more relaxed, and more aware—even a bit wiser." In contrast, Ann recorded less movement and seemed to accomplish fewer changes in her teaching. Students, assessments, and the time of year were not right for her. She had seemingly not become more self-directing but asked, instead, for "more guidance in actual teaching circumstances."

Fay seems to have been more successful in changing her teaching— perhaps as a result of her adapting her role character to suit her own ends. As she wrote, "I'm getting used to being different." She had previously often felt confused and frustrated when teaching English, possibly through lack either of direction at school or of actual pre-service training and experience. While she still experienced some misgivings, she felt that there had been actual improvements in her teaching. She reported feeling the need to be more adventurous, despite the possibility of failure and temporary disorganization in class. She was now using "Nothing ventured, nothing gained" as her teaching motto. Fay seemed to be worrying less about her daily success as a teacher. As evinced by her responses to this exercise, Fixed-Role Treatment can help teachers to realize that each lesson can be a limited venture, without their whole teaching career always being "on the line."

As Fay became more attuned to the relevance for her students of what she taught, she noted that this "other concern" led to a paradoxical increase in her own self-understanding. This gain, however, may have been due not only to my suggested changes in teaching strategies, but also to her beginning to share stories of teaching with another teacher at her school. This teacher's "functional approach to teaching language" made more sense after Fay observed a poetry lesson taught by this teacher in which her students were featured by reading poems aloud, using their own interpretations. Fay saw this as a very promising approach which helped reconcile for her the competing claims of school assessment and student involvement. Fay was led to try similar activities in her own class. More importantly than her successful implementation of any of the techniques that were embodied in her alternative teaching scenario, Fay was beginning to make her own choices. The wider range of possible teaching strategies that had been suggested had helped to release her own sense of possibility.

Fay welcomed the greater self-confidence that she experienced after seeing some of the alternatives work for her. She felt that other changes were now needed in her lessons. She wanted to cater to increased class interest and to provide greater variety in activities, including more relaxed talk. She realized that these changes would take more time to explore than the present experience could encompass. She felt that greater sharing of her lessons with other teachers would be helpful. Fay had originally sought help to change her teaching and, once her own alternative scenario had been launched, she offered a similar opportunity to Ann.

Ann did not report increased feelings of satisfaction and self-confidence as a result of her Fixed-Role Treatment. She remained reluctant to try the new teaching strategies that had been suggested. She still felt extremely limited by her classes. She described her "nonachieving" class of boys as rigidly resisting any alteration to their routine. Unfortunately, another class that would have been more responsive to change was caught up, as indicated above, in required assessment procedures. Her eighth-grade class, however, had successfully completed an autobiography during school. This had not been set for homework and had helped to break the link between writing and punishment. But Ann still saw this class as unsettled and requiring very close supervision. She found it difficult to attempt my suggestions with her two tenth-grade classes. These classes were due to leave school in four weeks, and she was intent on just surviving her first year. For her, it was a case of the wrong time of year with the wrong classes. Like many of the above 15 teachers, she felt that her influence as an instructor was limited.

The initial greater connectedness of the constructs within Fay's system of understandings may have been an important factor in her reported greater success. In addition, the fact that she had initially sought help would have led to some changes, regardless of whether or not the help itself did materialize. Fay's very conception of herself as a teacher "on the move" and then undertaking a Fixed-Role Treatment constituted events that were likely to bring about a series of positive revisions in her teaching. Seeking change is itself an event of great significance. Ann was still grappling to move beyond the realization that she had problems in her teaching. And this is only the first step. If teachers do not come to believe that change is possible, their classroom renewal may be postponed. What we do not look for we may not find.

CONCLUSION

Teachers invent and look upon the world of teaching from a particular vantage point, one that provides their way of interpreting and making sense of events and of actions in the classroom. Construed as it is from a given perspective, any teaching can always be varied, while ever higher levels of self-consciousness can be attained. At crucial times, as when they feel "stuck" or ineffective, teachers need help to stretch their vision and to expand their perspectives. By first knowing their own frames of reference and then by struggling to look at things in other ways, teachers can change.

Together with Fay and Ann, I explored the development of a clinical model of in-service teacher education in which perspectival development and changes in "meaning making" are emphasized. This, however, is not a simple way to promote teacher development. Whereas some humanistic writers may portray learning as a process of painless and almost limitless personal growth, from a Kellyan perspective, the process of continuing to learn to teach is often hard and sometimes costly—even though help may be provided in the form of possible alternatives. The individual teacher's own struggle to construe events more effectively forms the basis for the further development or enrichment of his or her personal set of understandings. The goal of transformative teacher education is not the easy reproduction of any ready-made package of knowledge but, rather, the continued recreation of personal meaning.

To achieve this end, teachers' visions need to be acknowledged and then acted upon by teacher educators who can help to prompt their further development by means of written self-characterization and other forms of discursive self-representation. However, while serving as critical friends and colleagues, teacher educators should avoid appearing too much like Hesse's Pablo—or like Momus! This Greek god was the impatient critic of his fellow gods and blamed Vulcan for making humankind without inserting windows into their chests. This would have allowed whatever they thought or felt to be brought easily to light. If Momus had had his way,

> Nothing more would have been wanting, in order to take a man's character but to have . . . gone . . . and looked in,—(and) viewed the soul stark naked; . . . then taken your pen and ink and set down nothing but what you had seen. (Sterne, 1950, p. 75)

But this is an advantage not to be had either by magician or teacher educator:

> Our minds shine not through the body, but we are wrapt up here in a dark covering of uncrystallized flesh and blood; so that, if we would come to (their) specific character . . . we must go some other way to work. (p. 76)

Self-characterization and Fixed-Role Treatment provide other ways of looking inward with teachers so that we can share in their lived experience of teaching and of discerning how it may be changed. As Britton (1970) concluded, as teacher educators and those traditionally charged with providing in-service teacher education, we cannot afford to underestimate our role, either as a means of helping teachers to organize and consolidate their accumulated experience of teaching or our value in interacting with them to create fresh perceptions. Nor can we afford to ignore the limits of our role. No theory or set of procedures that we devise can capture all the ingenuities of teaching. Whether enacted with others or explored in writing, something more is always wanting. Immersed in the stories of two groups of seventeen teachers, I have returned in my writing to their themes repeatedly over the years to rethink and reformulate my constructs of teacher education—and will do so again.

REFERENCES

Bannister, D., & Fransella, F. (1980). *Inquiring man: The psychology of personal constructs.* Harmondsworth, UK: Penguin.

Bonarius, J. C. J. (1970). Fixed role therapy. *British Journal of Medical Psychology, 43,* 213–219.

Britton, J. (1970). *Language and learning.* London: Allen Lane.

Calderhead, J. (1988). Conceptualizing and evaluating teachers' professional learning. Paper Research in Teacher Education Workshop, Moray House, Edinburgh, May.

Crockett, W. H., & Meisel, P. (1974). Construct connectedness, strength of disconfirmation and impression change. *Journal of Personality, 42,* 290–299.

Day, C. (1984). Teachers' thinking—Intentions and practice. In R. Halkes & J. K. Olson (Eds.), *Teaching thinking: A new perspective on persisting problems in education.* Lisse, The Netherlands: Swets and Zeitlinger.

Diamond, C. T. P. (1979). *The constructs, classroom practices and effectiveness of grade ten teachers of written expression.* Unpublished doctoral thesis, University of Queensland, Department of Education, Brisbane, Australia.

Diamond, C. T. P. (1985). The use of fixed role treatment in teaching. *Psychology in the Schools, 20*(1), 74–82.

Diamond, C. T. P. (1991). *Teacher education as transformation: A psychological perspective.* Milton Keynes, UK: Open University Press.

Greene, M. (1978). The question of personal reality. *Teachers College Record, 80,* 23–25.

Hesse, H. (1963). *Steppenwolf* (B. Creighton, Trans.). New York: Holt.

Jackson, P. W. (1968). *Life in classrooms.* New York: Holt.

James, W. (1892). *Psychology: The briefer course.* New York: Henry Holt.

Judy, S. (1975). *The English teacher's handbook.* Cambridge, MA: Winthrop.

Judy, S. (1979). *Explorations in the teaching of English.* Cambridge, MA: Winthrop.

Karst, T. O., & Trexler, L. D. (1970). Initial study using fixed-role therapy. *Journal of Consulting and Clinical Psychology, 34,* 363–366.

Kelly, G. A. (1955). *The psychology of personal constructs* (Vols. 1–2). New York: W. W. Norton.

Kohl, H. (1973). *Reading: How to.* Harmondsworth, UK: Penguin.

Nias, J. (1991). "Primary teachers talking": A reflexive account of longitudinal research. In G. Walford (Ed.), *Doing educational research.* London: Routledge.

Radley, A. R. (1974). The effect of role enactment upon construed alternatives. *British Journal of Medical Psychology, 47,* 313–320.

Raphael, F. (1976). *The glittering prizes.* Harmondsworth, UK: Penguin.

Shulman, L. S. (1983). Autonomy and obligation. In L. S. Shulman & G. Sykes (Eds.), *Handbook of teaching and policy.* New York: Longman.

Sterne, L. (1950). *The life and times of Tristram Shandy.* New York: Modern Library.

APPENDIX A

SELF-CHARACTERIZATIONS

Fay

As a teacher of English, Fay feels there are many areas of concern in her teaching methods and content that need attention.

There seems to be so much that students need to learn that it is difficult to choose material that is appropriate for them. Often she is not quite sure if the method being used is effective, wasting time, or counterproductive. When viewed at different times, she forms different opinions on this.

Within the classroom, she is aware of certain deficiencies and, according to mood, irritability, and pressure, remedies these when convenient, e.g.:

1. supervision of individual students' work—is it close enough?
2. individual attention.

3. "reinforcing" after giving back essays, comprehension, set work (drawing on errors and using these two show better ways of writing).

Generally, she is concerned that each student does as well as s/he can (most of the time), and derives a great deal of pleasure from seeing a student master a particular technique. It is often found that student dissatisfaction is often caused by lack of preparation for that particular class period, e.g., not reading something carefully enough. This often leads to misunderstanding, which, in turn, leads to irritability.

With regards to certain areas, having never been taught "how to teach English," she finds a lot of difficulty: e.g., poetry and creative writing. How does someone motivate and stimulate students so that they feel inspired to write a piece from their own desire? She feels there must be better ways of teaching certain topics—how does one teach grammar and punctuation in an interesting manner? What are the more interesting ways of teaching children how to write?

Book reviews seem to be a big bugbear—no matter how she attempts to teach students to write reviews (she has tried many levels), only those who are capable write satisfactory reviews. She feels that she should be a lot stricter on her classes—making students hand in rough copies, correcting, rewriting, etc.—yet all this is time consuming. She would like to be able to get students to analyze a book/article and read between the lines but is not sure how to go about it.

Another area of concern is trying to get students to communicate orally in front of a class—for example, oral assessment in the form of an impromptu talk, prepared talk, conversations, dialogues. Her lessons seem to be dull and uninteresting—and time consuming.

Ann

As an English teacher, Ann is still "finding her feet." In teaching English, she finds the main difficulty is the fact that in her discipline there is no definitive content or reference point. Unlike most other subjects, there is no text to pick up, digest, or recapitulate. Ann, unlike most, has unfortunately no innate entry in English, as she is not and never has been a big reader. Therefore, she is still searching for "right" or best teaching methods, for the most appropriate and necessary content, and possibly most importantly, finding out many things about herself. These three things are still being assessed, with a definite opinion and decision still, if ever, to be made.

Probably Ann's greatest problem is ignorance of what to teach. Fine, each class must do a novel, but what is taught with a novel? Does she teach who is telling the story—in other words, a detailed account of the author and his works? Does she teach what story is being told? A summary of events? Does she teach what the author is saying? What theme or deep philosophical, socially relevant message is s/he giving? Or does she teach how the story is told, how characters are introduced and presented, how the plot is paced, how the climax is reached, how the author has put everything together to make the story a success, or an absolute failure? Is someone supposed to tell Ann the answers to these questions, or is she to blunder through to find out for herself?

Another of Ann's problems would be an ignorance or lack of knowledge of the skills of achievement of certain grade levels. Is it enough for the grade ten boy to be able to get his message across, or does he need in his essay to have an introduction, conclusion, and nice neat paragraphs, with topic sentences in the middle? In the classroom, one of Ann's biggest difficulties is in the line of motivation; because Ann has always had an interest in the field of drama and has always been motivated herself, this seems to be passed on to her students, as in this field she has had very enjoyable, rewarding teaching/learning experiences. However, for other genres, such as the novel, motivation can become a problem. A novel that will interest grade ten boys may be chosen, but Ann is not really excited about it. This also shows in relation to age differences. The upper school student is generally more interesting and understandable to Ann and, therefore, seems easier to talk to, easier to get interested and motivated. In the junior school, grade ten boys, and especially grade eights, are much harder to motivate. Ann will make all sorts of suggestions of interesting orals, but whether it is because the students cannot be bothered or because Ann's talks are above their heads, or most probably because what one finds interesting differs greatly from that which interests another, she is not successful. Perhaps why is not to be discovered.

Probably the best thing Ann could do to overcome these problems is first to realize that she has them. After this, she needs to do some serious thinking about herself, possibly some talking to her seniors for suggestions. Most importantly, she must become determined to improve herself and to overcome these problems in order to help herself and, of course, her students.

APPENDIX B

FIXED-ROLE SKETCHES

Fay

Here is a teaching sketch of a person by the name of (Carole Spencer). In some way she is, of course, a quite different kind of teacher from you. In other ways, I suppose, she may be a little like you. But whether she is or isn't is not important. Let's go over this together. Please read the enclosed role. What's your impression of this teacher (Carole Spencer)? Does she sound like the kind of teacher you would like to know? Does she sound like a real teacher?

For the next five consecutive teaching days, I want you to do something unusual. I want you to ACT as if you were (Carole Spencer). We will work it out together. For five teaching days, try to forget that you are (Fay) or that you ever were. You ARE (Carole Spencer). You ACT like her! You THINK like her! You TALK to your pupils and other teachers the way you think she would talk! You DO the things you think she would do! You HAVE HER INTERESTS and you ENJOY the things she would enjoy in class!

Now I know this is going to seem very artificial. We expect that. You will have to keep thinking about the way (Carole) would do things in class, rather than the way (Fay) might want to do them.

You might say that we are sending (Fay) off for a week of seminars. In the meantime, (Carole) will take over. Other people may not know it, but (Fay) will not even be around. Of course, you will have to let people keep on calling you (Fay), but you will see yourself as (Carole). After five consecutive teaching days, (Fay) will come back refreshed.

Teaching Scenario

As a teacher of English, Carole relishes being with people—the other learner teachers and her own developing classes. She really looks forward to hearing what her pupils can share with her and their friends as they talk to their classes. Her tenth graders have really responded to their reenactment of the trial in *To Kill a Mockingbird*. As they swapped the written versions of their roles, her resident punctuation and spelling committee of experts was invaluable. One class prepares a regular spelling test—she writes her answers on the overhead projector and then the class helps her to correct her answers. They really learned a lot when she wrote on one of her own topics in front of them—all in the heat of creation! Carole has a wide variety of interests, and naturally recommends and personally endorses books (and music) she has enjoyed. She energizes her classes by reading aloud exciting passages from a favorite novel (or recounting a film version of it), or rendering a short lyric that captures some of her own recent feelings. A lot of writing flows from all this talking and shared reading. They often collaborate in preparing different versions of the beginning or conclusion or omitted scenes from the class novel. Carole often discusses her classroom "try-outs" with other teachers. They also share in planning a coming unit of work or test. This stimulates and lessens her preparation. She found Stephen Judy's (1979) 22 alternatives to the study of grammar very helpful, and is turning her class on to a greater awareness of their language and that of the media. Herbert Kohl's (1973) *Reading: How To* (Penguin), was a real breakthrough. She heard about it first through the English Teachers' Association of Queensland. Carole is always doing new things in her teaching. Most of all, she keeps involving her classes, touching their personal concerns with her teaching. Of course, not everything works—just most of it!

The copy of (Carole's) teaching is for you to keep. Keep it with you all the time and read it over at least three different times a day, say when you first get to school, during the lunch hour, and after school. For the present—for five consecutive teaching days—ACT OUT the part of (Carole Spencer). Eat it, sleep it, feel it, TEACH IT!

Ann

Here is a teaching sketch of a person by the name of (Jill Hartley). In some ways she is, of course, a quite different kind of teacher from you. In other ways, I suppose, she may be a little like you. But whether she is or isn't is not important. Let's go over this together. Please read the enclosed role. What's your impression of this teacher (Jill Harley)? Does she sound like the kind of teacher you would like to know? Does she sound like a real teacher?

For the next five consecutive teaching days, I want you to do something unusual. I want you to ACT as if you were (Jill Hartley). We will work it out together. For five teaching days, try to forget that you are (Ann) or that you ever were. You ARE (Jill Hartley). You ACT like her! You THINK like her! You TALK to your pupils and other teachers the way you think she would talk! You DO the things you think she would do! You HAVE HER INTERESTS and you ENJOY the things she would enjoy in class!

Now I know this is going to seem very artificial. We expect that. You will have to keep thinking about the way (Jill) would do things in class, rather than the way (Ann) might want to do them.

You might say that we are sending (Ann) off for a week of seminars. In the meantime, (Jill) will take over. Other people may not know it, but (Ann) will not even be around. Of course, you will have to let people keep calling you (Ann), but you will see yourself as (Jill). After five consecutive teaching days, (Ann) will come back refreshed.

Teaching Scenario

As a teacher of English, Jill runs most of her classes as very busy writing workshops. Her grade eights pooled their favorite children's books, and then together they began writing a series of short, simple stories that younger brothers and sisters could enjoy while in the local preschool. Out came all the modern, sci-fi versions of *The Magic Pudding*. Whoever heard of Alice in Australialand, puzzling over curious mammals and "curiouser" people? Notions about survival led the class into reading *Walkabout*. Jill has found that her younger classes can easily prepare a brochure (a sheet of paper folded in four and stood on its former long side) that helps them focus their reading. The first page contains an introductory "blurb" or "come-on," the second and third a list for further activities based on the book, and the fourth suggestions for further reading. This means that next year's new classes will be able to pursue these brochures or recommendations from the year before. Some of her students have become respected critics among their peers!

Jill uses lots of "getting to know you" activities at the beginning of each year. The students devise their OWN shield crest and motto, and then enjoy sharing with her. Jill found Stephen Judy's (1979) *Explorations in the Teaching of English* was full of things to try. She is currently reading Judy's (1975) *English Teachers' Handbook* for other ideas and resources. Jill's grade eleven class is in the middle of writing a popular thriller in small groups.

She found a list of characteristics of the best seller (often made into a movie) and, with the class, plotted their own short novel in the best Fleming–Maclean tradition. Her class is picking up a sense of craft and is more appreciative of the skill of the Bronte sisters. Next year she will use Mary Shelley's *Frankenstein*, and they'll produce a modern, "altered states" version. Maybe a musical version for the school concert.

Jill is always "setting up" a new teaching venture. The success of *My Brother Jack* as a "lead in" to *Great Expectations*, and of *Lord of the Flies* to *A Separate Peace* has propelled her into planning a unit on "Growing Up in Australia." Ann is enlisting the help of all her classes. They'll probably share a lot of the projects with their corresponding pen pal class in Los Angeles. Jill's interest in recent Australian fiction has really been triggered by the current vogue for Australian cinema. Yes, Jill and her classes are busy writing. She calls it "STORYING," the making (writing) and taking (reading) of stories. She must remember to arrange the exhibition of her grade eights' book covers—from line drawings to superimposed stills. She hopes the library will let her have the foyer space again. They also promised to get multiple copies of that Puffin (*The Wheel on the School*) for her grade eights. They liked the school's motto: "First to dream and then to do." And so did Jill!

The copy of (Jill's) teaching sketch is for you to keep. Keep it with you all the time and read it over at least three different times a day, say when you first get to school, during the lunch hour, and after school. For the present—for five consecutive teaching days—ACT OUT the part of (Jill Hartley). Eat it, sleep it, feel it, TEACH IT!

Response to Diamond: "In-Service Education as Something More: A Personal Construct Approach"

James Britton
Professor Emeritus, University of London

Pat Diamond reminds us that the process of learning is, at its most fundamental level, one of learning on the job and that, before long, learning and performance itself become indistinguishable. School learning has relied so heavily upon language, spoken and written, that we tend to forget that other modes of learning are possible. Michael Polanyi reminds us of what is involved in learning to swim or to ride a bicycle or dance a polka—and in broad, general terms: "The shaping of our consciousness is impelled to move from . . . incoherence to comprehension, by an intellectual discomfort similar to that by which our eyes are impelled to make clear and coherent the things we see" (Polanyi, 1958, p. 100).

It is a part of the strength of Kelly's (1955) theory of personal constructs that he sees that their existence does not depend upon their being verbalized. Learning in school is, in the first instance, "learning how to do," and this may sometimes be mistaken for the further process of knowing what it is we have learned. Performance is a stronger evidence of many forms of ability than verbal specification. Much learning in the secondary schools is "rote learning," and many of the modes of assessment in use may encourage it.

Learning to read and learning to write are good examples of "learning on the job." Tacit processes play a major part in those capacities: In general, it is only when those processes have failed that direct teaching can help, and then it is only within the context of sustained student performance. We must realize that in taking part in rule-governed behavior, individuals can internalize implicit rules by

67

means indistinguishable from the modes in which those rules were socially derived and continue to be socially adjusted. On the other hand, your traditional teacher may come along, observe the behavior, analyze to throw up the rules, and then teach the resulting rules as a recipe. Such a method of encouraging change in practicing teachers is particularly damaging. Teaching is *par excellence* something to be learned on the job—it is itself, in fact, a process of life-long learning. Behaviorists may define learning as a special kind of behavior— "behavior-changing behavior"—but Kelly (1955) responds with the view that learning is "human behavior at its most typically human."

As teachers we need to understand, from performance, how to carry out the processes we want students to learn, but we also need to know, more fully than they do, what tacit processes are involved and what obstacles or inhibitions may prevent them from operating. There is much that I can learn only from my experience—from my interactions with colleagues and students, from life in my family and in my social groups.

Teaching is an interactive process at all stages: from kindergarten to in-service courses for teachers. Kelly's Sociality Corollary spells out the boundaries of what is possible: "To the extent that one person construes the construction processes of another, he may play a role in a social process involving the other person" (Kelly, 1955, p. 95). This cuts both ways: Where courses are prescribed, sociality may be denied by the course member; where they are voluntary, they may be teaching only to be converted. The first requirement, then, is a teacher's sense of need, of something more that could be achieved. Fixed-role therapy is one method of responding, but how does it compare with alternative courses of action?

D. Bannister, certainly one of the leading British exponents of Kelly's philosophy, said of Fixed-Role Therapy: "It is in no way a panacea—rather it is a moderately useful technique when the psychotherapy has become circular and some trigger for movement is required" (Bannister & Fransella, 1971, p. 132). The method is introduced, moreover, with the caution: "But the construct theory psychotherapist would retain throughout the view that the client is essentially an experimental scientist in his own right" (p. 132). Kelly (1969) himself underlines the fact that:

> Fixed Role Therapy is . . . not a panacea, but an experiment. In fact we have learned that if it is presented as a panacea it fails its purpose and the client does not get on with the life process of finding out for himself. . . . The only valid way to live one's life is to get on with it. . . . Man lives best when he commits himself to getting on with his life." (p. 64).

Pat Diamond would, I am confident, agree with the views I have quoted. It is a matter, therefore, of deciding when it is useful to interrupt for a time the process of "finding out for oneself" and take on an associated view of one's assigned task. Kelly reminds us that what is involved is "make believe"—a role familiar from most people's childhood.

I suppose, in the end, I am in favor of "getting on with one's life" in the classroom while the problems that presents us with continue to lead to solutions.

REFERENCES

Bannister, D., & Fransella, F. (1971). *Inquiring man*. New York: Penguin.

Kelly, G. (1955). *The psychology of personal constructs* (Vol. 1). New York: W. W. Norton.

Kelly, G. (1969). The autobiography of a theory. In B. Maher (Ed.), *Clinical psychology and personality* (p. 64). Somerset, NJ: John Wiley & Sons.

Maher, B. (Ed.). (1969). *Clinical psychology and personality: The selected papers of George Kelly*. Somerset, NJ: John Wiley & Sons.

Polanyi, M. (1958). *Personal knowledge*. New York: Routledge and Kegan Paul.

4

Understanding Teacher Change from a Vygotskian Perspective

Laura M. W. Martin
Children's Television Workshop

At the end of an intensive five-day staff development workshop in inquiry-based teaching methods, the workshop's teacher-participants were asked how motivated they were to introduce new inquiry techniques into their classroom routines. Virtually everyone rated their motivation at the highest level. A year later, the records of ongoing observations in their classrooms were analyzed to see whether the workshop had led to changes in the ways those teachers organized their lessons. Although several teachers had tried to apply more open-ended, hands-on techniques, most had not assimilated anything new they had learned into their old routines. Furthermore, teachers misremembered the purpose of the workshop. They recalled simply learning how to use some new math and science materials.

The phenomenon of transforming information is not a surprising or unfamiliar one. We are always redigesting information at a later point in time after we have gained new kinds of experience. In the case of teachers, stages of development in adopting innovation have been well documented, specifically, according to the Concerns-Based Adoption Model (Hall, Wallace & Dossett, 1973). The mechanisms of this development process and the conditions that support it, however, are not as well understood. This kind of "resistance" to change—that is, not putting the principles of training into practice—will be addressed in the present chapter.

Changes in an adult's thinking are often taken for granted or seen as the responsibility of the individual. Still, many new studies in the area of expertise and in the use of new technologies in the workplace are beginning to focus on the social context of cognitive development in adults (Scribner & Cole, 1981; Scribner, 1984; Martin & Scribner, 1990). This work has shown that such factors as the social distribution of tasks can lead to differences in the technical concepts adults develop about particular job content (e.g., Scribner, DiBello, Kindred & Zazanis, 1991). Much of the current work on adult development is informed by the theories of L. S. Vygotsky, the Soviet psychologist who died in 1934 at the age of 38. From a Vygotskian perspective, resistance to change can be viewed as a failure to "appropriate" a particular socially defined goal. This failure can arise for reasons that will be examined below.

Vygotsky's work has received a lot of attention recently (Moll, 1990; Rogoff, 1990) because it seems to provide analytic tools for situations that are otherwise hard to understand and describe. These include performance differences by individuals on similar tasks in different settings, and learning in nonformal (i.e., nonschool) settings. While Vygotsky is known best for his work on child development, he was concerned with psychology in general. The core ideas of his theory have been extended by his students and followers and applied to adult development (Leont'ev, 1981; Zinchenko, 1985). Some of these core ideas concern the historical and cultural setting for learning, the everyday or scientific origins of concepts, and the role of others in an individual's intellectual growth.

Introducing new practices into teaching routines is a particularly interesting activity to examine from a Vygotskian point of view. In order to understand why this is so, the following section will review some of the general premises of Vygotsky's theory that relate to questions arising around the topic of teacher change. The results of three teacher training projects will also be described to show how this perspective helps us understand the mechanisms at work in them.

SOME VYGOTSKIAN PRINCIPLES OF INTELLECTUAL CHANGE

In his writings, Vygotsky described fundamental principles of learning and development. Vygotsky was primarily concerned with the development of what he called "higher" mental functions, such as voluntary memory, selective attention, and problem solving—the functions that define the human species. Consistent with a Marxist perspective, the higher mental functions are seen to arise from the activity by which humans control their physical and social environment: labor and the creation of culture. They entail the mastery of physical and psychological tools (including language), which have evolved over the course of history. On the individual level, each child develops higher psychological functions through interactions with others and through internalizing the tools of the culture. The biological possibilities of the species are the platform for growth.

The kind of complex mental processes that arise from engaging in culturally structured activities are ones that are voluntary, reflective, or conscious and, in some senses, tutored. Vygotsky felt that "those forms of social life that have the most profound consequences for mental life . . . lie primarily in the symbolic–communicative spheres of activity in which humans collectively produce new means for regulating their behavior" (Scribner, 1985, p. 123).

For Vygotsky, then, complex thinking is a product of our enculturation. For this reason, his theory is sometimes referred to as sociohistorical or sociocultural theory. This view differs from the Piagetian approach to the construction of knowledge, in which the individual is said to develop generalized intellectual abilities by assimilating formal properties of objects. Instead, the Vygotskian view is that complex thinking arises from the particular patterns of information exchange in which individuals engage, and which are signified as meaningful by the society that surrounds the individual. Patterns acquire meaning to individuals as they participate and partake in a set of practices and as they learn to make use of a culture's tools. In interaction with objects and others, individuals come to organize their thought. (Vygotsky did not write much about affect as a component of learning, although his work implies that affect is an important component of motivation.)

Reflection, a critical component of higher mental functioning, is something that is promoted and supported by the cultural patterns of interchange in which an individual engages. Reflection distinguishes between what happens in intuitive thought processes that children, for example, engage in naturally and the "scientific" thinking promoted in formal instructional settings. In instructional settings such as school or even—as we are now coming to realize in the case of adults— workplaces, abstract rules, algorithms, technical vocabulary, and conceptual terms are applied to concrete experiences. In some cases, abstractions are introduced in special situations arranged to illustrate particular concepts, such as when students are given problems to solve in a science lab. These more abstract representations of experience are what then allow the learner to detect new examples of a concept as well as to solve new problems using a general rule.

Complex or higher order thinking always exists, for Vygotsky, on two planes: the interpsychological (between people) and the intrapsychological (within the individual). What this means is that the mental processes people come to construct in their own minds always have their origins in interchanges between people. Research that looks at how teachers engage with students, for example, shows that students gradually assume more and more of the problem-solving behavior that the teacher initially carried out in the instructional situation (Wertsch, Minick & Arns, 1984; Newman, Griffin & Cole, 1989). Other examples from the research show many types of individual intellectual skills resulting from mentally "distributed" experiences with others (e.g., Rubtsov, 1992).

How information is conveyed from the interpsychological plane to the intrapsychological is explained by the idea that the individual learning process takes place in a "zone of proximal development," a "zone" of developmental sensitivity. In the zone, for example, when novices join in activity with more skilled individuals to complete a task, collaborative activity in relation to the goal of the task is subsequently internalized by the novices. In cooperative work, the experts and the novices are actually both changed by the interaction. The experts' information is "appropriated" in a unique way by the novices according to their own past experiences. At the same time, the experts have their teaching techniques modified by the novices. Of course, when experts are given a chance to articulate what went on in a lesson and to compare it to other situations they may have experienced, they have an even better chance of scientifically modifying their practices. This is an example of promoting their own reflection as learners.

The concept of a zone of proximal development arose from Vygotsky's investigations into the nature of children's differing intellectual performance and has been extended to analyze instructional situations (e.g., Newman et al., 1989). According to Vygotsky, in order to understand the development of thinking, it is necessary to look at the process of development, not simply the outcome, as we might in an exam or sample observation. It is also necessary to understand development on a number of levels, including the social. Thus the zone of proximal development is not a technique or a state the child achieves, but "the dynamic region of sensitivity in which the transition from interpsychological to intrapsychological can be made" (Wertsch, 1985, p. 67).

What is learned, exactly, in the types of zones that Vygotsky analyzed? Facts? Strategies? Mental habits? The answer is, essentially, human behavior, mental activity that is communicated through tools of abstraction. This allows a person not to copy the external (social) pattern, but to transform it and to be transformed by it, to acquire and create culture (see Cole, 1985).

Like Piaget, Vygotsky did not prescribe psychological or intellectual training methods, for children or adults. Instead, he outlined research methods that relate to teaching methods. His main criticism of Piaget, in fact, was the Piaget neglected the role of the adult in his account of development. In his own experiments, Vygotsky looked carefully at the interactions between adult and child to see how information is acquired by the child and how specific interventions reveal what the child is learning. Vygotsky's followers used these observations to design relevant applications in pedagogy, curriculum, and assessment (e.g., Davydov, 1975; Aidarova, 1982; Brown & Ferrara, 1985; Rubtsov, 1992).

Understanding a teacher's intellectual development, however, may be different from understanding that of a child. In observing teachers, we are looking at learning on the job, and at how fairly sophisticated thinking tools are transformed rather than acquired.

An important school of thought concerned with learning at the workplace grows directly out of Vygotsky's theory. The approach is called Activity Theory and was initially elaborated by Vygotsky's colleague, A. N. Leont'ev (1981). Activity as the core unit of analysis in psychological functioning is an idea that also derives from Marxist theory and that takes into account the relation between social institutions and individual development. Vygotsky emphasized this relation throughout his work and conducted some experimental research on the topic (Luria, 1976). Although Vygotsky himself concentrated more on studying individual cognitive processes than on social institutions, he described the need to understand the specific historical and social forces that impact an individual's development. So, for example, the technical sophistication of a society, the social distribution of the tools of knowledge, the demands of work, and types of personal encounters permitted in a culture are all seen as giving shape to an individual's thinking.

Activity Theory claims that an activity (such as completing a job or teaching a lesson) is a unit that implies a socially defined goal and the execution of some specific actions that have evolved or have been created to attain that goal (Leont'ev, 1981; Wertsch, 1979). It involves patterns of communication with others related to the setting and the goal, and thus, mastery of a set of symbolic tools (such as language) or perhaps material tools (such as a hammer or a computer). In an activity, each of these elements influences what the individual learns, carries out, and practices.

At the same time, neither Activity Theory nor Vygotsky's theory in general claims that intellectual functioning and thoughtful action are entirely due to external causes. They describe an interplay between internal development and external constraints, between creative thought and established knowledge. Furthermore, they state that as individuals engage in activity, they transform the work and their own understanding.

ISSUES OF TEACHER CHANGE

Following this brief overview of Vygotskian theory, we can see why teacher training is such an interesting activity to study. First, for Vygotsky and for researchers working in his tradition, examining the role of the teacher in any given instructional situation is critical because the "expert" communicates cultural expectations and new possibilities to the learner that account, in large measure, for learning. Studying the teacher as learner is a particular challenge because the "student" is both an expert and a novice simultaneously. Does the reflectivity of teachers as professionals apply to their own training? What are the characteristics of the cognitive transformation process for people in the business of cognitive change? How do teacher trainers contribute or fail to contribute to the internalization of information?

Another reason why teacher training is interesting to study is that teaching is clearly both a scientific and an intuitive activity. According to our theory, if we understand the intuitive origins and formal origins of different aspects of teaching practices, it should help us understand how to support change in a systematic way, through reaching teachers in their own zone of sensitivity.

Methods for training teachers that accommodate essential Vygotskian principles of learning have been designed but have not been fully studied. The principle value of the Vygotskian perspective here, then, is to help us understand what happens as people change their ways of working or as others try to help them change (see Newman et al., 1989; Moll, 1990). This might mean looking closely at teachers over a period of time as they interact with students and each other in the workplace. It might also mean documenting teachers' understandings of their professional practices and their feelings as learners and instructors.

The research described below presents the results of several teacher training projects. As I describe the outcomes of each, we will see how they are consistent with a Vygotskian account.

ILLUSTRATIVE RESEARCH PROJECTS

In 1983, I began conducting research on a series of projects that were designed to introduce new ideas, techniques, and technologies to teachers. With fellow research team members, I had the opportunity to observe closely as teachers began to use various innovations, both in their own staff development sessions and with their students.

The research had several goals. First, we wanted to identify patterns in the information we collected about teachers' implementation of new techniques. Second, we wanted to understand what supported teachers' adoption of these particular techniques the technologies. Third, we wanted to examine some of the difficulties that arise as teachers tried to change their practices.

The research was primarily observational but in one case utilized structured questionnaires and interview forms. In all cases, we observed a very wide range of instructional approaches that were not easily characterized. We also saw a wide range of responses to training.

The Influence of Institutional Factors on Individual Teacher Change

In 1985, Bank Street College of Education began the Mathematics, Science and Technology Teacher Education (MASTTE) Project to help teachers and staff developers become acquainted with principles of inquiry-based instruction. As they learned to use a multimedia science package and understand the key concepts covered, project participants also learned equipment management and resource planning.

The training participants were 83 individuals who varied widely with respect to their backgrounds and their experience in teaching science. They were elementary and middle school teachers and staff developers from districts and schools across the country.

Despite the extensive experience of some of the teachers, the principles of inquiry-based instruction covered during training were new to many of them. After one week of intensive training sessions, though, teachers returned to their districts with at least some idea of how to proceed in using the materials they learned about and how to develop a broader base for innovation in their science and math programs. In fact, each participant left the training week with specific plans for making the transition to using the new approaches.

The teachers also had reassurances that the project staff and local staff developers would be available to them for consultant support. Over the next three years, researchers collected information about developments at the sites through structured interviews and observations, as well as through teacher and trainer logs and questionnaires.

When we analyzed the data we had collected (Martin, 1987, 1988), we found that the aptitudes of individuals did not account for the difficulties schools were having in organizing effective inquiry-based instruction. Nor did individual teachers' skills or motivations account for how well they understood the purposes of the training week. Rather, the "skills" and understandings of teachers to a great degree depended on the setting in which the teachers found themselves.

Isolation was a big problem. Where the school system's structure prevented supportive contact, the efforts of imaginative teachers to provide meaningful experiences for children were thwarted, and innovations failed to flourish in the classroom. Where people worked together, the pull of old routines was counterbalanced. When the usual working circumstances were supportive of them and when teachers were given the chance to develop their expertise in a new domain, they showed a lot of creativity. In addition, the plans that participants made during training often became useless because of changes in staffing, changes in scheduling, and misunderstandings between teacher and administrators.

From the MASTTE study, we were able to identify features of school systems that, in effect, produced buffers to the forces that characteristically undermine change in a teacher's workplace. Specifically, we found that more extensive inquiry-based programs were catalyzed by the training in sites that had:

- district-level goals for introducing new science approaches to teachers and official approval for teacher experimentation with the program;
- staff developers who had contact with the teachers in their classrooms and with district administrators in their offices;
- administrations and parent bodies informed about the program;
- teams of teachers trained and working together in buildings (staff developers were also more effective when they worked together).

Many successful models for supporting inquiry activities evolved, but all shared these characteristics. In none of these successful cases did the implementation plan represent any one person's idea. Rather, collective growth and development was the rule; usually teachers, specialty teachers, staff developers, and administrators all contributed to the decisions about the development of the program. From the project point of view, of course, this pattern was fortunate: The project staff could not depend on a few successful solitary classrooms to spread the program or to help them understand how to support change.

In sum, institutional factors are a central part of the root system of learning, both for the adult and for the child. As Vygotsky's theory predicts, these larger social factors have to be included in the analysis of training success and failure.

Intuitive and Scientific Concepts of Instruction

The sociohistorical school emphasizes the role of reflection in the development of thinking and practice. Vygotsky and others define such awareness as the basis of scientific or conceptual reasoning. Through deliberate analysis, professional canons are changed and new ones enter the practice.

In the case of teaching, however, the stuff of reflection—classroom interaction—is not easily reflected upon. The situational constraints and historical work patterns in schools mean that teachers' daily practices actually may work against taking a scientific approach, in Vygotsky's sense. These patterns may also work against learning on the job. Because of time pressures, teacher-centered instructional methods, and lack of support staff, the repertoires teachers develop are often constructed upon unanalyzed experiences of instructing students. The second project I will discuss illustrates how the goals of a teacher training program need to be sustained by reflection and analysis on the part of the participants.

For the past four years, a progressive New York private school, in conjunction with New York University, has been conducting summer teacher training in the Investigative-Colloquium Model (I-CM). The I-CM method, developed by B. Lansdown (Lansdown, Blackwood & Brandwein, 1971) and G. Tokieda, is a "Vygotskian" technique of using discussion to help children's conceptual development in science. NYU and the partner private school are working to assess I-CM systematically and to refine the training model.

I-CM has been introduced widely outside of this particular project and has been used for years by a cadre of teachers quite successfully, according to their own evaluations. The technique, however, is difficult to carry out well, in part because it depends on the teacher responding to fairly subtle linguistic cues among the children. Carrying out a successful lesson depends on the teacher phrasing comments carefully and rephrasing children's remarks strategically. Furthermore, part of the way teachers know they are being effective with I-CM is to assess children's contributions during a "colloquium" discussion, by analyzing the depth and nature of their comments and questions. Informally, this is how teachers usually get a sense of where their students stand. With I-CM, this fairly intuitive assessment process is intended to become systematic and quite deliberate.

During the project evaluation, trainers reported that the teachers who began to use the I-CM technique with their classes would happily use a lesson guide like a script. Now, it is common for teachers beginning to master a technique to follow the rules closely before feeling comfortable about improvising, but in this case teachers were experiencing something a bit different. Ordinarily, in the initial stages of innovative programs, teachers will express anxiety and insecurity about the new method as they try to replicate what they saw demonstrated in training. Rather than feeling insecure, though, the I-CM teachers had very positive feelings about what they were doing, felt clear about it, and did not seem to think their scripted approach was problematic. In short, the point of their training—to learn to foster children's creative interpretation of data and facilitate their discoveries—was being simplified. From their inflexibility, we would say that the teachers had developed a nonscientific concept about the technique.

This simultaneously rigid yet positive attitude teachers adopt is complicated to understand. What we see in the I-CM project is that there is something about trying things out in the classroom that prevents teachers' daily experiences and more intellectual understandings from becoming integrated. The classroom situation seems actually to promote adhering unreflectively to whatever strategy works.

Our theory suggests two possible explanations. One relates to the job setting. The circumstances under which teachers do their learning, the times they get feedback about their efforts, are when they are "on stage." This does not allow them a chance to reflect on or assimilate the meaning of students' responses for their own work. Yinger has discussed how good teachers are like ad lib performance artists, inviting student challenges and choosing to take on difficult material to keep themselves toned (Yinger, 1987). If these rapid-fire conditions are teachers' only place to improve their performance, however, there is a problem.

Another reason for the power of the classroom experience over reflection relates to teachers' training experiences. Davydov (1975), Galperin (1969), and others working in the Vygotskian tradition suggest that traditional short-term methods of imparting information to teachers can result in the development of concepts that are less scientific and therefore less flexible than ones developed through more extended experiences such as apprenticeships. In a short time period, teachers may only have time to learn new terms but not fully learn their application. This may also lead the teachers to be reactive rather than reflective once they are back in the classroom.

Vygotsky's theory distinguishes between children's everyday, or intuitive, concepts and their "scientific," or generalized, concepts.

The difference between them rests on how they are acquired, either naturally or as a result of analysis and reflection. For teacher training, this distinction raises the question of whether practices built on different bases (experiential or analyzed) are equally flexible to apply in daily problem-solving situations.

Teachers' Zones of Proximal Development

We usually use the notion of a "zone of proximal development" when talking about a child learning a new cognitive skill. But we might also apply this notion to the conditions under which an adult learns new things. This application is not obvious because adults have already mastered many types of "higher" functions. Since they have been through school, for example, adults can think conceptually in many domains. They can also extract information very well from print and other abstract notation systems, and they are experienced problem solvers. It seems as though adults should be able to construct understanding on their own and apply whatever they have learned to their work.

In the case of acquiring subject matter understanding, such might be the case. But, I would claim, acquiring new teaching practices really means learning new communication strategies and new ways to organize informative environments. Skillfulness in these activities depends on a reflective approach. It also involves the teacher in a dynamic learning process with others, specifically, colleagues as well as students.

In the third project I will review, five teachers were partners with researchers in developing computer-based science literacy activities for children. The activities were focused on addressing some common difficulties teachers encounter in science instruction. The difficulties identified for the project were:

- the need to help children perceive the relevance of science;
- motivating children to organize their inquiries; and
- the general lack of variation in children's language.

Previous work we had done suggested that teachers who were less comfortable with science, and who therefore arranged these activities less often, were relatively more comfortable expanding on language-based science activities than they were developing hands-on activities using measuring, charting, graphing, counting, calculating, and other data representation systems. Applying the notion of a zone of proximal development, we tried to begin with what the teachers were likely to manage well, namely language arts-based activities, and then move them along into other types of activities.

The problem of children's language, originally phrased by one teacher as a problem of "limited vocabulary," formed the basis for the set of activities I will focus on here. The language issue is an interesting one because, according to the many interviews I have conducted, the perception is characteristic of teachers with traditional training or many years of experience working with traditional science textbooks. These teachers are used to beginning a lesson by introducing vocabulary. They do not feel comfortable tackling a subject, especially in science, without having children familiar with the scientific terms and labels. These teachers tell you they cannot explain anything, nor can the children tackle a topic, unless a technical vocabulary is first established.

A contrasting view is held by many educators, Vygotskian and otherwise, trying to promote inquiry-based learning. They view vocabulary as something that should arise from children's activities. The activities should provoke the need for verbal precision, discrimination, and effective communication. Their needs should drive the search for words. If learning the vocabulary comes before the inquiry, the concept behind the term may never come to be usefully applied because it is not fully understood.

We wanted to work with the teachers' starting points and move them along, so we first began by recasting the problem. Instead of emphasizing the problem as residing within the child ("lack of vocabulary"), we called it the problem of the lack of variation in children's language, which permitted us to focus on promoting language use through new experiences.

Using material that was at first more and then less familiar to the children, we devised a series of referential communication games. These exercises had the objective of getting the children (and the teacher) to see that using the explicit terms concisely could help them to be understood. We also organized an exercise for the class that illustrated how expressing their observations clearly can help their reasoning process. In another unit, the children completed a play about a scientific adventure, which was tied into the concept of changing one's point of view in problem solving.

The class we were working with happened to be the lowest track fifth-grade class in a school with few resources. Furthermore, teacher morale was low. Under the conditions we established, however, the children were able to generate rich yet specific descriptions with their language, create descriptive metaphors for events they observed, and articulate the purposes of the exercises we organized.

As the weeks went by, the teacher, who resisted our efforts to have her conduct the experimental lessons herself, saw that her students were able to express themselves in ways she had not seen them do before. She acknowledged that the program was attempting something new and useful. Although the project was primarily a design project and did not include long-range follow-up for the participating teachers, we had hoped to create some potential for change. We had hoped to leave the teacher equipped with a set of ideas on how to organize activities to produce different verbal responses among the children that she could build on. By developing instructional models and by showing her that her students were capable of unexpected competencies, we hoped to provide an experience she could draw on in the future.

We tried to construct activities that addressed the teacher's own concerns about children's language, yet encourage her to adapt her agenda in a way that illustrated the contextual nature of the children's language patterns. We were able to succeed with the children, but we only succeeded up to a point in changing the teacher's understanding. To the end, for example, she apologized for the fact that the children were talking so much, which told us she had missed part of the point of our work.

Although we may have provided some new insights for her, we did not change this teacher's practice because, in the school, there was little opportunity to work together beyond the time of our little demonstration. Furthermore, no one else in the school was working on these problems.

If the change literature is correct (see Guskey, 1986), and if the idea of a zone of proximal development has substance, the demonstration we provided this teacher might well be a first step to getting her to try something new. But much more ongoing outreach was needed.

Clearly, a good idea alone is insufficient to cause changes in teachers' perceptions and pedagogical practices. The subsequent sustaining steps, as we have described above, depend on larger changes in the teacher's milieu, as well as the relation of the staff developer to the individual teacher. As our theory tells us, the nature of a person's interactions with others is key to his or her internalization of new information.

CONCLUSIONS

In our research we found that, with few exceptions, teachers are learners and that the learning happens at their workplace. That is, authentic understanding of the new methods was gained in the course of practice, as teachers developed new questions and concerns about their work. But, although the value of various new strategies was universally recognized and appreciated during the training, "resistance" often followed. New ideas were not put into practice by every teacher who was trained.

The ideas discussed in this chapter point to the fact that the bases for creating changes in teaching practices cannot be understood by looking at individual teacher characteristics, the nature of the innovation, or contact with new ideas alone. Rather, particular district and school organizations and teachers' professional interactions allowed certain teachers to apply understanding and awareness and to expand their programs and repertoires to meet children's needs.

The research literature seems to tell us that the success of new teaching methods depends on the teachers' notions, the children's misconceptions, and the structure of particular activities. But when we inject a Vygotskian approach into our analysis that looks at teachers' working conditions, the structure of training, and teachers' interactions with colleagues, we can better account for individual differences among teachers. We may also gain some better insight about useful program adjustments.

Sustaining experiments such as the MASTTE Project required the involvement of others besides the teacher, as well as a wide support system for the teacher's good intentions and insights. Explanations for differences in teachers' thinking were found in the structure of their workplace, the school. There, among colleagues and strong traditions, teachers defined their professional goals and developed their practices.

In the case of the I-CM training, the situation we observed suggested that teachers cannot integrate theory with practice to create new, flexible understandings simply by doing what we think of as their "job." The job involves more than classroom performance: It encompasses professional development. Teachers need opportunities to analyze their experiences, to hear about those of others, and to exchange ideas. Otherwise, their experiences may remain unexamined and, as such, inflexible. Ironically, the more sound the ideas are initially, the more teachers will attempt to preserve them rigidly.

On the third project we reviewed, we learned that teachers, like other learners, cannot develop or reflect on learning in a setting where new ideas are not given time to take hold. Again, without time and support for constructive interaction, there is no chance that the teacher will appropriate the new information. If, instead, we focus our attention on the individual teacher's "flexibility" or "aptitude" to explain the success of our training programs, we are in danger of overlooking critical factors that influence pedagogical change.

The lessons these studies point to is that we need to think about ways to design measures and models that take broader social and cultural features into account in individual classrooms. We need to support extended learning opportunities so that teachers' concrete experiences and abstract understandings can become fully integrated. We need to begin with teachers' actual concerns and support their reflection and professional communication. We also need more studies that link the system-level factors with specific changes in teachers' intellectual patterns.

Studying change within the teaching profession means looking at a special kind of cultural development. As Vygotsky's work suggests, the structure and substance of teaching activity, which takes place in an enormously complex interactional setting, powerfully shapes adult learning and, in turn, children's learning as well.

REFERENCES

Aidarova, L. (1982). Child development and education. Moscow: Progress Publishers.

Brown, A. L., & Ferrara, R. (1985). Diagnosing zones of proximal development. In J. V. Wertsch (Ed.), Culture, communication, and cognition. New York: Cambridge University Press.

Cole, M. (1985). The zone of proximal development: Where culture and cognition create each other. In J. V. Wertsch (Ed.), Culture, communication, and cognition. New York: Cambridge University Press.

Davydov, V. V. (1975). The psychological characteristics of the "prenumerical" period of mathematics instruction. In E. G. Begle, J. Kilpatrick, J. W. Wilson, & I. Wirszup (Eds.), Soviet studies in the psychology of learning and teaching mathematics, VII. Chicago, IL: University of Chicago Press.

Hall, G. E., Wallace, R. C., Jr., & Dossett, W. A. (1973). A developmental conceptualization of the adoption process within educational institutions. Austin: University of Texas, Research and Development Center for Teacher Education.

Galperin, P. Y. (1969). Stages in the development of mental acts. In M. Cole & I. Maltzman (Eds.), A handbook of contemporary Soviet psychology. New York: Basic Books.

Guskey, T. R. (1986). Staff development and the process of teacher change. Educational Researcher, 15(5), 5–12.

Lansdown, B., Blackwood, P. E., & Brandwein, P. F. (1971). Teaching elementary science through investigation and colloquium. New York: Harcourt Brace Jovanovich.

Leont'ev, A. N. (1981). Problems of the development of mind. Moscow: Progress Publishers.

Luria, A. R. (1976). Cognitive development. Cambridge, MA: Harvard University Press.

Martin, L. M. W. (1988, April). System-wide factors in sustaining technology-based inquiry environments. Paper presented at the American Educational Research Association Meetings. New Orleans, LA.

Martin, L. M. W. (1987). Teachers' adoption of multimedia technologies for science and mathematics instruction. In R. Pea & K. Sheingold (Eds.), *Mirrors of the mind: Patterns of experience in educational computing.* Norwood, NJ: Ablex.

Martin, L. M. W., & Scribner, S. (1990). Laboratory for Cognitive Studies of Work: A case study of the intellectual implications of a new technology. Teachers College Record, 92(4), 582–602.

Moll, L. (Ed.). (1990). *Vygotsky and education: Instructional implications of sociohistorical psychology.* New York: Cambridge University Press.

Newman, D., Griffin, P., & Cole, M. (1989). *The construction zone: Working for cognitive change in school.* New York: Cambridge University Press.

Rogoff, B. (1990). *Apprenticeship in thinking: Cognitive development in social context.* New York: Oxford University Press.

Rubtsov, V. V. (1992). *Learning in children: The organization and development of cooperative action.* Commack, NY: Nova Science.

Scribner, S. (1985). Vygotsky's use of history. In J. V. Wertsch (Ed.), *Culture, communication, and cognition.* New York: Cambridge University Press.

Scribner, S. (Ed.). (1984). Cognitive studies of work. *Quarterly Newsletter of the Laboratory of Comparative Human Cognition, 6,* Special Issue. La Jolla, CA: University of California, San Diego.

Scribner, S., & Cole, M. (1981). *The psychology of literacy.* Cambridge, MA: Harvard University Press.

Scribner, S., DiBello, L., Kindred, J., & Zazanis, E. (1991). *Coordinating two knowledge systems: A case study.* Unpublished manuscript. Laboratory for Cognitive Studies of Work, New York.

Wertsch, J. V. (1985). *Vygotsky and the social formation of mind.* Cambridge, MA: Harvard University Press.

Wertsch, J. V. (1979). *The concept of activity in Soviet psychology.* Armonk, NY: Sharpe.

Wertsch, J. V., Minick, N., & Arns, F. J. (1984). The creation of context in joint problem solving. In B. Rogoff & J. Lave (Eds.), *Everyday cognition: Its development in social contexts.* Cambridge, MA: Harvard University Press.

Yinger, R. J. (1987, April). Teaching by the seat of your pants: Improvisation in an algebra classroom. In C. Clark (Chair), *Studies of teachers' thinking-in-action.* Symposium presentation at American Educational Association Meetings, Washington, DC.

Zinchenko, V. P. (1985). Vygotsky's ideas about units for the analysis of mind. In J. V. Wertsch (Ed.), *Culture, communication, and cognition.* New York: Cambridge University Press.

Response to Martin:
"Understanding Teacher Change
from a Vygotskian Perspective"

Denis Newman
Bolt Beranek and Newman Inc.

The chapter by Laura Martin introduces a theoretical perspective that may be less familiar than the Piagetian or the behaviorist perspectives that have been very influential in education. The perspective is very timely, however, because the current attention to school restructuring and to changes in the role of the teacher from instructor to facilitator of student inquiry calls for simultaneous changes in what teachers know and how they organize their work.

The sociohistorical school—or, more popularly, the Vygotskian school—brings together the cognitive and the social in a way that helps address teacher change in the context of organizational change. Take as an example the radical changes that the National Council of Teachers of Mathematics (NCTM) have recently called for in the way teachers conduct math lessons. Students should be learning to solve problems, not just to perform computations; they should be able to communicate about math, not just absorb it. We can understand this call for reform from several theoretical points of view. The proposed standards are consistent with Piagetian constructivism, which has always argued that it is not sufficient to lecture and drill the students. Students need the opportunity to construct the math. But when we turn to putting the reforms into practice, we have to ask how these opportunities are constructed. In practice there has to be a reorganization of the classroom. The teacher reorders the discourse so the students can ask questions and, as a group, they can come to share words for the math concepts that emerge in class.

From the constructivist perspective, this new classroom atmosphere allows an internal process to go on in the student. From that perspective, it is the internal process that is important to learning math. How the setting is changed to allow it to happen falls outside the theory itself. From the Vygotskian perspective, on the other hand, the change in organization of the math classroom is just as interesting as the transformation of thinking. The organizational change is not just an external condition for internal construction; it is the occasion for "interpsychological" construction. Since, from this point of view, new concepts originate in the interaction among people, new ways of interacting, discussing, questioning, and so on can create new "construction zones" for the class (Newman, Griffin, & Cole, 1989). As a research paradigm for studying teacher development, the advantage of the Vygotskian perspective is that the resulting changes in the classroom, what happens in the interaction between the teacher and the student, are the core. The internal construction by the student occurs in the context of the social interaction, not in isolation.

In a manner of speaking, the new classroom organization is a "zone of proximal development." That is, insofar as students are engaged in the interaction, they are operating within the zone of their capabilities. The teacher leads the discussion to some extent, reflecting on what the students say, rephrasing, encouraging students to ask questions, and so on. The students are engaged in problem solving supported by the teacher. The task of solving a math problem at the board, for example, is initially too difficult for the students to perform at their seats on their own. We can say the teacher creates a zone in which the students can work effectively on the problem.

What happens in that zone, in the interaction between teacher and student, is the critical research issue from the Vygotskian perspective. It is not sufficient to say that the student gradually takes over more of the task. That is an oversimplification into which a lot of discussions of Vygotskian education fall. For example, we find researchers such as Collins, Brown, and Newman (1989) referring to "scaffolding and fading" as a feature of a form of teaching they call "cognitive apprenticeship." In this process, the teacher starts out with a fairly high level of support, perhaps doing most of the task for the student, and gradually fades into the background as the student is able to take over more of the task components. As a recommendation for practice, the notion of scaffolding and fading implies that the goal of the student's work is entirely determined by the teacher, which is not necessarily the case with a zone of proximal development. Given a particular kind of support, different students may move in different directions, not just more or less closely to a fixed end-point. For example, students are able to invent new algorithms for solving computations if the teacher gives help in conceptualizing the problem. In this case, the "scaffold" does not lead to a predetermined result but to an invention that may not have been anticipated. That is, there is interactive construction and the teacher is not simply relinquishing predefined task components. As a framework for research, the notion of fading begs the question as to what actually happens in the zone. How does the student come to understand the task? how is what is relevant communicated? what parts of the task can the student be engaged in? how is the task transformed as the concepts are acquired? and so on. The point of the zone concept is to focus research on the construction of new knowledge as observed within the "interpsychologically" constructed task.

As a research program, the Vygotskian theory has particular relevance to the current reform movement. But what about it as a teaching practice? Is there a Vygotskian practice (as there is a Piagetian practice)? Is there a Vygotskian way of training teachers, and is it related to what it might mean to be a Vygotskian teacher?

It is quite striking in reading the Martin chapter that the only reference to a teaching method is one published two decades ago (and is now out of print). The Investigation-Colloquium Model (Lansdown, Blackwood, & Brandwein, 1971) is being pursued by a small number of teachers. There is practically no research being done to document or evaluate this practice. It would seem to be on its last legs. Perhaps an approach with Marxist roots is a poor candidate for widespread dissemination in this post-Cold War era. But one of the core Marxist ideas turns out to be quite useful in applying theory to practice. The idea is to remove the dualism of culture and cognition and of external stimulus and internal construction. The removal of this dualism is not achieved by denying the internal (as in behaviorism) or denying the external (as in some forms of radical constructivism). The focus is on the transformation of one into the other. This is where the relevance of Vygotsky to school reform is strong: in the focus on changes in practice that are simultaneously cognitive and organizational.

The core ideas of the Vygotskian approach are getting more play than the scant attention to the I-CM seems to indicate. There is growing interest in a notion of a "community of practice" as a basis for learning (Lave & Wenger, 1991), an approach consistent with Martin's concern for the conditions under which teachers reflect on what they have put into practice. Schoenfeld (in press), for example, points to the importance of the classroom as an intellectual community to which college students contribute in the process of collaborative problem solving. The teacher plays a role of interpreter and mediator. Likewise, Lampert (1986) describes the interactive construction of math concepts in her elementary classroom. In both cases, the classroom community is the locus of construction as students are drawn into the socially consti- tuted practice of mathematical reasoning. The social discourse in these classrooms, like the colloquium in the I-CM, is the occasion for reflection and the locus of conceptual change. Martin's perspective on teacher training also highlights the importance of the community of teachers. We cannot take individual teachers, "train" them, and send them back to the classroom. We must find ways to break down the isolation of teachers. A new practice must be developed in the schools, and a community must be maintained that continues to support it.

REFERENCES

Collins, A., Brown, J. S., & Newman, S. (1989). Cognitive apprenticeship: Teaching the craft of reading, writing, and mathematics. In L. B. Resnick (Ed.), *Cognition and instruction: Issues and agendas*. Hillsdale, NJ: Lawrence Erlbaum.

Lampert, M. (1986). Knowing, doing and teaching multiplication. *Cognition and Instruction, 3,* 305–342.

Lansdown, B., Blackwood, P. E., & Brandwein, P. F. (1971). *Teaching elementary science through investigation and colloquium.* New York: Harcourt, Brace and Jovanovich.

Lave, J., & Wenger, E. (1991). *Situated learning: Legitimate peripheral participation.* Cambridge, UK: Cambridge University Press.

Newman, D., Griffin, P., & Cole, M. (1989). *The construction zone: Working for cognitive change in school.* Cambridge, UK: Cambridge University Press.

Schoenfeld, A. (in press). On mathematics as sensemaking: An informal attack on the unfortunate divorce of formal and informal mathematics. In D. N. Perkins, J. Segal, & J. Voss (Eds.), *Informal reasoning and education.* Hillsdale, NJ: Lawrence Erlbaum.

5

Teaching in a Chaotic New Physics World: Teaching as a Dialogue with Reality

Jan D. Sinnott
Psychology Department
Towson State University

It is axiomatic that we live in a time of rapid social change, and that individuals often become teachers in order to become change agents for individuals or society. The "new" sciences—new physics, chaos theory in mathematics, new biology, new cognitive science—focus on mechanisms for dynamic effects, that is, for changes over time. Those who train teachers and who attempt to teach—aware that these happen within the parameters of a given society—might gain useful insights about teaching and learning by examining the new sciences. What do the new sciences have to say about change and induction of change, about teaching and learning?

This chapter examines very briefly four "new" sciences and their implications for the teaching/learning process. These new science models seldom have been used to inform institutional change and seldom have been applied to education, yet they have structures that would lend themselves to such an application. The first focus of this chapter will be on new physics and quantum theory, where concentration will be on ideas about the nature of reality. Next the focus will shift to the new biology, concentrating on its theories of cooperative evolution and brain development. Third, the new mathematics will be examined, especially chaos theory. Finally, the chapter will investigate new cognitive sciences, concentrating on theories of Piagetian post-formal thought. One key idea of each theory will be discussed as an example of its potential richness for classroom teaching. Each theory's potential impact on methods of teaching will be analyzed. Some practical application for teaching and teacher training will be outlined.

It will be argued that one main theme that links the new sciences' focus on change is that social, physical, or personal reality is partly *constructed* by the knower as reality is known, through principles of emergent structures, that is, order hidden within chaos. Teachers who can embrace this dialogue quality of reality empower their students to live fully and adaptively in this time of rapid change. They also more easily survive the changes in their own schools.

NEW PHYSICS MODELS AND TEACHING

Although new physics ideas (e.g., Herbert, 1986; Jeans, 1981; Pagels, 1982; Sinnott, 1981; Sinnott, 1984; Wolf, 1981) have made a tremendous impact on science, technology, and philosophy, they have had a limited impact on the social sciences and everyday life. This may be true in part because new physics concepts are more difficult to grasp since they describe the less familiar "big picture" reality. They differ from Newtonian physics concepts in that they go beyond our everyday familiar reality. However, in times of change, or when one is trying to bring about change, the breadth of the big picture is needed since small-scale descriptions have proved inadequate.

New physics ideas also seem somewhat alien to us because they do not necessarily concur with our shared Western cultural myths about reality (Campbell, 1988). In fact, these ideas are widely respected *because* they overarch cultural considerations. Until we are motivated by desperation, curiosity, or cognitive shifts to explore multiple views of reality, most of us will probably avoid the challenge of new physics ideas.

In my earlier work I have described new physics ideas related to developmental psychology, change, and cognition (e.g., Sinnott, 1981, 1984, 1989a–c). A table summarizing shifts in worldviews, from Newtonian to new physics ideas, is reprinted here. Notice that the shifts have huge implications for psychological reality. The nature of existence in psychological terms (i.e., identity), time (i.e., life span development), and causality (i.e., personal action, power, ability) all shift. Table 2 (Sinnott, 1984) describes the two worldviews in terms of interpersonal relations.

One conclusion that can be drawn from the new physics is that sometimes multiple contradictory views of truth are all "true" simultaneously, although they appear contradictory at first. It can be said that reality is therefore that view of truth to which we make a passionate commitment (Perry, 1975; Polanyi, 1971). Ideally, this commitment is made in awareness and with consciousness. We know

TABLE 1
Old physics/new physics concepts*

Old	New
Space is Euclidean.	Space is non-Euclidean, except in small regions.
Time and space are absolute.	Time and space are relative and better conceptualized as the space/time interval.
Space is uniform in nature.	Space is composed of lesser and greater resistances.
Events are located topologically on a flat surface.	Events are located topologically on the surface of a sphere.
Undisturbed movement is on a straight line.	Undisturbed movement is on a geodesic, i.e., by the laziest route.
Events are continuous.	Events are discontinuous.
No region of events exists which cannot be known.	Unknowable regions of events exist.
Observed events are stable.	Observed events are in motion, which must be taken into account in the observation.
Formation of scientific postulates proceeds from everyday activity through generalizations based on common sense, to abstractions.	Formation of scientific postulates also includes a stage characterized by resolution of contradictions inherent in the abstractions.
Causality is deterministic.	Causality is probabilistic, except in limited space/time cases.
Cause is antecedent to and contiguous with effect.	Cause is antecedent and contiguous to an event only in limiting cases. When events are grouped about a center, that center constitutes a cause.
Egocentrism is replaced by decentration during development of scientific methods.	Egocentrism and decentration are followed by taking ego into account in all calculations.
Concepts in natural laws conform to verbal conventions.	Concepts in natural laws may appear contradictory in terms of verbal conventions.
Universe is uniform.	Universe is nonuniform—either because it is continually expanding or because it is continually being created and negated.

From Sinnott, 1984.

that no one view of reality is, in Bronowski's (1976) words, the "God's eye view"; they are all limited by one's chosen vantage point or measuring tool. This argues that anything is known only within a region of tolerance, or of error, but not absolutely. When we *share* a vantage point (stand in the same context and history)—and only then— do we share a reality.

To create another personal or social reality (within limits), we need

TABLE 2
Applications: Interpersonal relations

Formalistic
- There is only one way to structure our relationship to reflect reality.
- Our relationship exists "out there" in reality.
- Our relationship involves only us, now.
- The relationship has just one "reality"—no need to match levels to understand.
- We can know the essence of each other.
- Role is more important than process.

Relativistic
- Our relations are logical within a set of "givens" that we choose to utilize.
- They are based on both our past relations to each other and our relations to other significant persons.
- Relating means knowing "where you're coming from" and interacting on that level.
- Relating is never knowing "you" completely, because in knowing you I am necessarily subjectively "creating" you.
- Relations are always "in process"; they cannot be described as stable until they end.

From Sinnott, 1984.

to change vantage points as individuals or groups. For example, in the physical world, from a small-scale local-space vantage point, parallel lines never converge. But change vantage points to the longer history and larger context of universal space, and parallel lines always converge!

The impact of a profound idea like that of new physics in the world of teaching can be monumental, whether we are speaking of classroom behavior, teachers confronting a changing society, development programs in Third World countries, or other education problems. From a new physics viewpoint, different incompatible realities are not necessarily to be narrowed to one correct truth; they may each have their own correct logic. From a new physics viewpoint, learning the truths of others can teach us greater flexibility and give us more tools for working with our construction of reality.

From a new physics viewpoint, the line between teacher and learner may be a vague one. Since several truths are simultaneously valid, dialogue is more appropriate than lecture. Awareness of the new physics ideas that truth is partly a choice of vantage points around which we build our reality lets the classroom teacher begin to allow students to use their abilities to construct and experience—and be responsible for—their intellectual lives. Such awareness lets the teacher see a changing society in a more benevolent way as a society shifting from one vantage point (e.g., "Cold War") to another (e.g., "Global Village"). This is a shift that the teacher may join, go beyond, incorporate into a larger shift, and point out to students. Meanwhile, the teacher prepares students to be flexible and to see future shifts in truth as normal rather than as aberrations.

What this means is that the teacher will see his or her role as one of bridging *multiple* valued realities/truths (D. Johnson, 1991). Accepting shifts in reality, bridging, and dialoguing between two "truths" is likely to lead to more permanent, useful, adaptive learning. Such learning is not sabotaged by a rigid worldview.

NEW BIOLOGY MODELS AND TRAINING

Proponents of the "new biology" include Augros and Stanciu (1987), Maturana and Varela (1988), and McLean (1988). Their work derives from the original data on which evolutionary theory was formed, and adds the new experimental data of modern medicine and biology to attempt to answer difficult biological questions. In doing so, they come to conclusions that stand evolutionary theory on its head. One of their basic arguments is that rather than modelling aggression or conflict, biological systems model synergy or cooperation. This means that species do not fight for the same niche in an environment; they evolve to fit a "free" space so that they can *prevent* conflict with another species. Interestingly, "higher," more evolutionary, recent brain centers (like the cortex and prefrontal cortex) do not so much *control* instinct or "lower" centers that are evolutionarily older. Instead, these provide theorists clever ways both to *help* lower centers reach their goals and to provide a sense of community and mutual goal setting between the organism and other organisms around it. The human immune system in this new biology model is more than an army that attacks invaders; it is a sense of wholeness, of mind and body emotional well-being. In the new biology, opposing parts or individuals seem meant to be synthetic rather than confrontational.

What might this finding imply for development models for teacher training? For one thing, it implies that, although biological entities are clearly individuals, they are also part of a larger whole. In this theory the "whole" does not subsume the individual or make the individual unimportant. It desperately needs the individual's specialness to reach its own goal. The part of individual provides the means; the whole provides a large part of the motivation and meaning. Empty evolutionary niches go quickly out of ecological balance because they have lost touch with their meaning. For example, immune systems having missing elements turn on the very body that sustains them. Over and over comes the clean biological message: each part is important; each part is related; each part obtains meaning through the interrelationship.

What does this theory suggest in an educational setting? It suggests that cooperative learning is desirable. Meacham and Emont (1989) have noted that most problem solving is social, not individual; yet classrooms operate as if individuals are alone, and *must* learn alone. Several authors (Johnson & Johnson, 1975; D. Johnson, 1991) and collaborators have demonstrated the value of cooperative learning and group work, but school systems seem slow to accept these ideas. Kohn (1987) has listed the detrimental effects of school competition. Yet in traditional classrooms, the act of getting help from a knowledgeable person to solve a problem is still often considered a sign of weakness. (When one gets to a business setting, cooperative work is "team building" and good.) The suggestion offered to education by the new biology seems to be to capitalize on students' belonging to a larger whole by letting them work together. The lesson of new biology may be like the lesson of the playground. If we each are alone, a bully is a threat; if we form some critical mass of compassion and mutual help, that bully mysteriously becomes less powerful. Teachers may find it worthwhile to try—in spite of pressures from their institutions—to be facilitators of a learning *team*, or *negotiators* between a community and a subject matter; in the spirit of the new biology.

CHAOS THEORY IN MATHEMATICS AND TEACHING

Chaos theory is a new mathematical model that has been used to describe phenomena as different as weather, the structure of coastlines, brain wave patterns, normal or abnormal heartbeat patterns, and the behavior of the mentally ill (Alper, 1989; Cavanaugh, 1989; Crutchfield, Farmer, Packard & Shaw, 1986; Gleick, 1987; Pool, 1989; Sinnott, 1990). Chaos theory describes the orderly and flexible nature of apparent disorder. It mathematically describes dynamic, complex systems with nonlinear equations. It describes commonalities of *process* over time which would otherwise appear *disorderly* if viewed at *one* time point.

One striking feature of chaotic systems is the way in which a tiny disturbance or "perturbation" can lead to complete rescaling of the entire pattern of the system. (This is termed "the butterfly effect" (Gleick, 1987) because weather forecasters using computer models have seen the "breeze" from a butterfly (the idiosyncratic perturbation) eventually lead to a whole new *direction* of wind movement even though the *pattern* of wind is unchanged!) Another feature of chaotic systems is the way a seemingly random set of events, after many repetitive interactions, can coalesce around a point in an apparently orderly way. The impression is of a dominant feature of some sort, analogous to a dominant personality trait or a hurricane eye. This is termed "strange attractors" (Gleick, 1987) because the point looks like it pulls in the events around it.

Think of chaos as "organized disorder," as opposed to sheer randomness, or disorganized disorder. In "orderly disorder," a flexible structure is hidden in events that only seem to be driven by change when examined in linear or one-time "slices." The hidden order unfolds gradually to make itself known when the longer term nonlinear pattern is observed. In true randomness, or "disorderly disorder," there is no hidden structure. Without some chaotic flexibility, some orderly readiness to fluctuate built into the system, a system (especially one like the heart or the brain) is too rigid to adapt and live. For one example, a rigid heartbeat pattern (no chaos) cannot effectively and efficiently correct for a small perturbing error like a skipped beat, so a heart attack occurs. For another example, a rigid brain wave pattern cannot respond effectively to an intellectual challenge, so poor performance results. Chaotic disorder is nonrandom and has a kind of potential to correct errors by use of the underlying, hidden corrective mechanism of the basic deeper pattern. Chaos is an order enfolded into apparent disorder; it is the pattern in the hologram, akin to the "implicate order" described by noted physical scientists Prigogene and Stengers (1984). Implicate order means that an orderly message is encoded within the surface and apparent disorder, so that the implied message can be unfolded and "read." Genetic material is another example of this implied message which is "unpacked," decoded, and read by the organism as the organism develops from its first cells to its full hereditary potential. But the unfolding makes even a very minor element powerful enough to create major effects.

Chaos theory gives a rationale for synchronous effects, those apparently unrelated events that "mysteriously" occur together. The system demonstrates entrainment in which one system locks on to the mode and pattern of another nearby system, so the minor event in one system can move the other systems with it.

What might such a theory as chaos imply? First, it suggests that there is more than one sort of disorder. Useful, chaotic disorder provides fresh options and room to correct for past errors; useless disorder provides nothing that seems meaningful, now or later. Second, it suggests the immense importance of each element in the system for the final outcome of the system as well as for the individual. Remember, a perturbation caused by the butterfly's wing can alter the weather pattern *and* let the butterfly fly! Third, it suggests the importance of openness to innovation to provide natural sorts of corrective devices for complex events.

What does this model suggest for teaching? First, if there are two types of disorder—useful and useless—the teachers must learn to foster creative disorder by tapping into deeper creative patterns. This insight would lead to greater adaptive flexibility for learners by giving them freedom to use *all* the tools for learning (all the pattern parts) they possess. Second, chaos theory points to the potentially tremendous importance of each person's contribution during the information exchange process. One individual can totally alter class dynamics. Could classes alter a society, the way one shift in wind can alter the scale of a weather pattern? If so, in a rapidly changing society, the teacher as a change agent can have real and far-reaching power through entrainment effects to influence change. One student can teach others, including the teacher, as teaching is best done through dialogue. This is a strong argument for interactive education. Third, chaos theory suggests to teachers that rigid adherence to methods or content is less than adaptive, while courting chaos is more creative and flexible. Willingness to hear the chaotic voice of intuition is important as a natural corrective device.

NEW COGNITIVE SCIENCE MODELS AND TEACHING

One new key area developing within cognitive science is called postformal thought. It includes cognitive epistemology (or the knowing of reality) and life-span development. Cognitive development is theorized to be accompanied by increases in social-cognitive experience and skills, and social interaction that leads to greater cognitive development. The ideas of others challenge the reality of the knower. Postformal Piagetian thought is one theory describing this development (Sinnott, 1984, 1989a–c, 1991a–c). Such cognitive approaches go beyond traditional information-processing approaches; postformal thought is a complex way of solving problems, one that develops with social experience, usually not before mature adulthood. It allows a person to solve problems even in situations where conflicted formal operational belief systems and priorities overlap. In postformal thought, the solver faces multiple conflicting ideas about "what is true." The solver realizes that it is not possible to "get outside the mind" to find out which "truth" is "TRUE," but that a solution must be found to the problem anyway. The solver then realizes that the truth system picked as true will *become* true, especially in relation to other people, as the solver lives it to a conclusion.

The main characteristics of these relativistic postformal cognitive operations (Sinnott, 1984) are: (1) self-reference, and (2) the ordering of formal operations. Self-reference is a general term for the ideas inherent in the new physics (Wolf, 1981) and alluded to by Hofstadter (1979) using the terms "self-referential games," "jumping out of the system," and "strange loops." The essential notion of self-reference is that we can never be completely free of the built-in limits of our system of knowing, and that *we come to know* that this very fact is true. This means that we take into account, in all our decisions about truth, the fact that all knowledge has a subjective component and therefore is, of necessity, incomplete. So, any logic we use is self-referential logic. Yet we must *act*, and do so by making a lower-level decision about the higher-level decision rules (nature of truth), then making decisions based on those rules. Once we come to *realize* what we are doing, we then can *consciously* use self-referential thought.

The second characteristic of postformal operations is the ordering of Piagetian formal operations. The higher-level postformal system of self-referential truth decisions gives order to lower-level formal truth and logic systems. One of these is somewhat subjectively chosen and imposed on data as "true." For example, Perry (1975) describes advanced college students as *deciding* a certain ethical system is "true," knowing full well that there is no absolute way of deciding the truth of an ethical system.

This is also the logic of the "new" physics (relativity theory and quantum mechanics) (Sinnott, 1981). New physics is the next step beyond Newtonian physics and is built on the logic of self-reference. It is reasonable that the development of logical processes themselves would follow that same progression (i.e., Newtonian logic, then new physics logic) to increasing complexity. As mentioned earlier, some characteristics that separate new physics thinking from earlier forms can be found in Table 1.

A new type of cognitive coordination occurs at the postformal level. Another kind of coordination of perspectives also occurs on an *emotional* level, taking place over developmental time (Labouvie-Vief, 1987). This coordination parallels the cognitive one, and is probably engaged in a circular interaction with it. Theorists expect that postformal thought is adaptive in a social situation with emotional and social components (Sinnott, 1984) because it is hypothesized to ease communication, to reduce information overload, and to permit greater flexibility and creativity of thought. The postformal thinker knows she/he is helping to create the eventual TRUTH of a social interaction by being a participant in it and choosing to hold a certain view of its truth. Postformal thought has an impact on one's view of self, the world, other persons, change over time, creativity, spirituality, learning and our connections with one another over time (Sinnott, 1981, 1984, 1989b, 1991a–c, 1992, in press a,b). It represents the way one knows or understands ideas such as those in the new sciences, that is, in all the models we have examined in this chapter.

What is the impact on teaching of such a view of cognitive processes? In earlier work, Lee (1991) has discussed some of the points of impact of this theory on the teaching process. L. Johnson (1991) has examined postformal thought as it relates to the teaching/learning process in international development programs. Both concluded that effective expert teachers and change agents show characteristics of postformal thought and complex cognitive processes. They can bridge across belief systems, entertain several views of truth, and work well in complex social realities. They can create the necessary chaos for the flexible change that must accompany learning. They can create cooperative learning environments in which dialogues between "teacher" and "learner" take place, dialogues which honor the truths of both parties. And by modeling such thought, permitting various perspectives, and challenging any Newtonian/conflict-based/inflexible worldviews of their students, they provide the best conditions for the development of postformal thought in students.

SPECIFIC IMPACT OF NEW SCIENCES' IDEAS ON TEACHING

Promoting Diversity and Creativity

Table 3 features some new science core principles. All new sciences make use of chaos, systems, and process ideas. The second column of Table 3 relates each principle to a specific way in which it promotes diversity and creativity through the mediating effects of teachers' behaviors. Table 4 contains a list of activities that can be consciously undertaken by teachers, students, parents, and administrators to encourage more openness to diversity with its concomitant states of conflict (cf. Sinnott, 1991a). Conflict and discomfort in the face of change are the largest barriers to classroom change because they lead to defensive, rigid stands.

The dynamic of change involves interacting elements that cross boundaries between self and society, as well as boundaries between aspects of self (McLean, 1988). Kenneth Gergen, in *The Structured Self* (Gergen, 1991), argues that the anguish of postmodern experience is

TABLE 3
New sciences as a framework for teaching diversity

10 Principles of New Science	Way They Promote Diversity
1. Change can only occur if the system includes *disorder* or *potential* or *unstructuredness*.	1. Teachers create disorder, challenge thought and rules, open up questions with "no" answers, reward students' adaptation of alternative ways to think, be, and see the world around them, challenge interpretations.
2. Systems construct their own reality.	2. Students can construct class rules, goals, value systems.
3. An "entity" is not necessarily the result of a boundary; it is also a "consistent set of relations with others."	3. Teachers examine class members' identities as they try new and consistent styles of relating to other people or things or knowledge or themselves.
4. Systems are synergistic.	4. Students explore knowledge cooperatively, not as competitors.
5. Systems that survive have "porous" boundaries.	5. Besides teaching criticism, teachers offer students a *good* thing about every theory, viewpoint, study, philosophy.
6. Systems go through predictable "life stages."	6. Students can be taught to honor—not to be anxious about—their normal stages of thinking, understanding, analysis. This permits them to learn from experiences rather than fight them.
7. Rigid systems are dying systems.	7. "True believers" of *any* theoretical, political, social stripe are the last gasps of a dying system. (When you're sure you're "right," you're history.) (Therefore, doubt this statement.)
8. To change, systems need other systems to interact with.	8. Because learning is a *social* experience, students learn to make good use of disagreements.
9. Systems strive for continuity.	9. Co-opting an example, idea or theory is easier than destroying it, and may let you see if it works.
10. Systems alter based on their context.	10. Teacher or student—remember the old saying: "Never eat with fools." Choose stimulating contexts.

due in part to the overwhelming number of interrelationships we experience between self and others in our lives. This leads us to *see* the relativistic and self-referential quality of our own decision making about our own identities. Awareness of our role in our creation of a self can either make us very uncomfortable, or lead us to a broader view of

TABLE 4

Methods for transforming classroom conflict experience into change experience

- Purposely attempt to shift perspectives so that some other reality about the problem can be explored.
- Consciously expect conflicts in the group and make them constructive.
- Consciously expect and accept intragroup conflict (at some level of intensity) as a routine experience.
- Consciously see ourselves as "all in this together."
- Posit that "no one is to blame for this problem."
- Assume that others act in the best way they know how (but that not all their actions need be tolerated even if they mean well).
- Consciously address facts about a conflict, but don't assume that others see the same "facts."
- Convincingly create a story around the conflict . . . and let the conflict show you its own solution.
- Enlarge the problem space by redefining the problem or its parameters.
- Generate many "crazy" solutions to the conflict.
- Shift from focusing on a concrete solution to focusing on finding a good process.

reality (Sinnott, 1991a–c). Indeed, the conscious creation of this complexity of awareness has been the goal of all learning and growth traditions, including those of religious, psychotherapeutic, and mystical traditions, for millennia.

Going even deeper to a more basic dynamic, philosophy has juxtaposed the worldview of objective, mechanical reality against the romantic worldview of reality that is moved by emotion and mystery (Gergen, 1991). It seems that the postmodern period in which we now live is a time to unite these worldviews in a fresh union of mind and heart, objectivist and romantic, self and society. The individual as a member of the culture constructs—together with the culture—a shared reality. The shared vision becomes objectively real. The individual and the group choose to live aspects of it and incorporate them. This shared construction inevitably leads to change. The core principles of the new sciences describe the patterns in ways that reality can be shaken up, reconstructed, and used as a reason for change.

The first principle noted in Table 3 is that *change can occur only if there is potential*. In teacher behaviors, this translates to opening up the meaning and possibility of things by, for example, asking questions that have no answers. Something as simple as "what is the right way to study for a test?" can lead to a discussion that shows there are many "right" ways (many realities). Since one can still choose one way to actually study, though, one need not be immobilized.

The second core principle is that *systems construct their reality with the outside world*. In teacher behavior, this can mean permission from the teacher for students to invent a course point system on which their grades are ultimately based (within the parameters of school requirements, of course). This highly charged negotiation situation *always* leads to a resolution, so students can see firsthand that diversity need not lead to immobilization or permanent indecision.

The third principle on the table is that *one need not be defined by a boundary, but may instead be defined by a set of relations to others.* Teacher behavior can nurture this principle and enhance change processes by creating situations in which students relate first one way, then another, to each other. In the author's high school, for example, students took turns being "those who keep order and clean up" and "those who are free not to think about order." Of course, all students quickly learned their world from multiple perspectives and became much better at creating the type of environment they wanted to live in!

Table 3's fourth principle is that *systems are synergistic.* Teachers who create multiperson learning experiences allow the many diverse systems to nourish each other in the classroom. Writing projects in which each person writes alone about a common topic, then shares that piece with others, lead to (at some point) a major leap forward in the quality of all papers and an awareness that each paper nevertheless remains unique. Principle 4 relates to Principle 5, in that the *systems that survive have "porous" boundaries and can admit new information.* The teacher's behavior is the best model for students trying to do this; the teacher can go with the "teachable moment," for example. But students doing the open writing exercise described above also quickly see that their papers will benefit from being open to others' input.

Teachers can demonstrate the sixth principle—that *systems go through predictable life stages*—by pointing out developmental stages in the life of a class. For example, the reassurance of knowing that other students initially feel anxiety about some subject and confusion over cooperative exercises, but later feel at ease, lets students feel safe enough to experiment with their thinking. The teacher can talk about personal experiences, too. This suggests that if the teacher "made it" through anxiety like theirs, they can, too.

Principle 7 is that *rigid systems are dying.* One of the most striking ways for teachers to teach this principle is for the teacher to be a rigid system. Students may be polite to a rigid teacher, but will see the teacher as irrelevant (a "fossil" in the terms of the author's school-age friends) and vow to live otherwise. More effective, and certainly better for the teacher, is to realistically abandon a project that is failing, acknowledging that it is time to try something else. The teacher may even invite the class to help think of that something else. This leads to Principle 8, which lets the *teacher promote change by getting greater input (greater potential)* about this project from others.

Systems do strive for continuity, though, according to Principle 9. The teacher can provide that continuity and still induce change by showing students how diverse ideas (old and new) link together. This linkage of ideas validates change and diversity while allowing the central project to continue.

The teacher, finally, can show that *systems change based on their context* (Principle 10). One of the most interesting ways to demonstrate this is to allow several groups to choose the same topic to write about, and to give relatively few guidelines. Groups quickly see that it is their particular "mix" that makes their product different from the other group's product.

More tools for creating conscious classroom tolerance of diversity and conflict along new science lines, thereby leading to acceptance of necessary change, are in Table 4.

Why Is Classroom Change Different?

The new science core principles outlined in this chapter predict some of the roadblocks to change in the classroom. Once again, see Table 3. The first principle is that change can only occur if the system has "space" for it. This space is "potential" or "unstructuredness." Most classrooms are nested in an organization with a fairly firm bureaucracy and are run in an authoritarian, rather than a dialogic, style. Time is to be filled by directed activity, not left open to possibility. There often is a "right" or "wrong" way to do things. Disorderly looking behavior is considered the sign of a poorly run classroom. All these attitudes and expectations militate against the potential necessary for change to occur. If systems construct their reality (#2), change comes hard when the reality is "we've always done it like this" and "we (not you) know what's best."

In Table 3, Principle 3 says that "identity" is a product of relations. Many teachers and schools still have only one type of relation with students, a hierarchical one where teachers have greater power. In a one-relation environment, possibilities for changes in identity are stillborn. Synergy (#4) is not easy to use if no surprises are admitted by the teacher who is considered to be the only authority figure.

Classroom interactions are too often limited to just a few, which means that change permitted by "porous boundaries" (#5) is fore-closed. Even the great diversity students can find by examination of *their own* reactions, responses, and group dynamics is often officially closed to inquiry, leading to stasis. The life stages of groups (#6) are often ignored in classrooms. For example, students are seldom honored for getting more knowledgeable, as people, as years go by, although a 30-year-old college sophomore is much *wiser* than a 20-year-old one! Rigid systems are enshrined in many classrooms where nothing changes.

Most classrooms forbid cooperative projects where knowledge is *really* shared. This means that there is no system/system interaction (#8), and change is less likely to occur. Since systems strive for continuity (#9), one way to ensure nonchange is to imply that change will be catastrophic to the "old order." In many school systems, this defensive posture is maintained consistently.

Finally, if systems alter based on a context (#10), one way to support change is to contextualize learning. Even today, many, if not most, activities in classrooms are devoid of context, existing for the sake of the classroom only. For example, papers are written to communicate with the teacher rather than with any real-life external audience. If the projects *were* also placed in a real-life context, the value of the exercise would be seen. For example, the writing assignment could be to write a newsletter about the students for parents. The students would see the value of writing and could practice looking at reality from the parents' perspectives.

The key element in letting classrooms be open to change—change inside the classes themselves, and change in the culture—may be to let them be led by teachers who are open to change. Persons who have experience as "change agents" in some other domain (for example, returning Peace Corps volunteers) might be invited to teach. Such teachers with a fresh outlook could bring new ways of seeing.

CONCLUSION

This chapter presents very brief descriptions of four "new science" models, along with several of their general philosophical implications and several of their implications for teaching. A summary of those points is in Table 5.

A key idea to note, in closing, is the clear convergence of implications of all four new science models concerning the teaching process in a changing society. The models' overriding message is that change is a dialogue, and that all voices matter. The models all suggest that we must change our traditional approaches to a greater use of dialogue and intuition if we expect our species to learn to survive in the world we are now constructing. And the construction of our world never ends.

TABLE 5
Summary table: Some potential implications of new sciences for teaching

Concept Applied to Teaching	Implication	Prescription for Teachers
From New Physics:		
• Relativity, quantum physics: Multiple contradictory realities can all be true depending on vantage points.	• Multiple truths are "true" depending on one's vantage point and choice.	• Prepare learners for multiple truths; bridge equally valid realities; have dialogues with learners.
From New Biology:		
• Cooperative evolution: Species don't fight for the same niche; they evolve to fit interrelated, nonoverlapping niches.	• Individual organisms are important as individuals *and* as somewhat irreplaceable members of a whole system.	• Use cooperative learning; be a fellow explorer with learners; limit competition in classroom; focus on individuals in synchrony with a larger whole.
From New Mathematics:		
• Chaos theory: Systems have adaptive disorder by design, which leads to unpredictable outcomes.	• Some disorder is nonrandom and is adaptive. • Systems that tolerate disorder survive. • Each system element has an impact on the whole.	• Foster creative disorder in the teaching process; use dialogue, as each individual's imput matters tremendously.
From New Cognitive Science:		
• Life span cognitive development and post-formal Piagetian thought: Mature knowers partly choose and construct TRUTH, especially social truth.	• The learned individual sees the relativity of realities and truth, but must make a passionate commitment to act, anyhow. This is postformal thought.	• Become a postformal thinker. Master teachers and good change agents are postformal thinkers, and teachers who relate well with adult learners are postformal.

REFERENCES

Alper, J. (1989). The chaotic brain: New models of behavior. *Psychology Today, 23,* 21.

Augros, R., & Stanciu, G. (1987). *The new biology.* Boston, MA: New Science Library.

Bronowski, J. (1976). *The ascent of man.* Boston, MA: Little, Brown Co.

Campbell, J. (1988). *The power of myth.* New York: Doubleday.

Cavanaugh, J. (1989, July). *The utility of concepts in chaos theory for psychological theory and research.* Paper presented at the Fourth Adult Development Symposium, Harvard University, Cambridge, MA.

Crutchfield, J. P., Farmer, J. D., Packard, N. H., & Shaw, R. S. (1986). Chaos. *Scientific American, 255,* 46–57.

Gergen, K. (1991). *The saturated self*. New York: Basic Books.

Gleick, J. (1987). *Chaos: Making a new science*. New York: Penguin.

Herbert, N. (1986). *Quantum reality*. New York: Doubleday.

Hofstadter, D. R. (1979). *Godel, Escher and Bach: An eternal golden braid*. New York: Basic Books.

Jeans, J. (1981). *Physics and philosophy*. New York: Dover.

Johnson, D. (1991, August). *Controversy and integrative negotiation*. Paper presented at the Annual American Psychological Association Conference, San Francisco, CA.

Johnson, D., & Johnson, R. (1975). *Learning together and alone*. Englewood Cliffs, NJ: Prentice-Hall.

Johnson, L. (1991). Postformal reasoning facilitates behavioral change: A case study of an international development project. In J. D. Sinnott & J. Cavanaugh (Eds.), *Bridging paradigms: Positive development in adulthood and cognitive aging* (pp. 59–72). New York: Praeger.

Kohn, A. (1987). *No contest*. Boston: Hougton Mifflin.

Labouvie-Vief, G. (1987, July). *Speaking about feelings: Symbolization and self-regulation through the lifespan*. Paper presented at the Third Beyond Formal Operations Symposium at Harvard University, Cambridge, MA.

Lee, D. (1991). Relativistic operations: A framework for conceptualizing teachers' problem solving. In J. D. Sinnott & J. Cavanaugh (Eds.), *Bridging paradigms: Positive development in adulthood and cognitive aging* (pp. 73–86). New York: Praeger.

Maturana, H., & Varela, F. (1988). *The tree of knowledge*. Boston, MA: New Science Library.

McLean, P. (1988, March). *Evolutionary biology*. Paper presented at the Gerontology Research Center, National Institute on Aging, NIH, Baltimore, MD.

Meacham, J., & Emont, N. C. (1989). The interpersonal basis of everyday problem solving. In J. D. Sinnott (Ed.), *Everyday problem solving*. New York: Praeger.

Pagels, H. R. (1982). *The cosmic code: Quantum physics as the language of nature*. New York: Simon & Schuster.

Perry, W. B. (1975). *Forms of intellectual and ethical development in the college years: A scheme*. New York: Holt, Rinehart, & Winston.

Polanyi, M. (1971). *Personal knowledge: Toward a postcritical philosophy*. Chicago, IL: University of Chicago Press.

Pool, R. (1989). Is it healthy to be chaotic? *Science, 243*, 604–607.

Prigogene, I., & Stengers, I. (1984). *Order out of chaos*. New York: Bantam.

Sinnott, J. D. (1981). The theory of relativity: A metatheory for development? *Human Development, 24*, 293–311.

Sinnott, J. D. (1984). Postformal reasoning: The relativistic stage. In M. Commons, F. Richards, & C. Armon (Eds.), *Beyond formal operations*. New York: Praeger.

Sinnott, J. D. (1989a). Adult differences in the use of postformal operations. In M. Commons, J. Sinnott, F. Richards, & C. Armon (Eds.), *Adult development: Comparisons and applications of developmental models*. New York: Praeger.

Sinnott, J. D. (1989b). Changing the known, knowing and changing. In D. Kramer & M. Bopp (Eds.), *Transformation in clinical and developmental psychology*. New York: Springer.

Sinnott, J. D. (1989c). *Everyday problem solving: Theory and application*. New York: Praeger.

Sinnott, J. D. (1990, April). *Yes, it's worth the trouble! Unique contributions from everyday cognitive studies*. Paper presented at 12th West Virginia University Conference on Lifespan Developmental Psychology: Mechanisms of Everyday Cognition, Morgantown, VA.

Sinnott, J. D. (1991a, July). *Conscious adult development: Complex thought and solving* our *intragroup conflicts*. Invited presentation, Sixth Adult Development Conference, Suffolk University, Boston, MA.

Sinnott, J. D. (1991b). Limits to problem solving: Emotion, intention, goal clarity, health, and other factors in postformal thought. In J. D. Sinnott & J. Cavanaugh (Eds.), *Bridging paradigms: Positive development in childhood and cognitive aging* (pp. 169–202). New York: Praeger.

Sinnott, J. D. (1991c). What do we do to help John? A case study of postformal problem solving in a family making decisions about an acutely psychotic member. In J. D. Sinnott & J. Cavanaugh (Eds.), *Bridging paradigms: Positive development in adulthood and cognitive aging* (pp. 203–220). New York: Praeger.

Sinnott, J. D. (1992, August). *Development and yearning: Cognitive aspects of spiritual development*. Paper presented at American Psychological Association Conference, Washington, DC.

Sinnott, J. D. (in press a). Creativity and postformal thought: Why the last stage is the creative stage. In C. Adams-Price (Ed.), *Creativity and aging: Theoretical and empirical approaches*. New York: Springer.

Sinnott, J. D. (Ed.) (in press b). *Interdisciplinary handbook of adult lifespan learning*. CT: Greenwood Press.

Wolf, F. A. (1981). *Taking the quantum leap*. New York: Harper and Row.

Response to Sinnott: "Teaching in a Chaotic New Physics World: Teaching as a Dialogue with Reality"

Diane M. Lee
University of Maryland, Baltimore County

In her chapter, Sinnott describes a number of pedagogical strategies that are consistent with new science paradigms and recent proposals for educational reform. In her argument, she prods us to see dimensions of our lived worlds in classrooms through a different lens, in ways we would not have noticed otherwise. In particular, Sinnott offers a theoretical basis for reconsidering dialogue, subjectivity, integration, and alternative methods of evaluation in education. It is toward these four aspects of pedagogy that I will direct my comments.

TEACHING AS A DIALOGIC PROCESS

In advocating a teaching style that is consonant with the new sciences, Sinnott asks teachers to surrender the traditional recitation mode and use dialogic approaches such as lecture–discussion formats and cooperative learning models. Many teachers, regardless of the age of their students, are abandoning their podiums and rearranging their rooms in ways that genuinely invite dialogue. For example, even when using direct instruction, many teachers replace chairs arranged in rows facing the teacher with large circles or horseshoe arrangements that foster face-to-face interaction. Small groups seated at tables are especially prominent in classes utilizing cooperative learning.

Frequently, when using cooperative learning, teachers begin by providing the background information and setting the activity while the group is in a large horseshoe arrangement, and then students move their seats to form smaller groups. Sometimes membership is designated by the teacher to maximize diversity; other times the students determine with whom they will work. Either way, every student is assigned a particular task. For example, one student may be responsible for recording the main ideas, another to ensure that each person speaks. A third is to see that consensus is achieved, while another is the spokesperson when the whole group reconvenes. In this way *everyone* has a part in the dialogue and *everyone* has responsibility for creating and sharing knowledge.

Sinnott suggests that in dialogue the "line between teacher and learner may be a vague one." I would emphasize that teachers have prime responsibility for orchestrating classroom conversations, for it is presumed they have deeper, broader, and more sophisticated understandings than do the students. Furthermore, the power to set the tone, limits, and range of allowable discourses inheres in the teacher's position. Use of this power of course varies and need not be authoritarian. The task is to surface what students know, lead them to more complex ways of thinking and knowledge as well as provide opportunities for them to participate in curricular decisions. Teachers do this when they encourage students to choose topics of study and make contracts designating the work to be done, when it is to be completed, and the final form evaluation will take.

SUBJECTIVITY IN TEACHING AND LEARNING

A second feature of teaching Sinnott mentions expands our thinking about context to include subjectivity. Sinnott urges teachers to go beyond tangible aspects of context to consider the intangible, that is, the tone or feeling of the classroom. In doing so, she emphasizes reunification of the affective and cognitive spheres of knowing and calls into question the very possibility of objective knowing.

In a class where subjectivity complements logic, personal values, beliefs, opinions, hopes, feelings, desires, and intuitions, enter into the dialogue. Tension exists, however, as teachers strive to balance the personal with the public.

To make safe spaces for the personal, many teachers have students write autobiographies, keep reflective journals, or participate in written conversations with them. In such writing, teachers reflect with students while refraining from any evaluative or corrective measures. The intent is to have students find their own words and make meaning of their experiences. As students write about their concerns, problems, and dilemmas, they are placed in the sphere of self-reference and self-awareness—a place where decision, conscience, and behavior are directed. Thus, in solitude and reflection, space for improvisation, creativity, risk, play, and what Sinnott describes as useful disorder are created.

Classrooms that are truly dialogic in orientation, that allow students to choose goals and the means for attaining those goals at a self-determined pace, and that bridge the public and private are controversial. Teachers and students alike are more vulnerable in situations that call for authenticity and probing of one's innermost thoughts and feelings. Openly challenging the accepted canons of authority demands that teachers and students confront a reality riddled with doubts and that they deal with contradiction, multiple perspectives, and uncertainty. This is a tenuous place to learn and to teach, yet it is within this tension that knowledge is constructed and thoughtful action decided upon.

DESIGNING AN INTEGRATED CURRICULUM

A third characteristic of teaching consonant with the new sciences is in the integrated curriculum. The integrated curriculum addresses the interrelations between subject areas and world realities. For example, mathematical computation may be integral to a chemistry experiment; science dioramas, models, and illustrations may be created in art class; and field trips to planetariums, hospitals, museums, science labs, and neighborhood recycling projects may help students make linkages between science presented in classrooms and science experienced in daily life situations.

Students are most likely to synthesize knowledge when learning is not bound and limited by a schedule of artificially separate courses or curricular boundaries. Yet this presents problems when curricular boundaries are eased and teachers must collaborate and plan together. Individual control must be abdicated in favor of cooperative team teaching. This may take more time, especially outside of regular class hours, and does present another task for already overworked teachers. The commitment is worth the additional effort, however, as such cross-disciplinary linkages provide broader bases of knowledge within which students may search for possible answers to problems they confront.

ALTERNATIVE EVALUATION MEASURES

Creating evaluation measures consistent with a new sciences approach involves using a combination of strategies and instruments to diagnose and assess students' progress. The traditional authority of multiple choice tests and single assessments is challenged when teachers and students assemble portfolios that contain a wide variety of students' work, teachers' anecdotal records, and students' self-evaluations. Also, involving students in their own evaluations and providing detailed, explanatory feedback should help them develop self-regulatory behaviors.

SUMMARY

Sinnott provides a way of seeing and listening that points toward maximal teacher and student involvement in the planning, implementation, and evaluation of classroom activities. Indeed, she urges teachers to recognize and realize the possibilities inherent in their practice, and thereby contributes a noteworthy dynamic to the dialogue on educational reform.

6

Why Teachers Change—
An Analysis of Consequences
and Rules*

Margaret E. Vaughan
Department of Psychology
Salem State College

Today, few people deny the role of consequences in determining why people do what they do. The principles of learning discovered in the animal laboratory have been demonstrated with a host of species under a myriad of conditions. There is no question: Behavior can be changed by altering its consequences. The literature, starting in the 1950s, is replete with examples. Through the systematic application of positive consequences, infants were taught to vocalize (Rheingold, Gewirtz, & Ross, 1959); cooperation between children was shaped and maintained (Azrin & Lindsley, 1956); stuttering was controlled (Flanagan, Goldiamond, & Azrin, 1958); mental patients were taught socially appropriate behavior (Ayllon & Michael, 1959); and adults were taught self-control (Goldiamond, 1965). These pioneering studies launched the field of psychology called behavior modification or, more recently, applied behavior analysis.

To be sure, applied behavior analysis has had its detractors. There were those who viewed the behavior modification movement of the 1960s with a great deal of suspicion. The concept of changing peoples' behavior by changing consequences seemed both shallow and dangerous. Some people believed that it was impossible to change behavior by simply administering M&M's, while others feared that attempts to do so foreshadowed the emergence of the world according to Orwell—

*I am indebted to Henry Owen, Director of Shore Educational Collaborative, who believed that the individual could make a difference and worked to create, for any one who wished, opportunities to do so.

113

1984. Fortunately, as behavior analysis evolved over the ensuing three decades, so did the general public's understanding of the approach and its usefulness. Today, physicians, psychologists, educators, and public policy makers rely on this approach to help people live more productive, happy lives.

A more serious criticism leveled against behavior analysis during these early years, however, has been more difficult to deal with. People within other branches of psychology took aim not at the application of learning principles, but at the underlying theory. The principles of learning, they argued, were relevant to only a small portion of human behavior. The really important human activities—receiving and processing information—overrode any effects of conditioning via consequences. Their point was this: People do not have to *experience* a particular set of circumstances to be altered by those circumstances; people can be *told* about a set of circumstances and, as a result, behave differently. In terms of explaining the latter method of behavior change, the critics claimed, behavior analytic theory was irrelevant.

The criticism stung. For the most part, behavior analysts had not addressed the effects of information when speculating about the causes of human behavior (however, see Skinner, 1957; Holz & Azrin, 1966). Clearly, if behavior analysis was to be taken seriously, it had to go beyond analyzing behavior change as a function of experiencing events to considering behavior change as a function of describing events.

Reformulating the Problem

Undoubtedly, behavior can be changed by a description of events. We listen to the radio, hear the traffic report and, as a result, take an alternate route home. We read books and newspapers and journals and find ourselves changing our opinion regarding the role of state government. We watch the evening news and decide it is best to stay out of the stock market. We talk to ourselves as we talk to others and behave differently as a function of what is said. The question is, how do descriptions of events come to control behavior?

For more than a decade, behavior analysts have been studying this question. In doing so, they have distinguished between contingency-shaped and rule-governed behavior. Contingency-shaped behavior refers to behavior that is changed by its consequences—experiencing events. Rule-governed behavior, on the other hand, refers to behavior that is changed by a rule—a description of events. This distinction has generated a great deal of research. But as the body of literature has grown, so has the disillusionment. Once viewed as the predominant form of human behavior, rule governance now appears to be fragile and, at best, difficult to produce. Apparently, just as our own experiences suggest, people follow rules very selectively (cf. Galizio, 1979; Matthews, Catania & Shimoff, 1985; Hayes, Brownstein, Haas & Greenway, 1986).

Unfortunately, all of the research in this area has been conducted in highly controlled laboratories, far removed from the complexities of daily life. Surely, people behave in more complex ways when confronted with the vagaries of day-to-day living? If the laboratory research is to be meaningful, corroborating evidence is needed from the world of everyday life.

A few years ago, a set of circumstances arose that allowed me to collect some of that evidence. I was able to study rule-governed behavior outside of the laboratory. This chapter describes my experience in working with teachers on changing their behavior in the classroom. I had the opportunity to offer rules describing change, as well as to arrange consequences to foster change. As a result, I learned a great deal about the relationship between contingency-shaped and rule-governed behavior. In particular, I learned something about how descriptions of events come to control behavior.

Setting the Stage

For the last five years I have worked as a consultant in several Massachusetts public schools, helping teachers control behavior-problem students in their classrooms. The childrens' behaviors ranged in severity from those who did not follow directions to those who were verbally or physically aggressive. Most of the teachers were in elementary education and worked with special education students (developmentally delayed or emotionally delayed) for either part or all of the school day. Some were first-year teachers and others were veterans who had taught for more than 20 years. My job was to advise these teachers on how to apply the principles of learning in their classrooms.

The first year I offered workshops. Hours were spent discussing various behavioral strategies that had been documented over and over again in the literature as being extremely effective in controlling disruptive students. The strategies were always based upon three very general principles of learning:

1. *The Principle of Reinforcement:* When you observe a student engaging in desirable behavior, immediately provide that student with some type of consequence that the student finds pleasing (e.g., praise, points, pats, attention). The desirable behavior will increase in frequency.

2. *The Principle of Extinction:* When you observe a student engaging in undesirable behavior that is not dangerous to himself or to others, ignore that child (e.g., walking away, avoiding eye contact) and attend to the children who are behaving appropriately. The undesirable behavior will decrease in frequency.

3. *The Principle of Punishment:* When you observe a student engaging in behavior that is dangerous to herself or to others, immediately follow that behavior with some consequence the student will find undesirable (e.g., removal from the playground, removal of all reinforcement, time-out, suspension). The undesirable behavior will decrease in frequency.

After discussing these principles at length, teachers gave classroom examples of disruptive student behavior. As a group, we discussed the procedures for handling the problems and outlined specific steps to take in implementing the strategies. The teachers were excited about trying the procedures, and I looked forward to visiting their classrooms to see how things were going. I was unprepared for what I found.

Fewer than one quarter of the teachers who had attended the workshops had actually implemented changes in their classroom. The excuses for not following through were bountiful. But the fact remained: Workshops were not effective in bringing about teacher change.

I abandoned workshops. I decided to work directly with individual teachers to determine firsthand what strategies led to the implementation of changes in the classroom. Since that first disappointing year, I have worked with close to 100 teachers individually. The observations and conclusions that follow are based upon my experience as a consultant with these teachers. This chapter is an exercise in interpretation.

RULES AND CONSEQUENCES: A HIERARCHY OF STRATEGIES TO FOSTER CHANGE

Consultants have at least two tasks: 1) to clarify problems and establish rules for change, and 2) to help implement the changes necessary to resolve the problems. Sometimes a consultant needs only to complete the former. But if he or she is interested in continuing to work as a consultant, eventually some of the problems must be resolved. In my case, the problem was ensuring that teachers effectively used the three principles of learning mentioned above (i.e., reinforcement, extinction, and punishment). As I worked with teachers, I began to develop strategies that address some of the factors that seemed to be hindering change. The strategies took the form of a hierarchy based upon the amounts of environmental support necessary for teacher change.

The simplest strategy consisted of describing to teachers what needed to be done (providing rules for action). The next strategy involved individualized instruction for teachers. The third level of intervention consisted of designing artificial antecedents for change, and the fourth level involved designing artificial consequences for change. If these interventions proved to be ineffective, then the last and most difficult strategy was required: teacher counseling. Only in retrospect did I see that this hierarchy represented, for practical purposes, how behavior is brought under the control of a description.

Providing a Rule

The easiest strategy, and the one I used initially with each teacher, was to simply describe to the teacher what needed to be done. My instructions took the form of a rule: If X, then Y. "Whenever Billy gets out of his seat, ignore him and randomly praise the other students who are in their seats and working. When Billy is in his seat, praise him, too." Simply put, a rule is an accurate description of what needs to be done, and when. As it turned out, the teachers who were able to immediately implement the rule were the teachers who were already doing what needed to be done. That is, the successful teachers knew how to ignore inappropriate behavior and reinforce appropriate behavior. They were ignoring and reinforcing behavior under other conditions with other children. For these teachers the rule served as encouragement to continue to do what they were already doing. It also served as a means of fostering generalization: Behave toward Billy as you behave toward Sally. In other words, these teachers were learning not so much *what* to do, but rather *when* to do it.

Unfortunately, few of the teachers had the necessary history that would allow them to benefit from the rules offered. Since they did not already know how effectively to ignore, reinforce and punish behavior, the rules were in a sense meaningless. Rules tell you *when* to do what you already know how to do. Rule following is a process of generalizing from one situation to another. Rules, or descriptions of events, will not generate novel behavior; rules can only evoke existing behavior but under novel or ambiguous conditions. The teachers who were able to follow the rules already understood the power of teacher attention as a consequence for shaping or maintaining student behavior. Unfortunately, this strategy reached only 13% of the teachers.

What hindered the other 87% from benefitting from the rules? Perhaps, sometimes, people do not change because they do not know how to change, even when a description of what needs to be done is provided. This point was made well by the philosopher Russell (1912/1961) at the turn of the century. He distinguished between two types of knowledge: "knowledge by description" and "knowledge by acquaintance." Put simply, there are two senses to the word "know": We know things if we can describe them, and we know things in a different way when we experience them. People can often describe quite clearly what needs to be done—knowledge by description—but are discouraged to find that they are unable to follow through and do what needs to be done. They lack knowledge by acquaintance. Being able to describe some behavior (e.g., how to ignore Billy) and being able to do what has been described (e.g., ignoring Billy) are two quite different skills. When a person shows knowledge by description, this does not imply knowledge by acquaintance (and vice versa). Experiencing an event is the only way a person can become "acquainted" with that event.

Individualized Instruction

To be acquainted with a rule means to have experienced the effects of engaging in the rule-specified behavior. There are at least three ways of becoming acquainted with a rule, one of which is through individualized instruction. This involves providing rules, modeling, cuing and feedback. First, teachers were asked to imitate my behavior. If, for example, a teacher did not know how to ignore undesirable behavior, I would ask him or her to watch me interact with a particular child. When the child talked out without raising her hand, I would look away and call on another student who did have her hand raised. If the disruptive student protested, I continued to interact with the other students who were behaving appropriately. Teachers were then asked to do the same and I gave them feedback. I would shake my head if they started to address the disruptive student and smile and praise them for ignoring the student. Cuing teachers when to ignore was as important as giving them immediate feedback on how well they did.

Although approximately 24% of the teachers were influenced by individualized instruction, it was a slow process. Often I had to visit the classroom several times. Not surprisingly, each teacher needed a good deal of feedback and encouragement. If left unsupervised for several weeks, it was not uncommon for teachers to resort to the old way of doing things. Many teachers reported that it was hard for them to give up their old practices. In effect, these teachers were being asked to behave in new ways even though the context, which was responsible for shaping and maintaining the old behavior in the first place, had not changed.

For example, when a student was acting out, the teacher's natural tendency was to reprimand the child. The immediate result was that the acting out stopped, if only temporarily, but long enough to serve as a powerful consequence for reprimanding. Reprimanding was strengthened. Unfortunately, so was acting out. (For some children, any kind of attention is better than no attention.) After being scolded, the child would go back to work, only to stop working again when the teacher's attention was directed elsewhere. To extinguish acting out in the long run, the teacher had to ignore it. But to ignore acting out effectively, the teacher had to sit through, at least initially, many minutes of aversiveness generated by the disruptive student. Sometimes this was just too much to ask of a teacher. Understandably, some teachers could not maintain rule following. They needed a more structured environment—a second way to develop knowledge by acquaintance.

III. Designing Artificial Antecedents for Change

Sometimes people do not change because they do not know how to change. Other times, people do not change because they cannot change. The powerful consequences maintaining the old way of doing things override current reasons for behaving in a different way. When teachers wanted to change but could not, the problem usually consisted of asking for changes that were too inconsistent with the way they normally behaved. In effect, teachers were being asked to interact with their students in new ways, but without any environmental support to facilitate the change. Simple rules for action were not enough. Nor was it enough for me to provide individual instruction—rules, models, cues and feedback—on an intermittent schedule over the course of several months. The context or environment needed to be changed, too. The classroom needed a major transformation. These teachers needed artificial antecedents for change (conspicuous rules and cues) infused into the classroom that would guide them toward achieving effective overall classroom management.

The eventual *modus operandi* was a student checklist (see Figure 1). Each student had an identical checklist taped to his or her desk. It was large enough for students and teacher to view easily. The checklist consisted of the daily routine listed vertically: for example, journal, science, math, recess, language arts, lunch, art, spelling, social studies, and free time. Points were awarded during each of these activities if the student engaged in specific classroom rules, which were listed

DAILY POINT SHEET

Date:_____   Name: _____

Academics:		Starts Work Quietly	Follows Directions	Stays On Task	Rasies Hand	Ignores Inappro. Behavior	
Journal	/4						/10
Science	/4						/10
Math	/4						/10
Recess/Gym		(Students must have at least 27 points)					/27
Language Art	/4						/10
Lunch		(Students must have at least 36 points)					/36
Art	/4						/10
Spelling	/4						/10
Soc. Studies	/4						/10
Free Time		(Students must have at least 63 points)					/63
					Total Points Earned:		**/70**

KEY TO POINTS:

Academics:

    4 — Completed work with 90% or better accuracy
    3 — Corrected work with 90% or better accuracy
    2 — Partially corrected work with less than 90%
    1 — Completed work with less than 90%, no correction attempted

Behavior:

Students may earn up to **6** point for appropriate behavior during each period. Students must have at least **90%** of the points possible before participating in recess, lunch, and free time.

Teacher's Signature: _____

Figure 6.1

horizontally across the top of the checklist: for example, starts work quietly, follows directions, stays on task, raises hand, and ignores inappropriate behavior of others. In addition, students could earn points (usually four) for completing their assignment with 90% or better accuracy. Fewer points were given for poorer quality work. The points were turned in at recess, lunch and immediately prior to dismissal at the end of the school day. If the students earned 90% of all the points possible prior to each of these breaks, he or she could choose among an array of activities or objects; computer time, jump rope, checkers, a new eraser or pencil, and so on. The ones with the most points were always the first to choose and the first to go to lunch or recess, or to be dismissed. Everything in the classroom was now contingent upon appropriate behavior, including teacher attention.

The students were always given a choice: "You may either do your math now or during recess." In this way, children were being taught responsibility and teachers were being taught how to take control of their classrooms. My job was to ensure that the system was used, and to provide feedback and encouragement to the teachers.

The overall purpose of the system was to teach teachers how to encourage positive behavior and ignore inappropriate behavior throughout the day. It gently forced immediate positive changes in the interaction between student and teacher and brought consistency to the way things were done in the classroom. The teachers had to award points regularly to ensure that students who were behaving well could earn free time or some other reward. Teachers were reminded to give points by the conspicuous checklist on each student's desk. The consequence for teachers who consistently gave points was having control of a smoothly run classroom. The classrooms were literally transformed; students were working and teachers were teaching.

It is worth noting that, by definition, all educational systems are based upon artificial motivational systems: grades, honor rolls, student of the week, etc. But for some students, these artificial consequences found in a regular classroom are too delayed. By providing more immediate consequences—enriching the system—for desirable student behavior, teachers can make a remarkable difference with even the most recalcitrant student. Eventually, of course, such a system must be phased out; the real world does not consist of checklists for conduct. But many of these students require this system for some time in order to overcome their considerable histories of floundering and failure. In fact, many teachers who only needed rules or modest individual instruction to gain control over their students often incorporated checklists too, for this very reason.

Designing artificial antecedents was effective with approximately 28% of the teachers, who were quickly sold on the approach. They began to read articles, chapters, and books that clarified and supported the approach they were using. Indeed, at this point they often began to teach other teachers the strategy they were using. This is an important point, as it provided them with positive feedback from colleagues.

Unfortunately, this still left approximately 35% of the teachers who did not follow through on any of the above interventions and who resisted any major shift in their teaching strategies. Perhaps this outcome underscores an important misconception about human nature. It is often argued that people can spontaneously behave in new ways because they are thinking, rational beings. The argument goes that, when presented with relevant information, regardless of what their histories have taught them, people will change accordingly. But if this were true, why are people often unable to change? Although it is hoped that information alone is sufficient to provide the needed motivation, the sad fact is that information is not motivation. Information of rules are of little use if motivation is lacking. For some teachers, the consequences of being brought under the control of artificial antecedents were not effective. Changes in student behavior did not serve as motivation. These teachers required additional consequences for change—a third way to develop knowledge by acquaintance.

Designing Artificial Consequences for Change

When confronting teachers who were unmotivated to maintain a new system of control in their classrooms, I initially wrote them off. I was always left wondering, though, was there any way of reaching them? Clearly, the problem was to figure out a way to motivate the teachers to experiment in the classroom—and to motivate myself to stay with them.

The three strategies already described relied on improved student behavior—progress toward understanding a concept, staying on task, staying in their seats, following directions, and so on—as motivation for teachers to change. The contingency was this: If you behave this way, your students will behave more appropriately. Unfortunately, not all teachers were motivated enough by student progress to overcome powerful competing contingencies. Sometimes people cannot change unless there are conspicuous, artificial consequences that override the consequences for current behavior. This point was made forcefully a few years ago.

In one school, I worked independently with ten teachers, five of whom were unmotivated to modify their classroom behavior. I eventually became frustrated and left the school. But in the next school I worked in, the administration was very interested in my activities and the activities of their teachers. I met with the administration frequently to report on what was happening with the problem students. Under these conditions, the percentage of teachers working toward change increased significantly, to almost 90%. I believe the overriding factor was the role of the administration. They were holding me *and* their teachers accountable. As a result, I had little tendency to give up on any teachers, and the teachers had little tendency to give up on any students. None of us wanted a bad evaluation from our supervisors. Unfortunately, the use of implied or explicit threats (e.g., criticism in front of colleagues, loss of job) to evoke change is hardly what anyone wants to encourage. Despite its effectiveness, instilling fear as a means of control is hardly an attractive method of soliciting change, especially with its potential side effects: aggression, escape, or revolt (Azrin & Holz, 1966).

However, when frustrated by the inability to bring about change, school administrators and teachers, like the rest of us, find themselves relying on threats to motivate others. But threats ultimately must be accompanied by punishment in order to control others. In public schools, this kind of follow-through is often very difficult to achieve. It is virtually impossible to fire a veteran teacher or, for that matter, to temporarily remove a student from the classroom. Once established that there is little follow-through, all future threats are useless. It is a paradox that threats continue to be the method of choice.

The opposite of a threat is, of course, an incentive. However, for many school systems, effective incentives have been bargained away. Tenure remains one conspicuous exception. But it is not often used as effectively as it could be in encouraging teacher change. More to the point, administrators have little say in terms of what teachers do in their classrooms once tenure is granted. Arranging incentives such as increased salary, grants, and stipends based upon student performance would enhance teachers' commitment to real change in the classroom and feelings of self-worth. Unfortunately, few school administrators take advantage of them. Change is not rewarded.

There are several reasons for this, but the most frequently voiced is that incentives are not necessary. "Why should we pay teachers more money to do what they should already be doing? Teachers *should want* to do what needs to be done." This argument raises an interesting issue and points to one final strategy for fostering change. Why are some teachers not motivated to do everything possible to ensure that students learn? This question has many answers, all of which point to powerful competing contingencies.

Counseling

For some teachers, change in the classroom was not the highest priority. Other issues in their lives were more important. Some teachers were unmotivated to change because they were unhappy, or preoccupied, or simply perceived the world differently than I did. My experience in counseling teachers was limited, but some points need to be made about this experience in terms of the current discussion.

Some of these teachers' concerns were related to work. The overall school atmosphere was poor and unsupportive. Teachers did not like the administration, or the administration did not like them. Some believed that the administration had little interest in what they did in the classroom or how they did it.

Some teachers expressed concerns that were more personal. A few teachers were struggling with events like cancer, divorce, and death. Yet others simply did not like their disruptive students and found it impossible to work with them. Moreover, they believed that if they complained enough about the disruptive student, the student would be moved eventually to a more restrictive environment. The problem would no longer be theirs.

Another obvious source of difficulty was the advice given and the advice giver. Some teachers simply did not like the advice; they did not believe it. These teachers believed that students behave as they do because of their genetic makeup, character, or personality. They would not accept the proposition that consequences play a major role in determining what students do. I argued that explanations in terms of genetics, personalities, mental deficiencies, and emotions were useful in characterizing students, but were impotent in terms of providing a constructive course of action. But some teachers remained skeptical. They did not believe that every student could learn. These teachers had a different view of teaching and learning. They failed to see teaching as changing behavior; rather, they viewed it as imparting knowledge. At another level, these same teachers resented an "outsider" telling them what they needed to do. Undoubtedly, they had a history of hearing too much advice from too many people, much of it contradictory. Or, worse, past advice served the advice giver rather than the person receiving the advice. More to the point, though, some teachers believed that I was the wrong gender or the wrong age.

Obviously, all of these issues needed to be addressed before any change could take place in the classrooms. Counseling sessions allowed teachers the opportunity to air their grievances, resentments and problems. But that was only the first step. Resolution was then necessary. Unfortunately, resolving these concerns was often beyond the scope of my job.

CONCLUSION

I began this chapter by discussing a theoretical issue currently debated in psychology: namely, how do descriptions of events come to control behavior? I presented the problem in terms of behavior change as a function of a description versus behavior change as a function of consequences. Although consequences are known to be important, many psychologists have argued in favor of descriptions as the most desirable form of intervention. Changing behavior by merely describing what needs to be done is far simpler, and far less intrusive, than altering consequences as a function of what is done. However, current literature suggests that the issue is more complicated (Hayes, 1989). Far from being separate entities, these two kinds of behavior are interrelated. Rule-governed behavior appears to be a product of contingency-shaped behavior. My work in the public schools has provided additional evidence, of a practical sort, for this proposition.

Here is the evidence: Rules are effective only when teachers already know how to engage in the behavior. Rules extend the conditions under which teachers engage in the described behavior, but rules cannot generate novel behavior. For teachers to learn a new way of interacting with their students, they need individual instruction; they need to develop contingency-shaped behavior. If the desirable change requires only slight alterations in teacher behavior, then modeling, cues, and feedback are sufficient interventions. If the change requires marked alterations in teacher behavior, more elaborate environmental supports are needed, such as artificial antecedents for change. With both of these strategies, teacher behavior is being brought under the control of a description. The process is slow and fragile, but essential for rule following to occur.

Both of these strategies are based upon desirable student behavior as an effective consequence for teacher change. However, if teachers are unmotivated by these natural consequences, additional external sources of control are necessary. Artificial consequences for teacher change are often effective in overriding the conditions that hinder change. When this strategy fails, however, the only recourse is counseling to help teachers articulate the competing contingencies that stand in the way of change, and then helping teachers resolve them. Once this is accomplished, rules alone could be effective in bring about teacher change.

In summary, for a description or rule to change behavior, a teacher must already be able to engage in the behavior and must find the consequence for doing so reinforcing. To generate new behavior, a teacher requires contingency shaping. This can take the form of individualized instruction, designing artificial antecedents or designing artificial consequences.

The degree to which teachers change as a function of a description is best viewed as a continuum, roughly broken into five categories.

1. Some teachers only need rules to begin experimenting in their classrooms. They are motivated to try something new, but require help in determining exactly what to do and when to do it.

2. Other teachers are motivated to change but have no experience in doing what needs to be done. That is, they can describe what to do but must be taught how to do it.

3. Another group of teachers can state the rule and can follow through, but they require environmental supports in the form of artificial antecedents that help maintain the new way of behavior (i.e., a student checklist).

4. There are still other teachers who are unmotivated to follow the rules given them. Their lack of motivation stems from the fact that student change is not an effective consequence. These teachers require an external, artificial source of motivation.

5. Finally, there are teachers who are unmotivated to follow the rules, even with additional environmental supports, because of competing contingencies that interfere with following them. These teachers require counseling.

Thus, in general terms, it seemed that either a teacher: (a) did not know *what* to change; (b) did not know *how* to change; (c) wanted to but *could not* change; (d) *did not want* to change; or (e) *did not care* about change.

Fostering change is the major job of a consultant or educator. We find ourselves lecturing on current literature and providing new rules to follow. We impart our knowledge of the subject matter and the methods by which it should be taught. We tell teachers what they must do to obtain the results we all agree are desirable. We are then surprised and frustrated to find teachers not following our advice. We cast about for reasons to explain this recalcitrance and, like teachers blaming their students, we blame ours. We call them lazy, unappreciative, and argue that they probably are having problems at home. Focusing on the resistance of teachers implies that the fault lies with them, just as teachers ultimately blame their students. But the most fruitful approach is to assume that the problem lies within us. It is our job to ensure change, not our students'.

I have learned several lessons working with teachers over the years. The most important lesson is this: When trying to change the behavior of someone else, more often than not, my behavior had to change first. The reward of doing so was being a teacher of teachers who was working in concert with the teachers of children.

REFERENCES

Ayllon, T., & Michael, J. (1959). The psychiatric nurse as a behavioral engineer. *Journal of the Experimental Analysis of Behavior, 2,* 323–334.

Azrin, N. H., & Holz, W. C. (1966). Punishment. In W. K. Honig (Ed.), *Operant behavior: Areas of research and application* (pp. 380–447). New York: Appleton-Century-Crofts.

Azrin, N. H., & Lindsley, O. R. (1956). The reinforcement of cooperation between children. *Journal of Abnormal and Social Psychology, 2,* 100–102.

Flanagan, B., Goldiamond, I., & Azrin, N. H. (1958). Operant stuttering: The control of stuttering behavior through response-contingent consequences. *Journal of the Experimental Analysis of Behavior, 1,* 173–178.

Galizio, M. (1979). Contingency-shaped and rule-governed behavior: Instructional control and human loss avoidance. *Journal of the Experimental Analysis of Behavior, 31,* 53–57.

Goldiamond, I. (1965). Self-control procedures in personal behavior. *Psychological Report, 17,* 851–868.

Hayes, S. C. (1989). *Rule-governed behavior: Cognition, contingencies, and instructional control.* New York: Plenum Press.

Hayes, S. C., Brownstein, A. J., Haas, J. R., & Greenway, D. E. (1986). Instructions, multiple schedules, and extinction: Distinguishing rule-governed from schedule-controlled behavior. *Journal of the Experimental Analysis of Behavior, 46,* 137–147.

Holz, W. C., & Azrin, N. H. (1966). Conditioning human verbal behavior. In W. K. Honig (Ed.), *Operant behavior: Areas of research and application* (pp. 790–826). New York: Appleton-Century-Crofts.

Matthews, B. A., Catania, A. C., & Shimoff, E. (1985). Effects of uninstructed verbal behavior on nonverbal responding: Contingency descriptions versus performance descriptions. *Journal of the Experimental Analysis of Behavior, 43,* 155–164.

Rheingold, H. L., Gewirtz, J. L., & Ross, H. W. (1959). Social conditioning of vocalizations in the infant. *Journal of Comparative and Physiological Psychology, 52,* 68–73.

Russell, B. (1961). Knowledge by acquaintance and knowledge by description. In R. E. Egner & L. E. Denonn (Eds.), *The basic writings of Bertrand Russell: 1903–1959* (pp. 217–224). New York: Simon and Schuster. (Original work published 1912)

Skinner, B. F. (1969). *Contingencies of reinforcement: A theoretical analysis.* New York: Appleton-Century-Crofts.

Skinner, B. F. (1957). *Verbal behavior.* New York: Appleton-Century-Crofts.

Response to Vaughan: "Why Teachers Change—An Analysis of Consequences and Rules"

Joan N. Steiner, Ph.D.
Menasha High School
Menasha, WI

In school settings, while working with mostly elementary special education teachers, Vaughan fostered change by offering teachers rules for describing behavior and arranging consequences. Even though Vaughan's study apparently involved primarily elementary school special education teachers, I—as a secondary teacher—related to her school settings experience.

At my high school during the last few years, children with behavior problems have been mainstreamed, as is the case in many U.S. schools today. Consequently, developmentally delayed and emotionally delayed students work side by side with other students in the classroom. What this means is that the special education teachers work as consultants with me, and sometimes we collaboratively plan and teach. As I read Vaughan's study, I wondered if the reason that mainstreaming problem students has worked so well is because special needs teachers and regular classroom teachers agreed among themselves to collaborate pedagogical efforts for the benefit of all students. For example, the teachers in my school feel that isolating students with specific learning problems tends to enhance the identified behavior problems. We have found that integrating these students tends to neutralize behavior problems in significant ways.

When special-needs students are mainstreamed and work with others, a growing number of students begin to realize that special-needs students are more like themselves than they are different. This may be due in part to the individual teacher in the classroom, but overall, I have found from my own experience and through hearing the experiences of other teachers that an empathy is fostered among students and teachers as they learn to work with people of varied backgrounds, talents, and interests.

In a heterogeneous classroom setting, students who have specific behavior problems observe others who do not share that problem. The negative behavior is not reinforced by others of a similar bent; instead, those who are well behaved serve as role models. Likewise, students with reading and writing problems actually benefit from working with students who are more fluent in their language. In this way, students have new models for learning, and the onus is not so explicitly on the teacher to do all the modeling.

From my own experience, tracking students from elementary school to high school reinforces expected behavior since children grow in ways to become whatever others expect of them. Students who are labeled by teachers, parents, and peers very often grow to meet those expectations. Under the heading "Principles of Learning," Vaughan addresses positive teacher reinforcement in her chapter, but what I have observed in my classroom experience is the negative reinforcement effects that occur when children are segregated. On the other hand, my experience has shown me that labels are less pronounced and tend to disappear as children with problems are mainstreamed.

Students aren't the only ones who suffer when classes are "tracked" by ability or behavioral issues; teachers are tracked, as well, by speciality or by class assignments. I wonder if the special education teachers noted in Vaughan's study worked with regular classroom teachers, or if they, too, were segregated from the rest of the faculty. I have found that when teachers talk across subject areas, grade levels, and tracks of students, they experience various perspectives that create situations through which they can work collaboratively toward common goals. Regular classroom teachers, like myself, benefit from conversations with specialists who offer other viewpoints.

When teachers face a top-down, externally imposed framework for change, such as that imposed when classrooms are segregated, they feel less important as people and as professionals. They feel manipulated, left out of the learning process, and diminished as change agents. This demoralizing effect prevents teachers from acting as catalysts in their own classrooms and, in turn, from empowering their students' learning. Thus, while external frameworks for teacher change attempt to stimulate lasting change, in reality such frameworks have little impact on long-range teacher change. My sense is that while, on one hand, Vaughan may be correct in helping teachers change student behavior by using rules, in another way such attempts are all too often thwarted from the outset because of the way the classrooms themselves are socially constructed by the administration. In this way, the problem becomes much more than an application of rules; it becomes a socio-political problem where certain segments of the school population (''regular'' students and teachers) are apparently deemed more valuable than other segments of the population (''special-needs'' students and teachers).

In recognizing these social factors, we come to understand that greater success in teacher change may be realized through the reflective-practitioner approach in working with teachers. Vaughan does not mention any of her attempts at this approach in her chapter. When teachers write about their own teaching philosophies, for example, they begin to trace the origins of their practice. Personal narrative is a powerful tool for learning change. My practice changed as a result of writing my own teaching philosophy. Prior to this, I had been conditioned to teach as I had been taught, which was not always grounded in learning theory. From this realization, I became involved with a network of colleagues with whom I shared ideas about theory and practice. In turn, I experimented with teaching practices, though change for me has occurred slowly.

7

To Serve, with Love: Liberation Theory and the Mystification of Teaching

Joseph Janangelo*
Loyola University of Chicago

In discussing the significance of teaching, Ira Shor concludes that "every human occupation must also become a preoccupation" (1987b, p. 81). Other liberation theorists agree. For example, Giroux and McLaren (1989) describe the intensity level necessary for transformative teaching. They critique former Education Secretary William J. Bennett's report, *American Education: Making It Work* (1988), for offering a "truncated vision" (p. xix) of pedagogical reform. For these critics, the qualities Bennett associates with good teaching are bereft of passion, difference, and liberatory force. They sound "as if they were taken from the scripts of the Mr. Rogers' children show" (p. xix). Bennett's ideas perpetuate the belief that "a good teacher is usually white and middle class" and "communicates effectively by finding a style least offensive to the majority" (p. xix). They also privilege a teacher who "vigorously avoids [posing] any serious challenge to prevailing accepted mores or the social relations that reinforce them" (p. xix).

This bleached image of teachers as white, middle-class, heterosexual Mr. Rogers clones, routinely training future victims or oppressors, offends liberation theorists who argue that "school is one of several

*The author wishes to thank the following people for their support and advice: Bruce Beiderwell, Lil Brannon, C. T. Patrick Diamond, Carmella Fiorelli, Kristine Hansen, Farrell J. Webb, and Molly Wingate. This chapter is decidated to Yola Janangelo who always teaches me about the irony of teaching.

agencies [used] to reproduce dominant ideology" (Shor & Freire, 1987, p. 175). Giroux and McLaren (1989) reject these neutralized images of teaching, and the ideologies inscribed within them. They claim that enacting this Mr. Rogers model "translates into teaching the so-called canon of Western virtues." This means "transmitting standardized and politically inoffensive content to students" in "morally neutral" ways, and equating teaching "with raising students' SAT scores and implementing tougher forms of classroom management" (p. xix). For these critics, Bennett's recommended formula for teaching transforms teachers from passionate intellectuals who work to change the world, to dispassionate, disinterested bureaucrats who tailor their pedagogy to perpetuate the dominant social order.

Giroux and McLaren (1989) argue that although the pedagogy of capitalism may work well in training privileged students to become the power elite, "teaching in the ghetto calls for an altogether different model" (p. xix). Disenfranchised students, these critics argue, don't need Mr. Rogers teaching them. They need dedicated individuals who teach to change the world. To this end, liberation theorists have composed reams of discourse detailing appropriate roles for teachers— ones they imagine will empower teachers to inspire social change.

While I agree with critics like Aronowitz, Freire, Giroux, McLaren, and Shor that educational reform is possible and desirable, I object to many of the roles they espouse to help teachers enact their theories. I see an irony in much of these critics' ideological stances. On the one hand, they offer a discourse which encourages teachers to change their behavior and become powerful "change agents" (Shor, 1987a, p. 1). On the other hand, their discourse is laden with reactionary and romantic tropes about teaching. These tropes portray teachers as muses who dedicate themselves selflessly to students, performers who entertain students while teaching them, prophets who dream about the future while ignoring the present, and martyrs who risk everything to fulfill their vision of "the calling." In this chapter, I argue that these tropes serve to delude teachers about their personal and professional responsibilities, to disempower them from making significant changes in their working conditions, and to discourage them from seeing themselves as worthy of better treatment by the academy. I also hope to show how liberation theory's images of teachers sometimes run dangerously close to the images of teachers celebrated in popular films. This proximity, I believe, leads students to conflate the actions and intentions of critical teachers with those of the liberal and charismatic superteachers portrayed in the media. After examining ways these theoretical and popular tropes interact to contribute to teachers' disempowered self-images, I will conclude by recounting a story about how damaging liberation theories can be.

LIBERATION THEORY PORTRAYS TEACHING AS A CALLING

By portraying teaching as a vocation rather than a career, liberation theory perpetuates two phenomena: the "myth of the calling," and the "muse syndrome." Both of these are antithetical to teacher empowerment.

The Myth of the Calling

The "myth of the calling" portrays teaching as a field to which one is spiritually drawn. For example, one of my students recently sought to enroll in a teacher-credential program. He showed me a school catalog which introduced its student teaching contract in the following manner:

> Here the student may begin to grasp the real meaning and value of teaching; a spark of enthusiasm which will carry him/her to great heights in teaching. . . . Suggestions are made in the spirit of helpfulness, recognizing mutual positions of trust in helping to prepare young people for the high calling of teaching. (*Student Teaching Contract*, 1990, p. 2)

This reference to teaching as a "high calling," one that transports individuals to "great heights" in teaching, exemplifies the way our profession is sometimes represented as a divine vocation.

While some liberation theorists ask us to embrace the myth of the calling, Shor and Freire (1987) assign teachers the "task of *demystifying* the dominant ideology" (p. 168). They argue that demystification cannot be accomplished by the system, or by those who agree with it. In their dedication to reform, "those [teachers] who believe in changing reality have to accomplish the transformation" (p. 168). Here, we are presented with a trope of belief and compulsory action—ideals that further the myth of the calling by portraying teaching as the special work of dedicated believers who know they have a sacred duty to perform.

In *Education Under Siege* (1985), Aronowitz and Giroux use this belief trope to argue that teachers should engage in a kind of *jihad* against illiteracy and social injustice. They want teachers to become "reflective practitioners" (p. 30) with human rights on their side. They claim that teachers should "be viewed as free men and women with a special dedication to the values of the intellect and the enhancement of the critical powers of the young" (p. 30). Here we confront the trope of free individuals who pursue their high calling whatever the costs. Fundamentally free of greed, pride, or self-interest, teachers are not portrayed as being primarily dedicated to self or family. Rather, they are seen as taking the veil of teaching in order to enact their "special dedication" to others.

This ideal of selfless dedication is given voice by Shor and Freire (1987): "In the liberating perspective, the teacher has the right but also the duty to challenge the status quo, especially in the questions of domination by sex, race, or class" (p. 174). Notice the word "duty." Ironically, while Shor and Freire do everything possible to ask teachers to be dialogic with students, they feel no qualms about dictating ideological imperatives to teachers. By portraying teachers as the educated elite who are integral parts of an exploitative system, they give teachers little choice but to answer the calling in order to expiate their guilt. To borrow Giroux's term (1988), these critics want teachers to become "transformative intellectuals" (p. 1) who transform things in concert with liberation theory's vision of the calling.

Any calling entails risks, and these critics know it. Giroux (Giroux & McLaren, 1989) argues that "a cultural politics has to be organized around a learned hope, a pedagogy formed amidst the realization of risks, struggles, and possibilities" (p. 151). But the battle is necessary since, "at risk is not only the future of our children, but the very fate of democracy itself" (p. 151). Suggesting that the advent of new social order hinges on individual acts of teacher change, this battle call fuses a rhetoric of Marine-like elitism (addressing teachers as though they are "a few good men and women" who are up to fighting the literacy battle), to an epic-like invocation of the gravity of their mission. In its flattery and urgency, this type of trope does more to inspire teachers to envision change than to educate them in ways of making it happen.

The Muse Syndrome

The second component of the "myth of the calling" is what I term the "muse syndrome." This trope exploits the idea of teacher selflessness in order to flatter teachers into ignoring their own needs and becoming inspirational forces for students. The ideology of the "muse syndrome" parallels the cult of individualism that informs the academy— one where emphasis on grading and individual achievement "reproduces an ideology in which the student experiences his or her difference from all others . . . proving that no matter what, 'the cream always rises to the top' " (Aronowitz & Giroux, 1985, p. 165). Arguing that some students enter into the educational process with socioeconomic advantages that have better prepared them to become "the cream," Aronowitz and Giroux urge teachers to become catalysts in their other students' lives. They do this by asking teachers to practice a pedagogy of "instrumentalism" (p. 196).

Aronowitz and Giroux (1985) argue that the discourse of educational reform has creatively "given way to the language of the instrumental" (p. 196). That is to say, instead of school being instrumental in the perpetuation of the dominant social order, teachers can intervene and become instrumental in students' questioning of that order. Like Dante's muse, Beatrice, teachers are portrayed as guiding students with knowledge and love. Of course, like Beatrice, teachers can never see all of paradise (read here as "the new social order") in this lifetime. That sight is reserved for the poets (read here as "the students"). According to the logic of the muse, it is for students to lead freer, less oppressed lives. A teacher's consolation is to know she has been instrumental in helping students reach that goal.

Implicit in this theory's suggestion that teachers become muses is the philosophical necessity of muses participating in their own obsolescence. In "The Withering Away of the Teacher," Ira Shor (1987a) describes this necessity:

One goal of liberatory learning is for the teacher to become expendable. At the start and along the way, the teacher is indispensable as a change agent. Yet, the need to create students into self-regulating subjects requires that the teacher as organizer fade as the students emerge. (p. 98)

In recruiting teachers to become muses, Shor asks them to be transformative individuals who dedicate their services to a clientele who will eventually outgrow them. While I agree with this idea from a pedagogical standpoint—I don't want students to be dependent on teachers for life—I do see significant problems with the muse role as it relates to teacher empowerment.

My concern is that students are, quite reasonably, more concerned with their needs than with those of their teachers. The problem, as I see it, is that when students outgrow teachers, they also tend to forget them. Sentimental reflections and individual expressions of gratitude aside, I am talking about the kind of remembrance that breeds students' political support when it comes to voting on school funding decisions or teacher workload or salary issues. Few students, however grateful to their teachers, will want to pay more taxes. I can accept Shor's suggestion of being a radical muse—inspiring students to change the world—but why must teachers' "withering away" often take place in the context of their receiving increased work responsibilities and decreased financial and insurance benefits? In its radicalism, could liberation theory go one step further? Could it train teachers in effective ways of lobbying for better working conditions? Could it show teachers ways of enlisting student and parental support to argue that better working conditions and wages for teachers will have a direct impact on the quality of their and their childrens' education? In asking teachers to dedicate themselves to students and then vanish silently from their lives like a humble muse, liberation theory mythologizes teaching as a sacred calling of silent nobility and perpetual sacrifice. This mythology may also keep teachers from being petty or selfish enough to make real-world demands for professional and institutional support that could help them do better jobs.

The fact that the image of the muse appears in the allegedly progressive discourse of liberation theory is ironic. We have seen this image glorified many times before in the more traditional discourse of Hollywood film. In the melodrama *Goodbye, Mr. Chips* (1939), Robert Donat plays the male muse *par excellence;* he is cast as a shy schoolmaster who devotes his life to "his boys." In *Tea and Sympathy* (1956), Deborah Kerr plays the female muse at her most self-sacrificial. She portrays a "faculty wife" who sleeps with a naïve college freshman in order to give him confidence in his sexuality. As the love-making lesson begins—once again we encounter Shor's concept of a dedicated instructor teaching so well that her pupil will not need her anymore— the muse, before withering away, makes one teacherly request: "Years from now when you talk about this—and you will—be kind."

While Kerr's self-sacrifice is exaggerated beyond anything suggested by liberation critics, one question remains. How can teachers equip themselves to make changes in their working conditions if they are content to be remembered and rewarded with the "kind" words (but not the votes and financial support) of those individuals they have served? In short, the "myth of the calling" and the "muse syndrome" delude teachers in several ways: They do not portray teaching as a reasonable career path to be explored by young people, but as an almost sacred vocation of absolute choice and eternal commitment to others; they do not encourage teachers to take an interest in worldly concerns that might enable them to communicate more effectively with administrators and politicians; and they overstate the degree of self-lessness that should be expected of teachers. In asking them to answer the call and to play the muse, liberation theory does teachers few favors.

LIBERATION THEORY PRIVILEGES PERFORMANCE-
ENHANCED PEDAGOGY

Not only do liberation theorists cast teachers in the role of muse, other tropes imply that teachers must become performers as well. In "A Little Laughter: The Resources of Comedy," Shor suggests that "an amusing milieu brings together intellectual and emotional experience" (1987a, p. 117). He claims that, in using humor, "the instructor comes down from the pedestal, in the process of withering away" (p. 116).

Although Shor (1987a) does not want teachers to become "clown-ish," he claims that, "comedy can be an unexpected landmark in the liberatory frontier" (p. 119). He sees laughter as "a potentially bonding experience for people" (p. 117), since students "can experience solidarity through song and comic moments" (p. 117). Suggesting that teachers use humor and music to bond students, Shor employs the traditional performative tropes for teaching that he claims to demystify and warn against. He also asks teachers to use the same rhetorical strategies as preachers and politicians who delude crowds by putting on a good show.

Yet teachers are not the only ones who are encouraged to use humor in the classroom. In the "mutual comedy between students and teachers . . . one of the funniest and most revealing moments . . . is the power of students to mock and mimic their superiors" (Shor & Freire, 1987, p. 117). Satire is a popular response to teacher domination, and "people satirize their oppressors through sarcasm, parody, *ad hominem* and *reductio*" (Shor, 1987a, p. 118). Presuming to identify the healthy and unhealthy uses of comedy, Shor (1987a) points out that there is

> . . . a dual resource available through comedy: appreciating popular satire as indigenous resistance and appreciating comedy as an influence on popular style. Both the form and content of the class can be healthily transformed by the dialectic assimilation of comedy. (p. 118)

Ironically, while celebrating students' ability to insightfully "mock and mimic their superiors," Shor and Freire (1987, p. 117) place restrictions on the "critical aesthetics" (p. 118) that teachers may employ. When talking to students, Freire writes, "I never use irony, but humor, yes" (p. 161). "For me, irony reveals a lack of security" and sarcasm "betrays an insecurity in the speaker" (p. 161). In warning against using irony—a form of comedy that students often appreciate and use—Freire suggests another comic model. He argues that "Humor is Chaplin" (p. 162). It should reveal the little tramp's vulnerability and charm. If teachers play the vulnerable tramp, all is well. But in employing more pointed kinds of humor, they reveal their "insecurity" (Shor & Freire, 1987, p. 161). Along with my resistance to seeing teachers' humor censored, I see several problems with this logic: Chaplin's humor can also be construed as pointed social commentary—think of *Modern Times*; the impulse to be entertaining may not come naturally to some teachers and could be misconstrued by students who see comedy in the classroom as unprofessional behavior; and by practicing a theatrically stylized pedagogy, teachers may delude students into believing that the learning process comes complete with amusing moments.

Despite the flaws in his logic, Shor (Shor & Freire, 1987) defends the value of entertainment-enhanced pedagogy:

> I've observed humorless classes taught by radical teachers who were plenty clear on their politics. They want to stimulate critical curiosity in the students, but their discourse was flat, without comedy and feeling. If students see the teacher bored, emotionless, or anxious . . . it is unlikely they will feel curiosity. They will think intellectual life is a drag. (p. 163)

While I don't advocate creating an "emotionally bleached classroom" (Shor & Freire, 1987, p. 163), I am not convinced by Shor's argument. As teachers wrestle with the decision about whether to be entertaining or not, I see little protection for them should their comedy be misunderstood or unappreciated by students, parents, and administrators.

In questioning the call for teachers to be entertaining, I am again reminded of teachers' cinematic counterparts. For example, there is Robin Williams' role as the charismatic English teacher in *Dead Poet's Society* (1989). There is also Edward James Olmos' role of the math teacher who is part muse, part taskmaster, and large part entertainer in *Stand and Deliver* (1987). But despite the many close-ups of students with enraptured expressions in both films, a teacher's comedy does not always receive praise. Consider the newspaper coverage of Jaime Escalante's (the teacher depicted in *Stand and Deliver*) departure from his East Los Angeles school district. One passage (Woo, 1991) praises Escalante:

> Educational experts say his hallmark is his thorough command of his subject and his unique classroom style. He entertains students as he leads them through the complexities of advanced mathematics, unabashedly using meat cleavers and funny hats to hold their attention while making a point. (p. B4)

However, as the story continues (Woo, 1991), a specter of doubt is raised:

> But the showmanship also has earned him some rebukes from fellow
> educators, who are concerned that the public now expects all teachers to
> be as flamboyant. "There is no formula" for a good teacher, United
> Teachers–Los Angeles President Helen Bernstein said recently, "What is
> sad is, now people think every teacher has to be a performer" like
> Escalante. (p. B4)

When pedagogical reform can be so easily trivialized as flamboyance
by peers and the press (notice that the journalist, and not Bernstein,
drew the explicit comparison between Escalante and a performer), I see
little protection for teachers who embrace performing as a pedagogical
necessity.

To my mind, the suggestion that teachers cultivate a performance-
enhanced pedagogy is flawed in numerous ways: It assumes that
comedic prowess is an essential component of creative teaching; it
suggests that teachers employ humor and song, while ignoring the fact
that these practices can be used to increase student oppression; it
attempts to censor teacher humor and restrict pedagogy, thus in-
fringing on the freedom to teach without being entertaining; and it
does not discuss how being entertaining can leave teachers vulnerable
to charges of unprofessional behavior. Finally, the call to be entertaining instills in teachers a need to be a charismatic superteacher—a
concept which is discussed in the next section.

LIBERATION THEORY EXAGGERATES THE SPIRITUAL DIMENSION OF TEACHING

Some liberation theorists ask teachers to become more than enabling
muses and able performers. They ask them to become part prophet and
part dreamer.

The Prophet

In discussing the roles liberation critics have drawn for teachers,
Charles Paine (1989) describes the call to be charismatic:

> The degree to which we are able to influence students depends a great
> deal upon charisma and power. Since the real value of emancipatory
> education can only be measured by the degree to which students are
> converted, . . . it is crucial that we set proper examples and engage in
> behaviors they would wish to pursue themselves. (p. 564)

In Paine's comment, we see a critique of this missionary call. "The assumption is that when students understand that they are oppressed . . . the light bulb will turn on, and they will become critical thinkers" (p. 561). Further instruction is now unnecessary "because the truth has been revealed to them" (p. 561). Describing how liberation theory argues that teachers know the truth and that their mission is to reveal it to students, Paine isolates, but does not interrogate, the central role model that liberation theory puts before teachers—that of the prophet.

In discussing pedagogy, Paine (1989) explains the teacher's prophetical impulse:

> The relativist teacher, as much as anyone else, is committed to his or her own beliefs, values, and loyalties about what is right and wrong in the world, and therefore feels as obliged to bring about change . . . by influencing the beliefs and values of other persons. (p. 563)

Here, teachers are transformed from change makers to evangelists: from selfless muses to charismatic prophets who teach in order to convert students to humanitarian purposes. And "if the teacher wishes to install such a vision in students, he or she must accept the role as manipulator" (Paine, 1989, p. 563).

Shor and Freire (1987) also advocate the prophetical stance. They cast the teacher as someone who, like John the Baptist, testifies to his/her vision: "What really happens . . . if you are a professor engaged in liberatory education is that you give a testimony of respect for freedom . . . (Shore & Freire, p. 34). Again, a strain of prophetical zeal (giving testimony) shows through. This testimony moves others to action. "Then in the last analysis, liberatory education must be understood as a moment or process or practice where we challenge the people to mobilize or organize themselves to get power" (Shor & Freire, 1987, p. 34).

Endorsing this philosophy, Freire (Shor & Freire, 1987) declares himself to be a prophet and shares his definition of the term:

> For me, being a "prophet" does not mean to be a crazy man with a dirty beard, or to be a crazy woman. It means to be strongly in the present . . . in such a way that foreseeing the future becomes a normal thing. . . . Imagination at this level is side-by-side with dreams. (p. 186)

The idea that teachers should foresee the future—that they should "anticipate tomorrow by dreaming today" (Shor & Freire, 1987, p. 187)—introduces an essential component of being a good prophet—the ability to dream.

The Dreamer

The romantic belief that teachers' dreams can help change the world is characterized as the mark of a true prophet. According to Shor and Freire, a liberatory teacher must be "committed to a political dream of social change," and "has to bring [that] . . . dream to places where [it] . . . is only a possibility" (1987, p. 95).

In asking teachers to share their dreams with others, Shor and Freire (1987) acknowledge that this process is intrinsically political. "Our project," they write, "involves anticipating a society different from the one we have now" (p. 185). It is a process in which "imagination can be exercised as a resource to expel dominant ideology and to open up some space in consciousness for transcendent thinking" (p. 185). By encouraging teachers to engage in "transcendent thinking" (after all, prophets are expected to think big), Shor and Freire pay little attention to the day-to-day constraints (e.g., time, budgetary, curricular) under which most teachers work. They also foster a notion of the teacher as dreamer—a mystical image that characterizes teachers as being somewhat detached from present-day reality.

As a dreamer, Freire exercises his right to give constant witness to his radicalism. "I have to make clear to them what my dream is, and I have to tell them that there are other dreams that I consider *bad!*" (Shor & Freire, 1987, pp. 156–157). At this point, when teachers place value judgments (*"bad"*) on the dreams of others, the teacher/prophet role is widened even further to include role models such as Socrates, Joan of Arc, Galileo, and Martin Luther King—individuals who felt compelled to speak out and risk their lives in order to "give testimony" (Shor & Freire, 1987, p. 34) to an "important truth" (Paine, 1989, p. 561).

That the ethos of these superteachers is indirectly put before teachers as role models is troubling enough. Who among us wants to be assassinated, threatened, burned at the stake, or excommunicated? But teachers are put at greater professional risk—especially at the elementary and secondary levels—by the inference that giving explicit testimony to their radicalism is, if not compulsory, essential to good teaching. As Freire admits, "if students have the right to bad dreams, I have the right to say that their dreams are bad" (Shor & Freire, 1987, p. 1757). And as Shor agrees, a pedagogy "demands that the teacher have goals and a point of view, one dream or another" (p. 157).

This suggestion that "bad" dreams should be judged and exposed puts teachers at a loss to communicate effectively with the majority of students and administrators. This is true because their theory does not honor the diversity of dreams held by all individuals in the classroom; it creates a simplistic dichotomy between capitalist and democratic dreams; it ignores the possibility that teachers and students may simultaneously hold several conflicting dreams; and by being so future-oriented, it does not keep teachers focused on present-day working conditions. Since prophets tend to be killed or seriously devalued in their lifetimes, this particular role model does not bode well for teachers who are eager to help change the world, but who would also like to live long and prosperously enough to realize the social benefits of their struggle.

LIBERATION THEORY ADVOCATES A ROMANTICIZED VISION OF TEACHER MARTYRDOM

In addition to asking teachers to be romantic dreamers, some liberation theorists advocate teacher martyrdom as an appropriate philosophical stance. Unlike the muse who is passive and silent, the martyr is aggressive—and sometimes militant—in her subversion of the status quo.

The Call to Militancy

Giroux makes the call to militancy when he argues that teachers should become transformative individuals who work to "exercise power over the conditions of their labor, and embody in their teaching a vision of a better and a more humane life" (Giroux & McLaren, 1989, p. xxiii). Here, we see the image of the prophet dreaming of change, forged to the glorified image of a worker struggling for it.

Although he espouses a dialogical pedagogy, McLaren (1988) leaves little room for disagreement as he outlines a transformative intellectual's duties:

> Quite clearly, the teacher as transformative intellectual must be committed to the following: teaching as an emancipatory practice; the creation of schools as democratic public spheres; the restoration of a community of shared progressive values; and the fostering of a common public discourse linked to the democratic imperatives of equality and social justice. (p. xviii)

Suggesting that teachers work "relentlessly" (p. xviii) to further democracy, McLaren issues imperatives that cast teachers as eternal strugglers and unrewarded workers.

It is in their work with students that teachers are asked to be more than militant. They are asked to become role models and teach in ways that elicit new recruits. Freire (1988) hopes that teachers will give students "the knowledge and social skills" to function as "critical agents" in society, and also "educate them for transformative action" (p. xxxiii). In asking teachers to recruit students as allies in social change, these theorists overestimate the influence that teachers can or should have over students. They also ignore the power and rights of students who do not want teachers to lead them to question the dominant social order, and exaggerate the amount of say teachers have in curriculum reform decisions.

For some critics, militancy necessitates noble suffering. Freire argues that teachers "must become militants in the *political* meaning of this word. . . . Something *more* than [an] 'activist' . . . a *critical* activist" (Shor & Freire, 1987, p. 50). For an activist to be critical, she must also be self-critical. Once again, the activist engages in self-scrutiny:

Ira: The militant, the critical activist, in teaching or elsewhere, examines even her or his own practice, not accepting ourselves as finished, reinventing ourselves as we reinvent society?
Paulo: Yes, yes, exactly! This is militancy. (p. 50)

Ascribing cosmological significance to militancy, Shor and Freire give their prose an epic sweep. They portray teacher empowerment on a large canvas—one in which the teacher/prophet achieves renewal by becoming a militant activist who constantly reinvents self and society.

To my mind, the call to militancy is flawed in many ways: It asks teachers to sacrifice everything for the cause, while giving them few strategies for self-protection; it issues moral imperatives—suggesting that teachers become role models for students—which fail to take into account that some teachers' alternative lifestyles may not be valued by students, school boards, or parents; it suggests that teachers employ strategies of social subversion with students who may support the status quo; and it asks teachers to become action-oriented, suggesting that change can be accomplished quickly rather than by extended training and dialogue.

The Martyr's Lore

Even more naïve than these critics' call for teacher militancy is their advocacy of teacher martyrdom. Writing prose that romanticizes teacher suffering and exploitation, these critics make the disturbing suggestion that good teachers should become martyrs and sacrifice themselves for others.

Liberation theorists know that martyrs—even willing ones—are sometimes plagued by doubts. Giroux and Simon (1989) ask the right question about what troubles some teachers: "How can we guard against the production of hopelessness when we take up an agenda of critique and social analysis" (pp. 250–251)? These critics also allude to a doubt that plagues teachers: "If we start questioning the givens of everyday life, won't this simply be overwhelming" (p. 251)? But too often, these lucid questions get glossed over in favor of a discourse that seeks to be more inspirational than practical.

In asking teachers to take risks, Shor and Freire (1987) offer them little more than a pep talk. They admit that having fear "is a manifestation of being alive," but that teachers must not let it become "immobilizing" (p. 55). "I must establish the limits, to 'cultivate' my fear. . . . To cultivate means to accept it" (pp. 55–56). Again, we see otherwise militant teachers stoically accepting their fates, cultivating their fear with humility and faith.

Society is comfortable with teachers bravely performing services in public and silently cultivating their fears in private. Sacrificing oneself for students can make one a popular teacher, and perhaps even a pop icon. Consider once again the press coverage of Jaime Escalante's departure from his school district. In paraphrasing Escalante, the journalist (Woo, 1991) wrote that, "In his view, the sole concern of teachers should be to help students get the best possible education" (p. B3). That "sole concern" translates into "coming into school early and staying late to tutor [at-risk] students," and calling parents "to assure their cooperation and soliciting community support" (p. B3). One of Escalante's students endorsed this perspective: " 'Most of us are sad' that Escalante is leaving, said senior calculus student Angela Fajardo. 'We are going to lose a great friend, a great man. He stays with us until 7 at night. No teacher does that' " (p. B4). In praising such selfless service, our culture creates intimidating, untenable role models for teachers who have additional work or child care responsibilities. Such praise also undermines the efforts of teachers who realize that the more they give their time to students outside of school, the more will be taken, unrewarded, and expected of them by their school districts.

Sounding somewhat like the kind of administrator he criticizes for being too conservative, Giroux (1983) also levels criticisms at teachers who do not give themselves totally to their students:

Recently, I heard a "radical" educator argue that teachers who rushed home early after school were, in fact, committing acts of resistance. She also claimed that teachers who do not adequately prepare for their classroom lessons were participating in a form of resistance as well. Of course, it is equally debatable that the teachers in question are simply

> lazy or care very little about teaching, that what is in fact being displayed
> is not resistance but inexcusable unprofessional and unethical behavior.
> (p. 109)

Although Giroux (1983) admits that "the behaviors displayed do not speak for themselves" and that we should "dig deeply into the specific historical and relational conditions out of which the behavior develops" (p. 109), one wonders whether the would be so hesitant in interpreting a student's purported act of resistance. I doubt it. I suspect that Giroux would rationalize and applaud a student's stated act of resistance as a creative response to school oppression. At any rate, he would grant the student a good deal more latitude of interpretation than he does to the teacher. While I agree that teachers bear more responsibility for the educational encounter than students do, I notice that some liberation critics occasionally lapse into an indirect, but insistent, form of teacher bashing. It is one in which most students are portrayed as being essentially well-meaning, fearful, misled, and misunderstood, while most teachers are portrayed as being intrinsically elitist, coercive, authoritarian, and lazy. Given these polarized images, I wonder why liberation critics, who purport to write in allegiance with teachers to inspire them to change, often create a discourse that portrays teachers as being in such dire need of change?

In asking teachers to change, Wallerstein (1987) outlines Freire's plan of action: that teachers "reflect on the relationship to the world in which they live [and] . . . insert themselves in history as subjects" (p. 34). In helping students become "subjects" in the world, teachers are again cast as individuals who are content to be martyred for a worthy cause. As teachers are encouraged to take risks, they hear nothing about creating strategies for their adequate protection and remuneration. The thinking presumably is that it would be crass and capitalistic for martyrs to think in those terms. In their zeal, liberation critics wax poetic about the future of their pedagogy. "Such education is a charmingly utopian challenge" filled with the "April hope of lowering . . . teacher burnout," and "the August desire of reknowing ourselves and history, in that vast arena of culture war called education" (Shor, 1987b, p. 26).

If teachers enlist in the "culture war" and resign themselves to possible martyrdom, they could receive a consolation prize. Giroux (1983) admits a hard truth—that being committed to radical transformation "always places the individual or the group in the position of losing a job, security, and in some cases friends" (p. 242). The "only consolation is to know that others are struggling as well . . . for our children. . . ." (p. 242). Suggesting that teachers find stature in shared oppression, Giroux tempts them to martyrdom with intimations of immortality. Like Shakespeare's Cleopatra, teachers are portrayed as having "immortal longings" in them—longings that compel them to suffer institutional ingratitude and exploitation in noble reverance for the cause.

This sense of *noblesse oblige* suffering exemplifies the kind of argument we should critique. No other profession, except for nursing, is asked to dedicate itself so selflessly to others. There is another irony here. Once teachers portray themselves as martyrs, it is inconsistent with their philosophy and image to make the real world requests that would help them live and perform their jobs better.

In short, I find the continuum from militancy to martyrdom unsatisfactory because it leads teachers to believe that self-sacrifice—both for students and for colleagues who have suffered before them—is part of the job; it breeds a cult of victimization and martyrdom that is falsely romanticized and ennobled; it suggests that teachers should suffer in silence, rather than voice their pain and oppression; it fosters divisiveness among peers by disseminating the lore of teacher sacrifice—one that suggests that teachers who devote much personal time to serving students are more committed to teaching than those who don't.

CONCLUSION: REFLECTIONS OF A
DISENCHANTED GIVING TREE

I began this chapter with an allusion to the film, *To Sir, with Love*, because it epitomizes my sense of what many liberation critics want for and from teachers as they ask them to change their politics and pedagogy. First, these critics ask teachers to give their time and attention unselfishly to students. They also ask teachers to answer the calling and become performers, muses, militants, and martyrs in the name of literacy. The message is that, in their militant missionary zeal, the focus of teachers' lives should be their students' and the ways that they can serve them with love. The larger assumption is that, if teachers make the appropriate pedagogical changes, large-scale educational reform will eventually be achieved. This is precisely the assumption I contest. In fact, I believe teachers should resist the call to martyrdom because it causes students to expect more of their teachers than they should.

That some students labor under the delusion that self-sacrifice comes naturally to teachers was dramatized for me last December. I had just finished teaching a graduate teacher-preparation course where many students placed significant demands on my time. They required tutoring, letters of recommendation, and advice on lesson plans and their student-teaching experiences. After the class ended, I had a grade complaint by a student who insisted that she deserved an "A" rather than the "A – " she had earned. At several points during our discussion, she became verbally abusive—saying that the conferences and extra time I devoted to her work "didn't matter" because she "didn't get an A and, besides, it was part of your job."

Mark, another student in the class, heard some of this discussion. He had come by to thank me for the extra help I had given him, and said he was "shocked" that a "great teacher" like me could be treated "so badly" by students. The next day he appeared with a token of thanks. His token was a copy of Shel Silverstein's children's book, *The Giving Tree* (1964). The book detailed a boy's relationship with an apple tree and was marketed as "an affecting interpretation of the gift of giving and a serene acceptance of another's capacity to love in return" (dust jacket). This synopsis appeared on the book's dust jacket:

> Every day the boy would come to the tree to eat her apples, swing from her branches, or slide down her trunk . . . and the tree was happy. But as the boy grew older he began to want more from the tree, and the tree gave and gave and gave.

Mark not only gave me the book, but he wrote a dedication on the title page that reads, "Thanks for being a 'tree' for so many."

On reflection, the image of the "giving tree" and Mark's comparison of it to me represents the essence of my struggle simultaneously to enact a liberatory pedagogy—to give myself over to my students—and to preserve reasonable working conditions for myself. It occurred to me that I had been a good and giving "tree" in that class. I had regularly met with students before and after class. I had come to school on nonteaching days specifically to see them, had them call me at home past 11 p.m. for conferences, and arranged conferences around their work schedules. And the more they took, the more I felt compelled to give because they "needed" me.

For example, a student named Derek asked if I would help him revise his personal statement for graduate school. I met him at 6 p.m., only to wait thirty minutes because he was late getting off from work. Should I mention that after our two-hour conference, he never said "thank you"? Or that after he lost his notes, I gave him a second conference for which he never said "thanks"? Through all this, I said nothing to Derek. In fact, I felt bad about being petty enough to want this kind of worldly recognition. However, months later when he came to me for another favor, I had changed my mind. When I asked him why he never said thank you, Derek surprised me. He said that it would "never occur" to him to "say thanks" to a teacher, and that he figured that a teacher "would just know" how grateful he was. Here, again, we see the functioning of the concept of teacher as omniscient muse. Derek saw me as someone whose very identity was derived from helping others and who could sustain himself on that knowledge alone.

After talking to Derek, I felt like the "giving tree," but also inferior to it. How dare I need or look for thanks for doing my job? Would Paulo Freire expect a thank you? Would Ira Shor? Why wasn't it enough to be a "'tree' for so many"? Unlike the "giving tree," my love was not endless. Nor was my ability to serve. I was a pretty miserable muse in every sense of the word.

My sense of inadequacy is intensified when I read the chronicles of teachers I admire. Jesus Christ and Buddha aside, I cannot compare my commitment to teaching to the brilliance and brilliant commitment of Freire (*Pedagogy of the Oppressed,* 1970), or to the profound vulnerability of Elbow (*Embracing Contraries: Explorations in Learning and Teaching,* 1986). Nor am I an eloquent champion of the oppressed and misunderstood like Mina Shaughnessy (*Errors and Expectations,* 1977) or Mike Rose (*Lives on the Boundary,* 1989). I feel inferior to these role models because often I am not up to the dimensions of their sacrifices, and I feel guilty because I am not sure that I want to be. I do not feel like serving my students *all* of the time. Sometimes I think it would be nice to have a raise, a sabbatical, and even an air-conditioned office.

I believe in some aspects of liberation pedagogy—its respect for students, emphasis on active learning, and holistic approach to instruction. But, in my more cynical moments, I wonder if the ideologies inherent in liberation theory's discourse of teacher change and empowerment need to be questioned. What if its discourse has sold teachers a flattering, yet delusory bill of goods? What if teaching is not a calling, but a profession that bears some resemblance to other, more worldly ones? What if Freire's militant missionary stance is not altogether functional or desirable when it comes to empowering teachers in North American schools? What if teachers are so flattered by the thought of being needed that they participate in their own exploitation? In speculating on an alternative ideology to the liberation paradigm, I wish to offer another image of teachers for consideration.

Suggestions Toward the Image of a More Passionate Teacher

I wish to argue for the emergence of a less mystical, more worldly, and more passionate kind of teacher. By the term "passionate," I do not just mean someone who is passionately involved in the education of students, but who is passionate about her own life. Instead of dedicating themselves to others, to militancy, or to martyrdom, teachers could dedicate themselves primarily to their children, their spouses, their parents, themselves, and their careers—perhaps not even in that order. Once teachers question the idea that their profession is a calling to be answered by a select (albeit suffering) few, they might see some of the ironies and inconsistencies in liberation theory's discourse for teacher empowerment.

For instance, if teachers truly want more power in shaping their teaching and working conditions, why would they express their right and desire to seek it in a discourse imbued with tropes of powerlessness and selfless service? In rethinking the muse syndrome, teachers might speculate on why they aspire to play seminal, yet decidedly supporting, roles in their students' lives. They might also ask why they feel it is unbecoming for them actively to seek students' political support when, as voters and alumni, students may be in positions to make teachers' working lives easier. As less sentimental, less giving souls, teachers might feel freer to ask for more worldly support. They might realize that the difference between being underpaid, exploited change-makers and becoming more fairly treated and financially secure ones could be a false dichotomy. As teachers cast off their roles as silent sufferers, they could find themselves in a better place to help their students and themselves.

But teachers are going to need new metaphors for the importance of teaching and for their roles as teachers if they are going to make their empowerment happen. Even Aronowitz and Giroux (1985) admit that "the basis for a radical pedagogy demands more than the development of a theory of resistance; it also needs to develop a new discourse" (p. 109) for change. They argue that the new discourse "will have to ground itself in a theoretical discourse that draws expansively from a number of radical traditions" (p. 109). To my mind, this discourse should draw selectively from a variety of philosophical traditions as well—ones that eschew tropes of martyrdom and selflessness. "Another idiom must emerge as part of the historical process of revolutionary transformation" (Shor & Freire, 1987, p. 182), and another epistemology as well. In their pedagogical discourse, teachers "must avoid dogmatism and disrespect" (Shor & Freire, 1987, p. 183). In their professional discourse, teachers should avoid self-flattery and self-deception. Avoiding these tendencies could mean the difference between teachers eventually achieving real change, and traditionally settling for small change.

REFERENCES

Aronowitz, S., & Giroux, H. A. (1985). *Education under siege: The conservative, liberal and radical debate over schooling.* South Hadley, MA: Bergin & Garvey.

Bennett, W. J. (1988). *American education: Making it work.* Washington, DC: U.S. Government Printing Office.

Elbow, P. (1986). *Embracing contraries: Explorations in learning and teaching.* New York: Oxford University Press.

Freire, P. (1970). *Pedagogy of the oppressed* (Myra Berman Ramons, Trans.). New York: The Continuum Press.

Freire, P. (1988). Introduction. In H. A. Giroux, *Teachers as Intellectuals: Toward a critical pedagogy of learning* (pp. xxvii–xxviii). South Hadley, MA: Bergin & Garvey.

Giroux, H. A. (1983). *Theory and resistance in education: A pedagogy of the opposition.* South Hadley, MA: Bergin & Garvey.

Giroux, H. A. (1988). *Teachers as intellectuals: Toward a critical pedagogy of learning.* South Hadley, MA: Bergin & Garvey.

Giroux, H. A., & McLaren, P. L. (1989). *Critical pedagogy, the state, and cultural struggle.* Albany, NY: State University of New York Press.

Giroux, H. A., & Simon, R. (1989). Popular culture and critical pedagogy: Everyday life as a basis for curriculum knowledge. In H. A. Giroux & P. L. McLaren (Eds.), *Critical pedagogy, the state, and cultural struggle.* Albany: State University of New York Press.

McLaren, P. L. (1988). Forward. In H. A. Giroux, *Teachers as intellectuals: Toward a critical pedagogy of learning.* South Hadley, MA: Bergin & Garvey.

Paine, C. (1989). Relativism, radical pedagogy, and the ideology of paralysis. *College English, 51*(6), 557–570.

Rose, M. (1989). *Lives on the boundary: The struggles and achievements of America's underprepared.* New York: The Free Press.

Shaughnessy, M. P. (1977). *Errors and expectations: A guide for the teacher of basic writing.* New York: Oxford University Press.

Shor, I. (1987a). *Critical teaching and everyday life.* Chicago, IL: University of Chicago Press.

Shor, I. (1987b). Educating the educators: A Freirian approach to the crisis in teacher education. In I. Shor (Ed.), *Friere for the classroom: A sourcebook for liberatory teachers.* Portsmouth, NH: Boynton/Cook.

Shor, I., & Freire, P. (1987). *A pedagogy for liberation: Dialogues on transforming education.* South Hadley, MA: Bergin & Garvey.

Silverstein, S. (1964). *The giving tree.* New York: Harper & Row.

Student teaching contract. (1990). St. Charles, MO: Lindenwood College.

Wallerstein, N. (1987). Problem-posing education: Freire's method for transformation. In I. Shor (Ed.), *Friere for the classroom: A sourcebook for liberatory teaching* (pp. 33–44). Portsmouth, NH: Boynton/Cook.

Woo, E. (1991, June). A calculated move: Jaime Escalante prepares to leave to teach in Sacramento. *Los Angeles Times,* pp. B1, B3, B4.

Response to Janangelo: "To Serve, with Love: Liberation Theory and the Mystification of Teaching"

Lil Brannon
University at Albany, SUNY

Arguments in favor of teachers' economic and institutional power are important to me, so I found Joseph Janangelo's essay provocative in its renderings of "teacher" images within narratives of liberatory pedagogy and popular culture. Although I will later challenge the assumptions and directions of Janangelo's argument, I too think it is a mistake to conflate images of critical teaching with liberal romantic images that have captured the popular imagination.

Dead Poet's Society offers an appealing image of the teacher because it works within the traditions of liberal values that American society understands. Here is a male teacher who works alone, without support from his colleagues who are, themselves, dreadfully boring people. He encourages his students to engage with him in meaningless romantic gestures, and all that happens to him is that he loses his job. The image of teacher here is of one who opposes the drudgery and oppression of educational authoritarianism. Yet he also works within traditions of American liberalism: namely, the rugged individual who strives against all odds to make a difference. The image of teaching as a calling, the image of teaching as inspirational, and the image of teacher as a lone prophet operate in our culture as a Romantic pedagogy, and this Romanticism is what Janangelo outlines in his essay—not my understanding of a critical or liberatory pedagogy.

Critical pedagogy is a sociopolitical educational commitment that challenges the conventional isolation of the teacher. Unlike the romantic teacher Janangelo describes, who works alone and must sacrifice and suffer in order to meet the demands of his calling, the critical teacher works within social alliances and with a critical understanding of the power relations within our culture. Although critical teachers, inasmuch as they are paid and/or licensed by federal and state agencies, are certainly constrained as to the ultimate effect their critical practice might have, critical teaching nonetheless aims to eliminate forms of oppression (including those that oppress teachers) by engaging in practices that create an active citizenry willing to pursue values of freedom and equality. The activities of a critical practice—self-realization, social critique, and cultural transformation—presume a dialectic between the individual and the communal, the local and the general. Popular media certainly have not portrayed this image of a critical teacher.

Janangelo rightly critiques the image of the Romantic teacher as a lonely martyr (albeit mistaken as the critical educator). The "call" for the male to take up a typically feminine role in our culture must be done in such a way that allows this role to be acceptable. The trope of "calling," its "seduction," is that it makes a place for men to take up teaching, yet all the while insuring that nothing ever changes. In other words, the Romantic trope reinscribes the feminine—teaching as service, teaching as woman—and, if men take it on, they will "profit" from it. They "profit" by sustaining the male image as the dominant social construct. What Janangelo fails to take up in his argument against the image of teacher as lonely martyr is how this image of masculinity operates to maintain systems of domination.

Janangelo's title "To Serve, with Love" foregrounds the basic problem. Janangelo finds problematic the "feminine" values of commitment and student-centeredness that work within and through this image of teacher. He prefers instead the masculinist tradition of "common sense" and pragmatism, emphasizing not the merely "domestic"—a feminine value—but rather the "breadwinner's" responsibility over the equally masculinist—but, for him, impractical—tradition of the romantic crusader, Don Quixote, whose lonely idealism proves his undoing—albeit a "noble" undoing. His pragmatist's image, in doing away with service, dedication, patience, and love as the dominant tropes for teaching, makes teaching fully a masculinist enterprise of power and self-interest, one that denies the contributions of women's work while reinscribing the invisibility of it.

While I find Janangelo's pragmatist image of teachers troubling, I also find troubling the image of a critical teacher in the works of Giroux, Freire, and Shor. I would argue that their notion of the critical teacher invokes the masculine heroic narrative of conquest—the teacher as critical Warrior, who only "fades away" in the sense that "old soldiers are unnecessary" once the battles have been successfully won and the people liberated. They retain values of commitment and student centeredness but masculinize them by emphasizing intellectual rigor and political aggression rather than empathy or effective consciousness raising. The critical teacher they imagine is a risk taker, one who bravely fights the forces of oppression—not one who naïvely tilts at windmills or offers himself up as sacrifice.

The image of liberatory teaching as resistance to the dominant culture, which these critical educators construct, therefore must be seen, as Glenn Hudak (1991) argues, within selective traditions of masculinity which have defined "teaching" and "teacher" in our culture. The image that Shor calls on—that of the teacher "withering away"—is important as a concept because the aim of critical teaching is for students to become self-directed agents within our culture. But "withering away" is problematic, not as Janangelo urges because teachers lose their power to effect changes in their own conditions, but as Hudak argues because the image of teacher that is evoked does not challenge the gender hierarchies that privilege male teachers. The male critical teacher, in effect, is allowed to maintain his privilege through a double move. In resisting the image of male teacher as the all-knowing, distant, imparter of knowledge, the male critical teacher gives up, on the one hand, the power of the authoritarian, conservative male teacher; yet, on the other hand, he paradoxically gains power by becoming the "star," the Bohemian male hero in the educational narrative mythos (*Dead Poet's Society; Stand and Deliver*). This is not to argue that the critical teacher is like Robin Williams in *Dead Poet's Society*, but rather that the male teacher "profits" from patriarchal structures that are maintained in the popular imagination, even as he attempts to resist those Romantic representations. A woman does not "gain" in the same way because, given the historical and social circumstances of women teachers, she is supposed to serve and accept her place. When critical educators argue that the role of the teacher is to become "expendable," to "fade from view," to create "self-regulating subjects," they also need to consider the historic conditions in which images of teacher are defined. The image of woman seems much less complicated to eradicate, for even in critical discourse, women remain, for the most part, invisible.

My concern as a critical teacher is how we might challenge these barriers to constructing new images of "teaching" and "teacher" by including the work of women who comprise over 80 percent of those who teach English and language arts K–12. I fear that by not recognizing who actually does the work of teaching, we are maintaining the very institutional structures and conditions that we wish to challenge. What I believe we need to examine are the institutional structures and practices that place the "teacher" at the bottom of the educational hierarchy, and how we maintain "teaching" as a "lesser calling" through our very practices.

Educational research, like all "disciplined" inquiry, has developed methodologies and discourses that "count" as knowledge, and it perpetuates these methodologies and discourses by educating future educational researchers and scholars. The power of discourses outside those "typical" of educational inquiry—the stories of teachers—that pose problems about the role educational research plays in the daily life of the classroom is often dismissed as merely anecdotal and certainly unscholarly. Yet without teachers becoming actively in- volved in constructing "selves," we maintain our privileged position and continue the objectification of "teacher." Instead of constructing alliances with teachers, the educational research enterprise is depen- dent on finding fault with what teachers do. The rhetoric of elitism and laziness about which Janangelo speaks permeates much of the talk about teaching, no matter what its political position.

The educational research enterprise, a predominantly male activity, is sustained by its own masculine image of objectivity, which, in effect and practice, means that (women) teachers never quite get it right. No wonder there are very few images of teachers as women, and the few that there are are typically not worthy of emulation. Teachers' stories, teachers' critical engagement with the material of their working conditions, might just offer a critique of educational research that challenges the social and political structures that sustain and cham- pion the "power" of the scholarly research paradigm itself.

REFERENCES

Hudak, G. (1991). *Doing our own work: A case study of "male" privilege and performance in the academy.* Unpublished manuscript, University at Albany, SUNY.
Stuckey, J. E. (1991). "The feminization of literacy." In C. M. Hurlbert and M. Blitz (Eds.), *Composition and resistance.* Portsmouth, NH: Boynton/Cook.

8

Tradition and Change in Computer-Supported Writing Environments: A Call for Action

Gail E. Hawisher
University of Illinois, Urbana-Champaign

Cynthia L. Selfe
Michigan Technological University

Traditions of pedagogy . . . derive from another time, another interpretation of culture, another conception of authority—one that looked at the process of education as a *transmission* of knowledge and values by those who knew more *to* those who knew less and knew it less expertly.

Jerome Bruner (1986, p. 122)

Computers, now a fact of life in English composition programs, have found their way into almost every aspect of college and high school writing curricula, with English courses often meeting in electronic classrooms where a computer is provided for each student. Educators have looked to these machines not only for help in teaching writing but also, and perhaps more importantly, for help in altering the politics and practices of literacy and composition classrooms as dynamic spaces in which teaching and learning take place.

Educators have expressed the hope, for example, that these machines can support learning spaces that are increasingly democratic (Moulthrop, 1991; Lanham, 1989); involve more students, including those who find traditional learning spaces less than conducive to learning (Hiltz, 1986; Spitzer, 1989); encourage increased equity within classes (Selfe, 1990a; Flores, 1990); provide spaces that are student-centered rather than teacher-centered (Cooper & Selfe, 1990); and provide forums in which students can take increased responsibility for their own learning (Barker & Kemp, 1990; Cooper & Selfe, 1990). Little systematic attention has been paid, however, to whether such fundamental—and politically based—changes can be realistically played out within the current educational system, a system in which forces of tradition—both cultural and educational—provide a powerful counterbalance to forces of change and reform. In fact, although great claims have been made for computers as agents of productive, democratic change, and although some research has been conducted, little evidence has been generated to support the notion that computers can—or will—serve as catalysts for the broader kinds of political reforms that would prove meaningful within our educational system. As a result, during the same period that some English professionals have looked to computers as possible allies in supporting fundamental pedagogical and political changes within literacy and composition programs, the daily instructional uses of computers in classrooms around the country have often belied the potential benefits of this alliance (Hawisher & Selfe, 1991).

This realization, which may surprise some educators, should not. As most technology critics (Braverman, 1974; Ohmann, 1985; Olson, 1987; Kramarae, 1988) remind us, computers, like other artifacts of our culture, are fundamentally shaped by our cultural values, and, as a result, reflect and support those values in fundamental ways—much like our educational system in general. Hence, computers, far from encouraging large-scale change, tend to support stasis within the existing educational system. Teachers who look forward to an alliance that might help them address some of the problems plaguing our educational system—not the least of which is the inequitable treatment of certain segments of students because of race, class, handicap, or gender—find that computers have arrived, but that the systemic problems linger.

Evidence of this pattern is easy to come by in English composition programs, especially—and ironically—in computer-supported programs. Electronic writing classes, with access to the dynamic power of word-processing software, the far-reaching connectivity of networks, the transformative contexts of desktop publishing, and other exciting instructional media, would seem to support a reconsideration of what it means to teach and learn. Yet departments of English in colleges and high schools frequently introduce computers into their programs without the careful research and planning that the use of new technology demands (Selfe, 1988). In doing so, they have ensured the continued marginalization and oppression of underrepresented minority groups and women within computer-supported educational contexts (Gomez, 1991). At the same time, English composition teachers, educated within programs that do not stress critical thinking about the design and implementation of instruction in computer-supported writing facilities, also resist—in many cases, at an unconscious level—

the fundamental changes that proponents of technology indicate are possible: student-centered rather than teacher-centered classes, the increased participation of marginalized students, expanded and increasingly democratic access to systems of publication and distribution, and the democratization of information.

Indeed, as some experts note, despite the climate for change that the use of computers would seem to suggest, teachers trained within the current educational system often resist any fundamental alteration of their instructional approaches and students' approaches to learning (Klem & Moran, in press). Such teachers, even with computer-supported writing classrooms that could support radical new kinds of teaching and learning, may favor more traditional approaches supplemented by lectures, assignments, and classroom strategies. This evidence, while indicating that change is generally difficult—and often only partially enacted—even within computer-supported classrooms, does not reveal much about why such patterns exist. Nor does it explain the underlying dynamics of tradition and change within the American educational system that, in turn, affect both the possibility for and the rate of change in literacy classrooms.

As we approach the 21st century and computers become increasingly ubiquitous in the American educational system, we might well ask ourselves whether English composition teachers can realistically continue to hope that technology can support fundamental change and reform within literacy classrooms and programs—or whether traditional notions of teaching and education, as shaped by our culture, and the cultural values built into the new technology will make such efforts difficult to undertake with any realistic chance of success. We might, in addition, ask ourselves how the process of using technology to support educational reform might begin and how it might proceed if teachers want to make their writing classes into centers for new kinds of learning that some experts claim possible with computer support. By scrutinizing some of the cultural forces involved in shaping traditions of teaching in American schools and some of the political dynamics involved in using computers to support fundamental educational reform in writing classes, this chapter seeks to provide a partial perspective on the role of electronic technology in educational approaches, in general, and in composition instruction, in particular. Our purpose is to think about forces of tradition and change, and how these forces relate to the possibility of creating positive electronically supported environments for writers.

In this chapter, we make the following basic argument about the forces of tradition, change, and education. We start with the assumption, drawing on Margaret Mead's (1970) work, that education is influenced at fundamental levels by cultural values. The American educational system, for example, is an institutional artifact of our larger culture and—as such—it ultimately reflects the changing values and needs of our society. However, we point out that this process of reflection takes some time to be instantiated. Indeed, the American educational system, given its institutional inertia, is relatively slow to respond to changing cultural needs. We cite, as evidence for this claim, the rhythm and pace of educational trends in this decade that, in part, are formulated as responses to changing cultural needs. This pace of change—as well as its depth—is due, to some degree, to the inherent conservatism of the educational system itself, a system designed to maintain and support the dominant ideological vision within our culture, to reflect the cultural values of generations past rather than the generation currently being taught.

Change connected to computer-supported literacy and composition programs, we note finally, is often addressed with a special degree of conservatism—in part, a reaction against the broad claims that computers can support radical, systemic-level changes in the values that shape teaching and learning in such programs. Hence, making meaningful changes within such programs can often prove, at least in some sites, both slower and more partial than change within nontechnological programs. As a result, we argue, literacy and composition teachers need to acknowledge that our reform efforts, especially when they are computer-supported, must proceed simultaneously on at least two levels if we hope for success: in local arenas—in the minds of individual teachers and students and within computer-supported learning spaces—and in the broader political arenas where social and political policy is made. Such a recognition, as Ira Shor (1987) points out in connection with theories of critical pedagogy, acknowledges that there is an important distinction to be made "between raising consciousness in the critical classroom and transforming society through political action" (p. xi). Both kinds of action are necessary to enact fundamental reforms, but local change in computer-supported classrooms "lays a base for transcendent change which will have to be fought for and won in multiple social arenas" (p. xiii).

We illustrate these arguments in a general context by looking at broad patterns of American educational thinking, and in a more particular context by tracing related movements in composition instruction. We demonstrate how the forces of tradition and change have shaped the current use of technology within composition programs and constrained the environments that a more reform-minded use of computers could help us support. In closing, and in keeping with the natural optimism of our profession, we provide a glimpse of two computer-supported learning spaces that teachers can make use of on a local level to support critical pedagogical aims. These spaces, we feel, retain a potential for supporting deep-seated, reform-minded changes in literacy instruction—at a local level—because, within them, teachers can use computers to support a critical pedagogy that calls into question the current educational system and the inequities that accompany the system. Teachers can, in Ira Shor's (1987) words, use these spaces to disrupt the "institutional decorum," to create localized teaching and learning spaces that are "active generators of critical thought" which are "eventually rich in possibilities" because of the particular students they serve (p. 19).

CULTURAL FRAMEWORKS FOR TEACHING AND LEARNING

To begin our discussion, the larger framework of cultural change and tradition provides a productive initial context for tracing the pace and depth of educational tradition and change. In fact, Margaret Mead (1970) argued more than 20 years ago in *Culture and Commitment*, the shape and direction of a culture ultimately determines the way in which it transmits information to succeeding generations, the way in which educational efforts are conducted within that culture. At that time, Mead wrote to describe three different cultural styles, distinguished by particular ways in which children are prepared for adulthood, with each style determined, in large part, by the degree of change that seems to mark a society.

The first, the "postfigurative," characterizes a society in which change is largely imperceptible and adults hand down the necessary knowledge to children. In a postfigurative culture the "future repeats the past"; the young child is born into a culture in which grandparents and parents expect the child's life to be a replica of theirs. According to Mead, "the essential characteristic of postfigurative cultures is the assumption, expressed by members of the older generation in their every act, that their way of life (however many changes may, in fact, be embodied in it) is unchanging, eternally the same" (Mead, 1970, p. 14). Education within such cultures privileges the passing down of traditional values and knowledge through an adult/teacher.

The second, the "cofigurative," marks a culture in which contemporary society is the model for the future and in which children learn primarily from their peers. Although Mead argues that most societies, when they incorporate notions of change, tend to rely on some form of learning from peers, few societies are characterized exclusively in this way. Cofigurative cultures often arise when some form of disruption is experienced by a society. Interestingly, as Mead (1970) notes, one such break with the old is often the "result of the development of new forms of technology in which the old are not expert. . . ." (p. 39). Instead of looking toward elders for expertise and role models in a changing world, then, young people look to their contemporaries for guidance in their choices.

The third cultural style, what Mead terms the "prefigurative," occurs in a society where change is so rapid that adults are trying to prepare children for experiences the adults themselves have never had. The prefigurative cultural style, Mead argues, prevails in a world where the "past, the culture that had shaped [young adults'] under-standing—their thoughts, their feelings, and their conception of the world—was no sure guide to the present. And the elders among them, bound to the past, [can] provide no models for the future" (p. 70).

Mead traces these broad patterns of cultural change particularly in terms of American culture, all the while setting her analysis within a global context. She claims the prefigurative culture characteristic of America in the 1970s—and, we maintain, the 1980s and 1990s—is symptomatic of a world changing so fast that it exists "without models and without precedent," a culture in which "neither parents nor teachers, lawyers, doctors, skilled workers, inventors, preachers, or prophets" (p. xx) can teach children what they need to know about the world. Mead notes that the immediate and dramatic needs our prefigurative culture faces—fueled by increasing world hunger, the continuing population explosion, the rapid explosion of technological knowledge, the threat of continued war, global communication—demand a new kind of social and educational response that privileges participatory input, ecological sensitivity, an appreciation for cultural diversity, and the intelligent use of technology, among other themes.

Given this dramatic—and, we think, essentially accurate—analysis, it is also important to understand that the changes that our culture has undergone, especially during this century, have been reflected only slowly and partially in those changes occurring within schools. In part, the rate of change is systemically determined. As members of a democratic nation, we are all familiar with the ongoing cycles of educational criticism and reform that punctuate American education: Some parts of the general public sense the extent of cultural change; these taxpayers note and speak up about the concomitant need for educational change; and—when the pressure becomes great enough within the culture—the educational system (schools, teacher education institutions, governmental institutions) begins to respond. Such change, however, given the magnitude of our education system and the ideological forces active within and around it, is ponderously slow rather than immediate, marked by inertia rather than nimble response, and partial rather than thorough. As Mead (1970) notes, this rate of change may not be sufficient to answer the immediate needs of our prefigurative society.

> We [the past generation] still holds the seats of power and command the resources and skills necessary to keep order and organize the kinds of societies we know about. We control the educational systems, the apprenticeship systems, the career ladders up which the young must climb, step by step. . . . We are still making do with what we know. (p. 72)

In making do with "what we know," we may have failed to cultivate the kind of forward-looking vision that is necessary for important educational changes to benefit our society and the education of our young.

PATTERNS OF TRADITION AND CHANGE IN AMERICAN EDUCATION

As we have indicated in the preceding section, change is manifested slowly and partially in the American educational system—especially, as Mead (1970) points out, because it reflects and responds to a generationally determined power structure. But change does eventually happen. And tracing such change—even through a necessarily brief and simplified analysis of common patterns of teaching and instruction, and common perceptions about these approaches—can be useful in understanding the relationship between tradition and change. During much of this century, for example, our population has continued to understand classrooms as places where teaching methods reflect the needs of a postfigurative society. In these learning spaces, the teacher has knowledge, and the students are perceived as "empty vessels" (Freire, 1990), receptables to be filled with the cultural information that the adult/teacher deems appropriate to pass along as intellectual currency. As they receive this information, students are expected to sit at desks bolted to the floor, hunched over their papers writing, while teachers are expected to patrol the room, walking up and down the aisles, often—as the stereotype went—with a ruler in hand. If this pattern was not strictly true of American classrooms as they developed later in this century, it has become our stereotypical vision, the one that most often portrayed in mass media images of classrooms, places in which memorization, recitation, and obedience are prized, all necessary behaviors for replicating a culture.

If teaching approaches in general were teacher-centered and postfigurative in their profile during the early part of the twentieth century, so too was most composition instruction. Teachers of writing were charged with passing along to students an accepted repertoire of composition skills that stressed the traditional modes of discourse (description, argument, narrative, exposition); typical organizational patterns for writing; and precision and correctness in language, usage, and mechanics (Berlin, 1988). This was a time when papers were assigned, graded, and returned by teachers who saw writing primarily as a medium through which the ideas of the mind were directly transferred and stored on paper, just as the ideas of the instructor were transferred to the *tabula rasa* of the student's mind. We are all perhaps only too familiar with the sort of writing instruction that accompanies this view of learning and writing.

Later in the century, the psychological theory of "behaviorism" had a profound influence on ideas of teaching and learning. Its essential belief that human beings could be shaped through conditioning—that by rewarding appropriate behavior teachers could improve students' learning—resulted in the profession's not viewing the student and the mind so much as a vessel to be filled with knowledge but rather as a highly developed organism that nevertheless reacts to stimuli and reinforcers. It was the teacher's job, in other words, to provide the sort of reinforcements that would produce the desired behavior. Some early computer-assisted instructional (CAI) programs that reinforce the student's choosing correct answers with an opportunity to proceed through the material are based on this model of learning. According to B. F. Skinner (1968), the behavior of students should be constructed not by the students so much as by the teacher—the teacher informs and shapes, building desired behavior in each student. In this way, classrooms remained teacher-centered and hence postfigurative in emphasis since the adult was still passing down the requisite knowledge—in this case, requisite behavior—of the culture.

Skinner (1968) fascinates those of us interested in electronic technology because he was also interested in programmed learning and teaching machines, both of which are often associated with computers. But the machines were not to be constructed in ways that might encourage students to explore; instead, they were to be programmed to reward correct answers. For Skinner, learning was not so much discovery on the part of students as it was the result of a teacher's "priming, prompting, and vanishing" (1986, p. 107), so that the student is finally able to demonstrate the learning independently. In a

1986 article, Skinner reaffirms the value of such programmed learning when he writes, "we do not learn by doing, as Aristotle maintained; we learn when what we do has reinforcing consequences. To teach is to arrange such consequences" (p. 107). Thus, successful teaching—and Skinner would advocate the use of computers—involves setting up the school environment in such a way that students can be promptly evaluated and go on to additional learning as soon as they are ready. Despite promoting a rather mechanized view of learning, behaviorism nevertheless looked to the individual student as the primary recipient of attention, with programmed learning texts or individual packets of learning materials designed to allow each student to proceed at his or her own pace.

During this time, the American culture was showing signs of dramatic change, with other educational experiments also influencing the schools. Among the many societal factors causing such upheaval, Mead (1970) mentions the explosion of scientific and manufacturing knowledge, the focus on nuclear families, and the increasing mobility of the population. As the pace of change increased in the culture, approaches to American education reflected change as well, but more slowly and only partially. Along with the rise of behaviorism, less emphasis was placed on transmitting knowledge from the adult generation to the generation of children, and more attention was paid to the development of individual children as problem solvers who could grapple with the challenges the culture was facing. During this period, progressive education with its emphasis on the student as doer and lifelong learner became perhaps the prime educational experiment of the century, embodying as it did values of a democratic society in which experience was prized. Yet both English teachers and society finally rejected the movement as a whole, resisting the dramatic changes of cross-disciplinary teaching that it brought to the profession and viewing it as undermining the sort of intellectual rigor necessary for young citizens to succeed in a competitive world (Applebee, 1974).

Emphasis on the child as learner, however, continued to receive attention in developmental learning theory. Because psychology is inevitably concerned with the development of individual human minds, it is perhaps not surprising that Jean Piaget (1968) similarly focused on the individual child. His research led him to the concept of egocentrism—a looking inward and an inability to sustain a viewpoint other than one's own—and to argue that it is characteristic of an early period in the child's development, gradually diminishing with the aid of the peer group as the child matures. In this view, the ideas and voices of others become important later rather than earlier in the child's development; the image is one of the child developing from inner to outer, gradually maturing into a thinking adult. An interesting aspect of Piagetian thought is the suggestion that talk with children should be diminished—that children don't learn through lectures. And although most teachers would agree with this last part, few would argue today that reduced talk between adults and children or between children and children leads to greater learning. Piaget was interested in the learner's engaging in action, in the child's doing, rather than merely being instructed through talk. Yet there is something in Piaget that precludes negotiation or transactions between individuals as meaning-making activities; there is a privileging, Jerome Bruner (1986) argues, of "unmediated conceptualism," that is, the idea that "knowledge is achieved principally by direct encounters with [the] world" (p. 61), rather than through talk or vicarious experience. Today, largely as a result of social constructionist theory, interaction among students and between students and texts within English classrooms is valued, with conversation prized in and of itself as a knowledge-making activity (Trimbur, 1989; Lloyd-Jones & Lunsford, 1989). But the recognition of interaction and conversation among students as a valued part of learning is a relatively new concept to American classrooms.

As the pace of change continued to accelerate during the twentieth century—not only in our own country but also worldwide—American moved increasingly toward a prefigurative society. In Mead's (1970) terms, the younger generation in our country (and elsewhere) faced a "world without models and without precedent" (p. xx) as they contemplated the "emergence of a world community" (p. 68) linked electronically by various media, worldwide travel opportunities, the increasing threat of nuclear destruction, and struggles with population control and food production. This culture was marked by a deepening generation gap, Mead continues, because "young people everywhere share a kind of experience that none of the elders ever had or will. Conversely, the older generation will never see repeated in the lives of young people their own unprecedented experience of sequentially emerging change" (p. 64). The American culture was becoming one in which adults could not teach children because they lacked experience in current problems. In response to these changes, among others, educational approaches eventually placed an increasing emphasis on social environments, having students learn in collaborative settings, and using group problem-solving methods—all characteristics, we might add, of the progressive education movement that was earlier rejected (Applebee, 1974). During this period, Jerome Bruner (1986) was beginning to develop a theory of learning that moved steadily toward social views of learning, and in the 1980s he refined a theory of educational development that was informed in a fundamental way by this focus on social relations. As Bruner wrote,

> It [a developmental theory of the future] will be motivated by the question of how to create a new generation that can prevent the world from dissolving into chaos and destroying itself. I think that its central technical concern will be how to create in the young an appreciation of the fact that many worlds are possible, that meaning and reality are created and not discovered, that negotiation is the art of constructing new meanings by which individuals can regulate their relations with each other. (p. 149)

Bruner is responding, as Mead had earlier, to the tremendous forces of change shaping our society, changes that are felt in our schools yet are often neglected as we continue to try to teach and educate our young as we ourselves were taught and educated.

These themes remain important features of English composition classes today, both computer-supported and otherwise. As Bruner has pointed out (1986), the ideas beginning to inform education in general—and, we would argue, writing classes in particular—seem increasingly indebted to the work of Lev Vygotsky and his social theories of learning. If for Piaget egocentrism was characteristic of the very young, for Vygotsky (1962) language from the start penetrates the child's psyche, exerting its socializing forces on the mind. According to Vygotsky, inner and egocentric speech mark a transition from "interpsychic" to "intrapsychic functioning," "from the social, collective activity of the child to more individualized activity" (p. 133). For Vygotsky and his colleagues, the main drive of the child's development is toward gradual individualization that can only come after socialization, and this entire process is reflected in the development of language. Vygotsky, partially perhaps in reaction to Pavlov's emphasis on the passive human organism blindly and predictably responding to the environment, set forth a theory that seems to be more compatible with the way we conceive of learning today and is in keeping with current theoretical views regarding social epistemic rhetoric and its classroom practices (Berlin, 1988). His view of the zone of proximal development, in which learning can pull development forward, provides a rich environment in which students can work together with their teachers to learn. Many English composition classes, in response to such theoretical work, have begun to feature an emphasis on rhetorical setting, collaborative writing and peer-response groups, and small group discussions.

THE LIMITATIONS OF CHANGE

This picture of cultural pressure and resultant educational change, while it helps identify some parts of the relationship between tradition and change, is far from the simple and necessarily reductive picture we have sketched. Given the size, intractability, and inherent conservatism of the American educational system, some much-needed changes have never occurred and, indeed, some needs within the system have become exacerbated during the last years of this century. Among the many problems—evidenced in English composition classrooms at least as frequently as they are in any other learning spaces—are the continued marginalization of individuals due to race, gender, age, or handicap; the silencing, intentional or unintentional, of certain segments of our population, such as the very poor; and the unequal distribution of power within economic and social groups represented in our classrooms.

These problems persist because they are systemic and politically determined, not only within the framework of our educational system, but also within that of our culture and its economy. As liberatory and critical educators sketch the problem, "schooling is a device through which a corporate society reproduces its class-based order . . . [and] recreates a stratified society by socializing each new generation into its place in the established order" (Shor, 1987, p. 2). To address the problems identified earlier, these educators maintain, we would have to change the very foundations of our culture through radical reform movements (cf. Freire, 1990; Shor, 1987). Such radical changes, of course, are unlikely; they face stiff and continuing resistance from a wide range of educators, politicians, administrators, and taxpayers who have vested power in the current cultural situation. Hence, efforts to initiate change that will address these problems are always partial, localized, and resisted by opposing forces within the educational system and the culture. As Shor points out, schools remain "battlefields for the conflicting interests of the state and the people" (p. 40), and, as such, continue to marginalize certain groups.

Even in composition classrooms—where a good many teachers would subscribe to a vision in which all students, regardless of their age, gender, handicap, or socioeconomic status, enjoy equal participation—some students remain marginal and only partially engaged. Women, for instance, given their cultural and family training, speak less than men and are interrupted more often in oral conversation (West & Zimmerman, 1983; Zimmerman & West, 1975). Students, informed by cultural experiences, continue to privilege the comments of individuals who can speak articulately and with authority because they have enjoyed enriched educational experience (Kramarae & Treichler, 1990). Students who speak English as a second language continue to fall behind those who speak English only (Gomez, 1991).

Recent and revived interest in the liberatory pedagogy of Paulo Freire (1990), or the critical pedagogies of Ira Shor (1987) and Ivan Illich (1971), attests to the recognition of such systemic ills and the need to initiate radical reform of the American educational system. However, the study of such radical approaches illustrates all the more sharply how change in the American educational system is often only partially realized. The problems we have identified have existed, in one form or another, to one degree or another, since the beginning of this century and show little sign of being productively addressed by partial educational reforms.

TRADITION, CHANGE, AND COMPUTER TECHNOLOGY IN ENGLISH COMPOSITION CLASSROOMS

In such a climate, then, it is little wonder that computer technology is still often used by teachers in primarily traditional ways and with little real impact on the educational system (Hawisher & Selfe, 1991). Identified as it has been—and continues to be—with a radical potential for restructuring human language activities (Heim, 1987; Selfe, 1989b; Turkle & Papert, 1990), connecting groups on a worldwide basis (Spitzer, 1989), exploding traditional classroom boundaries and constraints (Hiltz, 1986), changing the traditional teacher–student hegemony (Cooper & Selfe, 1990), and altering the very fabric of social and psychological interaction (Kiesler, Siegel, & McGuire, 1984), computer technology has the potential to be extraordinarily dangerous to existing systemic values within schools and, thus, to people who depend on the continued existence of the educational system for a livelihood. As a result, Joseph Weizenbaum (1976) reminds us, although computers seem to be a nexus of money, power, and creative energy that inspires change—given the strong conservative values inherent in the technology, and those cultural values that inform and shape its use—they are often used to "entrench and stabilize social and political structures" (p. 31) that might otherwise benefit from more radical and deep-seated reform.

This resistance to fundamental change and radical reform can be observed in a variety of sites, both within computer-supported composition classrooms and within our educational system as a whole. A closer look at several illustrative sites can help us understand more about the complicated relationships binding tradition and change within the American educational system.

One of the major hopes that educators have had for computers is that the machines could, somehow, help educators democratize classrooms. As the culturally informed reasoning went in the last decade, if we can put enough computers into enough schools, then all students—regardless of socioeconomic status, race, or gender—will have access to technology and, thus, to success through the technologically supported power structures of our culture. Impetus for the movement to integrate computers into the schools was prompted by at least two important cultural realizations: first, that our society would be increasingly dependent on technology; and second, that we were not providing equitable educational opportunities to all students within the existing system. As Wheelock and Dorman (1989) pointed out in their report for the Massachusetts Advocacy Commission, of those students who enrolled in secondary schools in 1980, 12.2% of white students dropped out of secondary schools, while 17% of Afro-American students, 18% of Hispanic students, and 29.2% of Native American studies did so.

When computers were introduced into schools during the succeeding years, however, the expected changes were only partial, and the resulting reforms no more than minimal. In fact, by the end of the 1980s, a number of educators (Cole & Griffin, 1987; Sheingold, Martin, & Endreweit, 1987) were noting alarming tends associated with computers. Mary Louise Gomez (1991) summarizes Cole and Griffin (1987):

- More computers are being placed in the hands of middle- and upper-class children than poor children;
- When computers are placed in the schools of poor children, they are used for rote drill and practice instead of the "cognitive enrichment" that they provide for middle- and upper-class students;
- Female students have less involvement than male students with computers in schools, irrespective of class and ethnicity. (pp. 43–44)

By the end of the 1980s, as this information suggests, computers were indeed present in every school, but they were being used in ways that sustained rather than changed the existing educational trends. This pattern was certainly true in terms of a continuing gender bias. As Emily Jessup (1991) points out, the "gender gap" (p. 338) in educational computing had—and continues to have—both a qualitative and quantitative side. Citing numerous research projects (cf. Gerver, 1989;

Hawkins, 1985; Becker, 1987), Jessup notes that in programs depending on computer support,

> at all levels of learning about computers—in school, in higher education, in further education, in training, in adult education classes, and in independent learning—women tend to be strongly underrepresented. The extent of their underrepresentation varies from sector to sector and to some extent from country to country, but the fact of it is so ubiquitous that the evidence tends to become monotonous. (p. 336)

Certainly some of the resistance to fundamental change during the last two decades has come from within the ranks of English composition teachers themselves, and this group provides a second site for examining the relationship between tradition and change. During the early 1980s, despite the promise of radical change associated with computers, English composition teachers continued to use the technology—and to write about their experiences—within highly traditional contexts from conservative educational purposes: among them, grading and evaluating papers (Marling, 1984; Jobst, 1984), providing drill and practice grammar tutorials (Holdstein, 1983; Falk, 1985), identifying stylistic problems (Neuwirth, Kaufer, & Geisler, 1984; Reid & Findlay, 1986), checking spelling (Zimmer, 1985; Harris & Cheek, 1984), providing practice with sentence combining (McCann, 1984), and overall helping students improve the quality of their writing (Duling, 1985; King, Birnbaum & Wageman, 1984; Montague, 1990).

The conservative trend in instructional strategies during this period was exacerbated by teacher education programs. At this point, most schools lacked teacher education programs that devoted time to examining technology from critical perspectives. Few teachers, moreover, had access to any postservice education that helped them think critically about the use of computers within instructional settings (Selfe, Rodrigues, & Oates, 1989). Without such education—and faced with administrators who demanded a speedy and cost-effective integration of computers into English programs (Selfe, 1988)—English composition teachers often resorted to the readily available computer-assisted software packages prepared by commercial vendors. The packages were frequently authored by software developers who had very little experience in the teaching of English. Moreover, as Paul LeBlanc (1990) points out, software packages—such as style and spelling checkers—often served highly conservative functions themselves, in that they reinforced the back-to-basics movement that supported (and continues to support) traditional authority structures within educational settings. Thus, teachers came to adopt computers but, nevertheless, resisted meaningful change by using computers to reinforce older and unproductive ways of thinking about learning. The computers were, in effect, no more than electronic versions of the printed grammar handbooks that came before them. Computers were seen, in essence, as a means of reducing student-generated error in composition and literacy classrooms. This approach, critical pedagogists would be quick to point out, is entirely congruent with the trend of capitalist cultures to replace the "error and unpredictability" generated by a human with the "reliability" associated with machines (Shor, 1987, p. 52).

A third site in which to examine forces of tradition and change and how they operated during the last decade is the computer-supported writing labs or classrooms that sprang up across the country during the last half of the 1980s. English composition teachers, by 1985, had begun to recognize some of the limitations of their earlier uses of computers and to realize that the technology could help them change—in dramatic ways—the local learning and teaching environments in which they functioned (Hawisher & Selfe, 1989). Change, however, was still slow in coming and continued to be partial at best. Hawisher noted as late as 1988 that teachers had yet to adjust their instructional strategies systematically and productively to these new spaces: "The real challenge of working in this context [a computer-supported writing classroom], then, is to devise a pedagogy that capitalizes on . . . computers . . . yet goes beyond what we have previously contrived" (Hawisher, 1988, p. 18).

During this period, English composition teachers, influenced by the social-epistemic movement, were learning to use word processing to support increased peer-group work in writing classrooms (Cyganowski, 1990; Skubikowski & Elder, 1990), design computer-based classrooms that encouraged collaborative work (Selfe & Wahlstrom, 1986), explore connections between reading and writing while learning how to use computers in pedagogically sound ways (Hawisher, 1990), and carry out research that looked at computer technology within broader social contexts (Herrmann, 1990). Despite the best intentions of teachers, however, the instructional change that accompanied computer use often remained "skin deep" and failed to address the fundamental, culturally derived problems of equitable student involvement, educational opportunity, and power differentials based on race, age, gender, and socioeconomic status.

Elizabeth Klem and Charles Moran (1992), observing two teachers and their classes in a computer-supported writing environment, commented on the relationship between tradition and change as it was played out in these classrooms. They identified several ways in which the forces of tradition, represented in part by teachers who invested in—and were comfortable with—the existing system, and the forces of change, represented in part by the disruptive potential inherent in the computer-supported classroom, came into opposition:

> What we had not anticipated was that we'd see in these new classrooms a persistent and deep-rooted conflict between the teachers' own goals and those built in to the new facility. It is generally thought that computers carry with them new pedagogies and that teachers will, in some undefined way, go along. Indeed, computers are often hailed as "The Catalyst for Broad Curricular Change" (Gilbert & Balestri, 1988). Our computer classrooms were designed, as noted above, to complement and reinforce the Writing Program's model of "good teaching." The room layout, with its notably absent teacher-place, privileged a workshop model of a writing class and aimed to cast the teacher as a fellow writer and editor—albeit the most experienced writer in the room—rather than as the center-of-the-class authority. Moreover, the network configuration sought to foster a class model in which much of the learning and writing happened as students collaborated on the in-process drafts.
>
> What we saw in our teachers' classes, however, was a fair amount of dissonance: a genuine clash between the kind of writing class envisioned by the teacher and the kind of writing class privileged by the computer-equipped classroom and its architecture. Because we were not attempting to measure student learning, we can not relate what we saw to what progress students made. We have to admit, though, that the tug-of-war between the teachers and their classroom was on-going and sometimes quite striking. The teachers' behavior did not change significantly as the semester progressed, nor did the teachers noticeably adapt their teaching styles to the new environment. (pp. 22–23)

What becomes evident even from this brief examination is that systemic change, especially meaningful change, has proven hard and slow—and perhaps impossible—to enact directly from within a classroom setting, whether or not technology is involved. Adding technology to the highly complex equation of education, at least in English composition classrooms, does not necessarily improve the chances for meaningful change in connection with equity and literacy instruction—even though educators have continued to hold great hopes for computers as democratizing influences.

TRADITION, CHANGE, AND THE CONTINUING STRUGGLE

Recognizing the difficulty in initiating and sustaining fundamental systemic change in education, however, offers no excuse for inaction, especially for professionals who face daily the continuing need for change and reform. As Henry Giroux and Paulo Freire (1987) point out, teachers who want to enact critical pedagogies of any sort must "steadfastly refuse to engage in a politics of withdrawal or cynicism" (p. xi). Indeed, it has become increasingly apparent to teachers of English composition and other literacy workers that educators much increase their participation in political arenas situated both nationally and locally if they hope to make any progress in addressing those fundamental literacy problems identified earlier in this chapter.

We have, during the last decade, made some progress—especially in getting educators to recognize some of the important links between literacy problems, the cultural forces that spawn these problems, and the shapes of the solutions needed to address such problems (cf. Lunsford, Moglen & Slevin, 1990; Berlin, 1988; Cooper & Holzman, 1989). We have also made some progress in getting English educators to think critically about the most effective ways to orchestrate learning at elementary, secondary, and college levels (Lloyd-Jones & Lunsford, 1989). As a result, the energies of the profession have been devoted, increasingly, toward thinking critically about pedagogy and designing instruction in classrooms that encourages students to challenge, through intellectual and critical analyses, "knowledge, perception, ideology, and socialization" (Shor, 1987, p. xi) as they have been defined within our culture. This stimulation of critical perspective, which can take place in composition and literacy classrooms, is designed, at least in part, to outfit students who can then work to change social policy through "groups, movements, and political arenas which influence social policy" (p. xiii), who can effectively resist a belief in the "mysterious invulnerability" of the "oppressive" and "incomprehensible" system we have constructed (p. 57).

In our prefigurative society, then, we have begun to realize that if young people are to do more than learn from their elders (in this case, their teachers), these elders must arrange learning spaces in such a way that allows students to challenge the status quo, question their roles in a society that continues to resist stasis. Some of this role questioning and learning can be facilitated through what we've learned from Piaget, who paved the way for a learner-centered classroom, and from Vygotsky, whose social views of learning have led us to peer-group work and collaboration. Such activities require students to think and learn from one another as well as from their teachers. In this sense, developmental theories of learning, coupled with an increased awareness of social and political influences on language and on literacy education, may help teachers respond to the patterns Mead documented and initiate local educational reforms based on their own classrooms.

One promising direction for these classroom-based reform efforts involves teachers who use computer technology within literacy and English composition programs to create new kinds of local, "micropolitical" (West & Zimmermann, 1983) spaces for teaching and learning that—when informed by critical and liberatory pedagogies—can help teachers resist the conservative values of education and disrupt "institutional decorum" (Shor, 1987, p. 19). Within these virtual spaces (existing only in the memory of a computer), we believe it is possible for students and teachers to work together to gain some critical perspective on systemic patterns and problems, and to develop a "democratic, entertaining and penetrating dialogue" (p. 32) that will prepare students to be "their own agents for social change" (p. 48). In this way, two particular kinds of such spaces—on-line conferences and hypertextual environments for writing—may yet prove to offer forums for positive and meaningful educational change in local educational sites.

On-Line Conferences as Local Sites for Change

Teachers who have had experience with on-line conferences as alternative forums for literacy education, for instance, have already claimed that these electronic conversations show promise as spaces that support critical teaching and learning. On-line conferences involve a relatively simple use of the technology that can best be described as an electronic letter drop, an on-line conversation, or an electronic bulletin board. Among the intriguing claims computer-using teachers make about such conferences and their use in literacy classrooms have been the following:

> Networks create an unusual opportunity to shift away from the traditional writing classroom because they create entirely new pedagogical dynamics. One of the most important is the creation of a written social context, an on-line discourse community, which presents totally new opportunities for effective instruction in writing. (Batson, 1988, p. 32)

> Although I thought I might resent students intruding into my own time after schoolhours, I find instead that I enjoy our correspondences [over the network]—that I get to know students better and they know me better, too, a benefit that transfers to our classroom. (Kinkead, 1988, p. 41)

> All the instructors in the pilot project [using an electronic conference for writing instruction] reported never having seen a group of first-year students, thrown randomly together by the registrar's computer, become as close as their students had. Students set up meetings in the library and

in campus computer labs, came early to class and stayed late, made plans together for the next semester, and exchanged addresses. The computer, far from making the class more impersonal, fostered a strikingly close community in one of the nation's largest universities. (Schriner and Rice, 1989, p. 476)

Once people have electronic access, their status, power, and prestige are communicated neither contextually . . . nor dynamically. . . . Thus, charismatic and high status people may have less influence, and group members may participate more equally in computer communication. (Kiesler, Siegel, & McGuire, 1984, p. 1125)

On the network, students can work collaboratively to brainstorm, solve problems, [and] experience writing as real communication with real people. . . . (Thompson, 1987, p. 92) Those people with powerful ideas will have more influence than those with powerful personalities. . . . The democratization fostered by computer conferencing has other consequences as well. Just as nonverbal clues are missing in conferencing, so too are clues about an individual's status and position. (Spitzer, 1986, p. 20)

Such claims appeal especially to composition teachers who hope to provide alternative forums for student-centered, collaborative writing that involve all members of their classes in active learning situations centering on written discourse. Often, these teachers are looking for nontraditional strategies to improve the learning of individuals who might be considered—or consider themselves—marginally involved in more traditional academic forums in the making of meaning within a classroom community. On-line conferences seem to offer alternative local sites for academic discussions and exchanges, forums that have the potential for encouraging new patterns of student involvement because they offer different conversational power structures than those characterizing traditional classrooms.

Much of the evidence available to us concerning computer-based conferences supports such beliefs. Reports of on-line discussions via networks, for example, indicate that such conferences may encourage more people to participate in group discussions and efforts than do similarly constructed face-to-face meetings (Fersko-Weiss, 1985; Kiesler et al., 1984; Pfaffenberger, 1986; Pullinger, 1986; Spitzer, 1989). Computer networks have also been reported to make conversations possible for writers and readers in different geographical locations (Holvig, 1987; Pfaffenberger, 1986; Spitzer, 1989); for individuals who are handicapped (Batson, 1988) or do not find it possible, because of age or economic constraints (Holvig, 1987; Ludtke, 1987) to get to a traditional classroom where they can participate in academic conversations; and for individuals who do not find the traditional classroom a conducive environment for contributing to intellectual discussions (Hiltz, 1986; Meeks, 1985).

Many communities of students who converse on-line would or could not have formed in traditional classrooms. Students in a suburb of Pittsburgh, for example, now use the BreadNet computer network to communicate with their peers on an Indian reservation in South Dakota (Schwartz, 1990). Deaf students at Gallaudet University (and now increasing numbers of students at such institutions as The University of Texas–Austin, the University of Minnesota, Texas Tech University, and Carnegie–Mellon University, among others) use a computer network in their English classes to converse in "real time" with their peers and their teachers (Batson, 1988); and at the New York Institute of Technology, over 200 university students living in remote locations attend classes on an electronic, computer-based network (Spitzer, 1989).

Computer-based conferences also have been found to minimize some cues of gender, race, position in established organizational hierarchies, social status, or appearance (Kiesler et al., 1984; Sproull & Kiesler, 1986). This ability to minimize social and hierarchical cues, in turn, contributes to increasingly egalitarian participation by individual group members engaged in a common task and the decreasing potential for group domination by individuals (Kiesler et al., 1984; Spitzer, 1986).

Hypertexts as Local Sites for Change

If computer-based conferences support both resistant and accommodative discourses, however, they still adhere closely to an existing set of genre conventions valorized by the dominant influences of our culture. A second promising area of exploration in computer use may involve even more potential for radical reform: It is called hypertext. Hypertext represents a way of structuring information (in the form of text, image, sound, and video) so that each reader of a "text" (and here, we use this term to refer to collections of information from several media) chooses the information he or she wants or needs to see and the sequence in which the information is accessed. Hypertexts, in other words, are dynamic collections of information, constructed electronically by each reader who charts a particular path through the text. The idea behind hypertext is to give readers choices about how to construct/ explore/create the text that they read and to expand readers' access to information by linking information bases in vast frameworks of electronic information that can be navigated at will.

The proponents of hypertext, for example, might construct an educational hypertext about the Civil War by linking various drafts of Crane's novel, *The Red Badge of Courage*, to published versions of Ulysses Grant's personal papers, and to Quaker Cyrus Pringle's diaries so that readers can move electronically from one text to another by pressing a button at any point in a text. These texts, in a vast web of additional connections, would then be linked electronically to critical commentary, films and still photography of the Civil War period; descriptions of social artifacts relating to northern and southern cultures; bibliographical sources that a study of the literary texts might inspire; biographies of well-known or little-known Civil War figures; maps and simulations of famous battles; oral renditions of contemporary or modern poems and songs dealing with war; databases of popular culture that survives from the period; and student commentary on the various components of this vast hypertext itself. Pure hypertexts—which have no beginnings, no middles, and no ends, until these elements are defined by a particular reader—are literally authored by every reader. So each reader of the Civil War hypertext would start at a different place and read or see a different text.

As Ted Nelson (1987) notes, hypertexts represent a new way of structuring information that allows authors to link bits of text (or still images or video images) in a rich web of associations that readers construct (or write) as they go along. Because a pure hypertext has no one point or beginning or ending (every piece of information is a potential beginning or ending point), readers create their own document as they read. Hypertext, its supporters claim (cf. McDaid, 1991; Moulthrop, 1991; Bolter, 1991), has the potential for being intellectually aligned with democratic ideals in ways that our print culture cannot be and has the potential for turning our notions of education upside-down and inside-out. Such a system, as Stuart Moulthrop (1989) suggests, assumes an intellectual world in which "diverse and even antithetical statements coexist within a single structure, each capable of emerging in the act of reading" (pp. 19–20). In this world, as Moulthrop (1989) continues, hypertexts may "force us to reformulate our notions of intellectual authority" (p. 27), to acknowledge that "discourse can no longer be limited to isolated 'works'" (p. 27), and to conceive of texts in which "students' questions have the same presence as teachers' glosses" (p. 27).

Given that hypertext radically changes our fundamental conceptions of genre and form, of text and gloss, of authorship and ownership, of canon and popular culture, the ideological implications of hypertexts for literacy educators and students are startling. There are scholars who see hypertext as a medium so radical in its conception that, when used in educational settings, it can provide teachers and students with a way of transforming existing cultural values and, thus, the venues for learning and thinking, into radically democratic spaces (cf. McDaid, 1991; Nelson, 1987; Lanham, 1990). If this is true, hypertext might, as some experts contend, prove to be a reformist tool in literacy classrooms, one that can open up local spaces for students to think in different and increasingly critical ways. Hypertexts, for example, are even now being used at various sites by reform-minded teachers to validate multiple interpretations of a text; to expand the range of texts and media to which we expose our students; to change in radical ways the nature of privilege associated with printed texts representing our dominant culture; and to preserve alternative representations of our world in film, oral histories, music, and image.

Sherry Turkle and Seymour Papert (1990), in a recent issue of Signs, suggest an additional reason for seeing hypertextual writing environments as productive alternative sites for literacy education. Their article deals with the learning styles of student programmers and the dominant ideological/epidemological assumptions that shape the education of these individuals. Turkle and Papert note that student programmers have traditionally been taught approaches to program construction that are formulated at fundamental levels in abstract, formal logic and are heavily dependent on representing such logical relationships abstractly—in the form of propositions within the rules of programming syntax. This "formal, propositional" way of "knowing" (p. 129), according to the authors, has come to constitute a "canonical style" (p. 133) of thinking and writing, a privileged way of relating ideas one to the other for those who enter the process of computer science. More importantly, in Turkle and Papert's words, this abstract propositional representation has become "literally synonymous with knowledge" (p. 129)—so synonymous, so transparent a lens for programmers, in fact, that they can barely see it anymore, so much it is now equated with "formal" and "logical" thinking. This way of representing knowledge has been given "a privileged status" (p. 133) for programmers and others in scientific or technological fields.

As an alternative way of coming to know the world of learning, Turkle and Papert (1990) suggest an approach they call "bricolage" (p. 135) in reference to the work of Claude Levi-Strauss (1968). Bricolage, as Turkle and Paper use it and as we use it here, refers to the construction of meaning through the arrangement and rearrangement of concrete, well-known materials, rather than through an abstraction of thought in representations of formal propositional logic. Bricoleurs get to know a subject by interacting with it physically; by manipulating materials, symbols, or icons in rich, associative patterns; by arranging and rearranging them constantly until they fit together in a satisfying or meaningful way. Bricoleurs reason "from within" (p. 144) to come to an understanding of a problem rather than reasoning with the help of a traditionally validated pattern of logical representation.

We are convinced that this distinction—between individuals who compose by representing ideas in abstract propositional representations (what composition teachers call writing sentences) and individuals who compose by arranging and rearranging concrete symbols into text blocs—holds as true for writers as it does for Turkle and Papert's programmers. Students who write in hypertextual composing environments such as StorySpace, for example, are taking advantage of what Jay Bolter (1991) calls a "writing space" that encourages the concrete manipulations of symbols, or icons that stand for text, rather than the representation of thought in abstract language structures. These students are manipulating ideas within this space in ways that they cannot do when working within the confines of the formal propositional structures characterizing linear writing tht we have privileged as composition teachers in most of the instruction that we carry out.

Who might benefit from the space in which to write a bricoleur? As Turkle and Papert (1990) point out, strict adherence to propositional logic—certainly as it is represented in linear writing—is best expressed in terms of Western male gender norms. Those writers who have succeeded with the canonical approaches to writing that we had been teaching within our classes have learned to cope with these norms. However, many women and men may prove even more adept at bricolage as a method of organizing and representing their thoughts, of thinking and writing in increasingly critical ways about communication and culture. We see hypertextual spaces, therefore, as local learning environments that may provide students and teachers radical intellectual alternatives to composition instruction as it has been approached in decades past.

THE POTENTIAL FOR CHANGE IN VIRTUAL TEACHING AND LEARNING SPACES

Even this brief overview of the virtual writing "spaces" created by on-line conferences and hypertext programs suggests how teachers might find them useful in supporting the aims of critical pedagogy and classroom-based reform. There are, moreover, additional reasons why these spaces have potential as sites within which teachers and students can develop critical perspectives on language and culture. To begin—because these new spaces exist on-line—we must recognize that reform-minded teachers and students can create and, to an extent, control these local, virtual spaces differently than they can control traditional classrooms.

Traditional classrooms, as artifacts of the educational system, represent writing and languaging spaces constrained in particular ways by the weight of history, the architecture of power, and the intellectual habits of both teachers and students. The elements of traditional classrooms serve to reflect and sustain a way of regulating power that many teachers consider antithetical within the conceptual framework of a liberatory pedagogy. For example, traditional classrooms privilege the teacher's space as a center of power. The teacher's location clearly designates the "front" of a room and is marked by furnishings appropriate to such a power center (lectern, blackboard, desk). At the same time, traditional classrooms also work to limit the power of students, in many cases, actually riveting desks to the floor to make sure that students must face the teacher at all times and restrict their independent movements and interpersonal conversations.

These realizations about classrooms as teaching and learning spaces, of course, are not new, nor do they come as a surprise to most teachers. Michel Foucault (1984) reminds us that the architecture of learning "spaces" (and other public spaces such as prisons, orphanages, or schools) is one of the many sites in which a culture plays out its collective notion of power and its exercise (pp. 239–256). Architecture, to Foucault (1979), represents a "technology" of power (p. 205), a way of "coding" (Foucault, 1984, p. 253) our cultural thinking about power. In light of this connection between architecture, power, and educational spaces, it is not hard to understand why teachers are often less than effective in instituting some classroom-based reforms. The overwhelming weight of tradition, of historical precedent, of intellectual habit generally hinders both teachers and students from experimenting in meaningful ways with the architecture of alternative learning spaces that might more effectively support critical education.

In contrast, reform-minded teachers who have had the opportunity to design virtual writing environments suggest that the inertia working against educational reform does not govern so inevitably in local computer-supported contexts. For one thing, given the relative lack of historical precedent connected with designing computer-supported facilities for English curricula, administrators are unsure of how these virtual spaces should look, what elements they should contain, or even where they are located (Selfe, 1990b). Often, for example, these spaces—because they do exist on-line—are hidden from the gaze of administrators and other teachers, thus offering reform-minded teachers and students some privacy and protection for experimental learning situations. Virtual learning spaces that are informed by a critical pedagogy, in fact, can be "invisible" to classroom visitors. Within what seems to be a "normal" classroom space, a virtual environment can exist within the memory of a single microcomputer. Within such a local educational environment, students can access both on-line conferences and hypertext webs and the alternative learning spaces these applications offer, and teachers can design and implement the activities characteristic of critical pedagogy. In a single networked environment, for example, a teacher can customize portions of the local learning space to support critical educational goals. This customization may involve articulating a specific educational agenda for this virtual space, creating forums that encourage the kinds of learning and teaching behaviors valued by this agenda, importing commercial software and authoring home-grown software that would support specific educational goals, and identifying assessment procedures for evaluating the new learning space.

Virtual environments are also still new enough to our discipline to inspire a sense of experimentation and exploration (cf. Cooper & Selfe, 1990; Levy, 1984; Fjermedal, 1986). Often, students and teachers see in these spaces reflections of the many on-line bulletin boards and discussions that have begun to flourish on the margins of academic communities. These on-line discussion environments are places in which faculty, students, experts, and nonexperts meet to talk about problems and issues of common interest. Characteristic of these language spaces is a value on what is said rather than on who is talking (hence, the frequent use of pseudonyms), an enlarged sense of access to information and dialogue (many such discussions have self-subscribe features), a lack of formal academic language, and a frankness disruptive to the "institutional decorum" of traditional academic sites (Shor, 1987, p. 19). These spaces offer, in other words, what Shor (1987) might call a localized site of "dysfunction" within the education system, one within which teachers and students can begin the process of developing a critical awareness by "reading closely, writing clearly, thinking critically, conceptualizing, and verbalizing" (p. 37) in connection with the problems posed by our culture.

CONCLUSION

With this chapter, we have tried to identify some of the forces that influence tradition and change in American education, in general, and in computer-supported composition classrooms, in particular. We have first tried to look at some of the larger forces shaping American education and teaching and then at some of the political dynamics of using computers to bring about educational reform in writing and literacy classes. Relying on the work of Margaret Mead, we have also tried to relate theories of cultural transmission—postfigurative, cofigurative, and prefigurative—to the world as we know it in the last decade of the 20th century. In so doing, we have touched upon various theories of learning of the past century and have examined them in the context of composition studies, especially as they relate to approaches that use electronic networks and hypermedia for instruction. As the profession has gradually come to value social theories of learning, we have also noted that, over the years, classroom practices have tended to downplay teacher-centered environments and moved to an increasing recognition of the importance of the individual student and, more recently, to small-group learning. The movement has not been a linear progression—indeed, many teachers today continue to use lecture as their primary teaching strategy—but it can be documented, with schools, teachers, and the attendant classroom practices interacting with other societal forces, and all the while resisting and responding to the many calls for change that persist. Throughout the chapter, we have also acknowledged that approaches to teaching are inextricably tied to the culture in which they exist, and that societies change more rapidly than do educational systems and dominant modes of teaching—especially in computer-supported composition programs, which often serve to encourage conservative reactionism.

Given these arguments, we advise reform-minded teachers to rethink the potential for change at local levels, within individual classrooms and computer-supported learning spaces. It is within these spaces, we are convinced, that educators can reflect in increasingly critical ways on their teaching and use of technology, and where they can create learning opportunities that will support students as they gain intellectual perspective on "language, thought, and culture" (Shor, 1987, p. 19). In closing, we suggest that two of the newer developments in writing classes—computer-based conferences and hypertext applications—may eventually contribute to meaningful change by providing spaces in which students can practice resistance through language activities (Cooper & Selfe, 1990).

But these same computer applications, given a lack of the critical consciousness that Freire (1990) described for us, can also be used by teachers—like the old CAI programs of the last decade—to confound reform, to replicate existing power structures and social patterns. We must remain vigilant, then, so that we do not use the new developments to support unwittingly the kind of environment that oppresses students, closing them off from learning rather than opening them to the exciting possibilities of a world we can only imagine. As Bruner (1986) suggests

> We are living through a cultural revolution that shapes our image of the future in a way that nobody, however titanic, could have foreseen a half-century ago. It is a revolution whose shape we cannot sense, although we already sense its depth. (p. 148)

Similarly, although we can only sense the future, Mead (1970) reminds us that, as teachers, we too must change. If we do not, if we fail to reconceive learning for our students, we will find our work as teachers unrewarded—we will find that our "devotion to teaching [is] betrayed by the young who cannot learn in the old ways" (p. 78). As the year 2000 approaches, we wonder which "traditions of pedagogy" will continue to persist into the 21st century and which will be left to the past, to the schools and the classrooms of the 1990s.

REFERENCES

Applebee, A. N. (1974). *Tradition and reform in the teaching of English: A history.* Urbana, IL: National Council of Teachers of English.

Barker, T. T., & Kemp, F. O. (1990). Network theory: A postmodern pedagogy for the writing classroom. In C. Handa (Ed.), *Computers and community: Teaching composition in the twenty-first century* (pp. 1–27). Portsmouth, NH: Boynton/Cook Heinemann.

Batson, T. (1988, February, March). The ENFI project: A networked classroom approach to writing construction. *Academic Computing,* 32–33, 55–56.

Becker, H. J. (1987). Using computers for instruction. *BYTE,* 149–162.

Berlin, J. (1988). Rhetoric and ideology in the writing class. *College English, 50*(5), 477–494.

Bolter, J. D. (1991). *Writing space: The computer, hypertext, and the history of writing.* Hillsdale, NJ: Lawrence Erlbaum.

Braverman, H. (1974). *Labor and monopoly capital: The degradation of work in the twentieth century.* New York: Monthly Review Press.

Bruner, J. (1986). *Actual minds, possible worlds.* Cambridge, MA: Harvard University Press.

Cole, M., & Griffin, P. (1987). *Contextual factors in education: Improving science and mathematics education for minorities and women* (Research Report). Madison, WI: University of Wisconsin–Madison.

Cooper, M. M., & Holzman, M. (1989). *Writing as a social action.* Portsmouth, NH: Boynton/Cook Heinemann.

Cooper, M. M., & Selfe, C. L. (1990). Computer conferences and learning: Authority, resistance, and internally persuasive discourse. *College English, 52*(8), 847–869.

Cyganowski, C. K. (1990). The computer classroom and collaborative learning: The impact on student writers. In C. Handa (Ed.), *Computers and community: Teaching composition in the twenty-first century* (pp. 68–88). Portsmouth, NH: Boynton/Cook Heinemann.

Duling, R. (1985). *Word processors and student writing: A study of their impact on revision, fluency, and quality of writing.* Doctoral dissertation, Michigan State University, Ann Arbor, MI.

Falk, C. J. (1985). English skills tutorials for sentence combining practice. *Computers and Composition, 2*(3), 2–4.

Fersko-Weiss, H. (1985, January). Electronic mail: The emerging connection. *Personal Computing,* pp. 71–79.

Fjermedal, G. (1986). *The tomorrow makers: A brave new world of living-brain machines.* New York: Random House.

Flores, M. J. (1990). Computer conferencing: Composing a feminist community of writers. In C. Handa (Ed.), *Computers and community: Teaching composition in the twenty-first century* (pp. 106–117). Portsmouth, NH: Boynton/Cook Heinemann.

Foucault, M. (1979). *Discipline and punish: The birth of the prison* (Alan Sheridan, Trans.). New York: Random House.

Foucault, M. (1984). Space, knowledge, and power. In P. Rabinow (Ed.), *The Foucault reader* (pp. 239–256). New York: Pantheon Books.

Freire, P. (1990). *Pedagogy of the oppressed* (Myra Bergman Ramos, Trans.). New York: The Continuum Publishing Company.

Gabriel, S. L., & Smithson, I. (Eds.). (1990). *Gender in the classroom: Power and pedagogy.* Urbana, IL: University of Illinois Press.

Gerver, E. (1989). Computers and gender. In T. Forester (Ed.), *Computers in the human context: Information technology, productivity, and people* (pp. 481–501). Cambridge, MA: Massachusetts Institute of Technology.

Gilbert, S. W., & Balestri, D. P. (1988). *Ivory towers, silicon basements.* McKinney, TX: Academic Computing Publications.

Giroux, H. A., & Freire, P. (1987). Series introduction. In D. Livingstone (Ed.), *Critical pedagogy and cultural power* (pp. xi–xvi). South Hadley, MA: Bergin & Garvey.

Gomez, M. L. (1991). The equitable teaching of composition. In G. E. Hawisher & C. L. Selfe (Eds.), *Evolving perspectives on computers and composition studies* (pp. 318–335). Urbana, IL, and Houghton, MI: The National Council of Teachers of English and Computers and Composition Press.

Harris, M., & Cheek, M. (1984). Computers across the curriculum: Using WRITER'S WORKBENCH for supplementary instruction. *Computers and Composition, 1*(2), 3–5.

Hawisher, G. E. (1988). Research update: Writing and word processing. *Computers and Composition, 5*(2), 7–28.

Hawisher, G. E. (1990). Reading and writing connections: Composition pedagogy and word processing. In D. H. Holdstein & C. L. Selfe (Eds.), *Computers and writing: Theory, research, practice* (pp. 71–83). New York: Modern Language Association.

Hawisher, G. E., & Selfe, S. L. (Eds.). (1989). *Critical perspectives on computers and composition studies.* New York: Teachers College Press.

Hawisher, G. E., & Selfe, S. L. (Eds.). (1991). *Evolving perspectives on computers and composition studies: Questions for the 1990s.* Urbana, IL, and Houghton, MI: The National Council of Teachers of English and Computers and Composition Press.

Hawkins, J. (1985). Computers and girls: Rethinking the issues. *Sex Roles, 13,* 165–180.

Heim, M. (1987). *Electric language: A philosophical study of word processing.* New Haven, CT: Yale University Press.

Herrmann, A. W. (1990). Computers and writing research: Shifting our "governing gaze." In D. H. Holdstein & C. L. Selfe (Eds.), *Computers and writing: Theory, research, practice* (pp. 124–134). New York: Modern Language Association.

Hiltz, S. R. (1986). The "virtual classroom": Using computer-mediated communication for university teaching. *Journal of Communication, 36*(2), 95–104.

Holdstein, D. (1983). The WRITEWELL series. *Computers and Composition, 1*(1), 7.

Holdstein, D. H., & Selfe, C. L. (Eds.). (1990). *Computers and writing: Theory, research, practice.* New York: Modern Language Association.

Holvig, K. C. (1987, November). *Voices across the wires through BreadNet and ClarkNet.* Paper presented at the Annual Meeting of the National Council of Teachers of English, Los Angeles, CA.

Illich, I. (1971). *Deschooling society.* New York: Harper and Row.

Jessup, E. (1991). Feminism and computers in composition instruction. In G. E. Hawisher & C. L. Selfe (Eds.), *Evolving perspectives on computers and composition studies: Questions for the 1990s* (pp. 336–355). Urbana, IL, and Houghton, MI: The National Council of Teachers of English and Computers and Composition Press.

Jobst, J. (1984). Computer-assisted grading of essays and reports. *Computers and Composition, 1*(2), 5.

Kiesler, S., Siegel, J., & McGuire, T. W. (1984). Social psychological aspects of computer-mediated communication. *American Psychologist, 39*(1), 1123–1134.

Kinkead, J. (1988). Wired: Computer networks in the English classroom. *English Journal, 77,* 39–41.

King, B., Birnbaum, J., & Wageman, J. (1984). Word processing and the basic college writer. In T. Martinez (Ed.), *The written word and the word processor.* Philadelphia, PA: Delaware Valley Writing Council.

Klem, E., & Moran, C. (1992). Teachers in a strange LANd: Learning to teach in a networked writing classroom. *Computers and Composition, 9*(3), 5–22.

Kramarae, C. (1988). *Technology and women's voices: Keeping in touch.* New York: Routledge & Kegan Paul.

Kramarae, C., & Treichler, P. A. (1990). Power relationships in the classroom. In S. L. Gabriel & I. Smithson (Eds.), *Gender in the classroom: Power and pedagogy* (pp. 41–59). Urbana, IL: University of Illinois Press.

Lanham, R. (1989). The electronic world: Literary study and the digital revolution. *New Literary History, 20*(2), 265–290.

Lanham, R. A. (1990). The extraordinary convergence: Democracy, technology, theory, and the university curriculum. *The South Atlantic Quarterly, 89*(1), 27–50.

LeBlanc, P. (1990). Competing ideologies in software design for computer-aided composition. *Computers and Composition, 7*(2), 8–19.

Levi-Strauss, C. (1968). *The savage mind.* Chicago, IL: University of Chicago Press.

Levy, S. (1984). *Hackers: Heroes of the computer revolution.* New York: Dell.

Lloyd-Jones, R., & Lunsford, A. A. (1989). *The English coalition conference: Democracy through language.* Urbana, IL: National Council of Teachers of English.

Ludtke, M. (1987, September). Great human power or magic: An innovative program sparks the writing of America's children. *Time,* p. 76.

Lunsford, A., Moglen, H., & Slevin, J. (Eds.). (1990). *The right to literacy.* New York: Modern Language Association.

Marling, W. (1984). Grading essays on a microcomputer. *College English, 46*(8), 797–810.

McCann, T. M. (1984). Sentence combining for the microcomputer. *Computers and Composition, 1*(3), 1.

McDaid, J. (1991). Toward an ecology of hypermedia. In G. E. Hawisher & C. L. Selfe (Eds.), *Evolving perspectives on computers and composition studies: Questions for the 1990s* (pp. 203–223). Urbana, IL, and Houghton, MI: The National Council for Teachers of English and Computers and Composition Press.

Mead, M. (1970). *Culture and commitment: The new relationships between the generations in the 1970s.* New York: Doubleday.

Meeks, B. (1985, December). Overview of conferencing systems. *BYTE,* pp. 169–184.

Montague, M. (1990). *Computers, cognition, and writing instruction.* Albany, NY: State University of New York Press.

Moulthrop, S. (1989). In the zones: Hypertext and the politics of interpretation. *Writing on the Edge, 1*(1), 18–27.

Moulthrop, S. (1991). The politics of hypertext. In G. E. Hawisher & C. L. Selfe (Eds.), *Evolving perspectives on computers and composition studies: Questions for the 1990s* (pp. 253–271). Urbana, IL, and Houghton, MI: The National Council of Teachers of English and Computers and Composition Press.

Nelson, T. (1987). *Computer lib/dream machines* (2nd ed.). Redmond, WA: Tempus Press.

Neuwirth, C., Kaufer, D. S., & Geisler, C. (1984). What is EPISTLE? *Computers and Composition, 1*(4), 1–2.

Ohmann, R. (1985). Literacy, technology, and monopoly capitalism. *College English, 47*(7), 675–689.

Olson, C. P. (1987). Who computes? In D. Livingstone (Ed.), *Critical pedagogy and cultural power* (pp. 179–204). South Hadley, MA: Bergin and Garvey.

Pfaffenberger, B. (1986). Research networks, scientific communication, and the personal computer. *IEEE Transactions on Professional Communication, PC-29*(1), 30–33.

Piaget, J. (1968). *Six psychological studies.* New York: Vintage Books.

Pullinger, J. D. (1986). Chit-chat to electronic journals: Computer conferencing supports scientific communication. *IEEE Transactions on Professional Communication, PC-29*(1), 23–29.

Reid, S., & Findlay, G. (1986). Writer's workbench analysis of holistically scored essays. *Computers and Composition, 3*(2), 6–32.

Schriner, D. K., & Rice, W. C. (1989, December). Computer conferencing and collaborative learning: A discourse community at work. *College Composition and Communication, 40,* 472–478.

Schwartz, J. (1990). Using an electronic network to play the scales of discourse. *English Journal, 79,* 16–24.

Selfe, C. L. (1988). Computers in English departments: The rhetoric of technopower. *ADE Bulletin, Fall*(90), 63–67.

Selfe, C. L. (1989a). *Creating a computer-supported writing facility: A blueprint for action.* Houghton, MI: Computers and Composition Press.

Selfe, C. L. (1989b). Redefining literacy: The multilayered grammars of computers. In G. E. Hawisher & C. L. Selfe (Eds.), *Critical perspectives on computers and composition studies* (pp. 3–15). New York: Teachers College Press.

Selfe, C. L. (1990a). Technology in the English classroom: Computers through the lens of feminist theory. In C. Handa (Ed.), *Computers and community: Teaching composition in the twenty-first century* (pp. 118–139). Portsmouth, NH: Boynton/Cook Heinemann.

Selfe, C. L. (1990b). English teachers and the humanization of computers: Networking communities of readers and writers. In G. E. Hawisher & A. O. Soter (Eds.), *On literacy and its teaching: Issues in English education* (pp. 190–205). Albany, NY: State University of New York Press.

Selfe, C. L. (1990c). Technology in the English classroom: Computers through the lens of feminist theory. In C. Handa (Ed.), *Computers and community: Teaching composition in the twenty-first century* (pp. 118–139). Portsmouth, NH: Boynton/Cook Heinemann.

Selfe, C. L., Rodrigues, D., & Oates, W. R. (Eds.). (1989). *Computers in English and the language arts: The challenge of teacher education.* Urbana, IL: National Council of Teachers of English.

Selfe, C. L., & Wahlstrom, B. J. (1986). An emerging rhetoric of collaboration: Computers, collaboration, and the composing process. *Collegiate Microcomputer, 4*(4), 289–295.

Sheingold, K., Martin, L. M. W., & Endreweit, M. W. (1987). Preparing urban teachers for the technological future. In R. D. Pea & K. Sheingold (Eds.), *Mirrors of the mind: Patterns of experience in educational computing* (pp. 67–85). Norwood, NJ: Ablex.

Shor, I. (1987). *Critical teaching and everyday life.* Chicago, IL: The University of Chicago Press.

Skinner, B. F. (1986). Programmed instruction revisited. *Phi Delta Kappan, 68*(2), 103–110.

Skinner, B. F. (1968). *Technology of teaching.* New York: Appleton-Century-Crofts.

Skubikowski, K., & Elder, J. (1990). Computers and the social contexts of writing. In C. Handa (Ed.), *Computers and community: Teaching composition in the twenty-first century* (pp. 89–105). Portsmouth, NH: Boynton/Cook Heinemann.

Spitzer, M. (1986). Writing style in computer conferences. *IEEE Transactions on Professional Communication, PC-29*(1), 19–22.

Spitzer, M. (1989). Computer conferencing: An emerging technology. In G. E. Hawisher & C. L. Selfe (Eds.), *Critical perspectives in computers and composition instruction* (pp. 187–200). New York: Teachers College Press.

Spitzer, M. (1990). Local and global networking: Implications for the future. In D. H. Holdstein & C. L. Selfe (Eds.), *Computers and writing: Theory, research, practice* (pp. 187–199). New York: Modern Language Association.

Sproull, L., & Kiesler, S. (1986). Reducing social context cues: Electronic mail in organization communication. *Management Science, 32*(11), 1492–1512.

Thompson, D. P. (1987). Teaching writing on a local area network. *T.H.E. Journal, 15,* 92–97.

Trimbur, J. (1989). Consensus and difference in collaborative learning. *College English, 51,* 602–616.

Turkle, S., & Papert, S. (1990). Epistemological pluralism: Styles and voices within the computer culture. *Signs: Journal of Women in Culture and Society, 16*(11), 128–157.

Vygotsky, L. (1962). *Thought and language.* Cambridge, MA: Massachusetts Institute of Technology.

West, C., & Zimmerman, D. H. (1983). Small insults: A study of interruptions in cross-sex communications between unacquainted persons. In B. Thorne, C. Kramarae, & N. Henly (Eds.), *Language, gender, and society* (pp. 103–118). Rowley, MA: Newbury House.

Wheelock, A., & Dorman, G. (1989). *Before it's too late.* Boston, MA: Massachusetts Advocacy Commission.

Zimmer, J. (1985). The continuing challenge: Computers and writing. *Computers and Composition, 2*(3), 4–6.

Zimmerman, D. H., & West, C. (1975). Sex roles, interruptions and silences in conversations. In B. Thorne & N. Henley (Eds.), *Language and sex: Difference and dominance* (pp. 105–129). Rowley, MA: Newbury House.

Response to Hawisher and Selfe: "Traditions and Change in Computer-Supported Writing Environments: A Call for Action"

Gary Graves
Frenchtown High School
Frenchtown, MT

Using Margaret Mead's work as a conceptual framework, Hawisher and Selfe have synthesized a wide range of thinking to explain many of the complexities and apparent contradictions surrounding computers in schools. The result is a rich, challenging, and intriguing new look at the subject of tradition and change in computer-supported classrooms.

The authors conclude that if we do not change how we teach, "we will find that our 'devotion to teaching [is] betrayed. . . .' " The foreboding conclusion to this wise and elegant analysis of current use of computers in education stuns me. In one sentence, the authors push the discussion of computer technology in education beyond the academic to another level—more emotional, perhaps even tragedic. Even though the discussion of computer-supported classrooms intrigued me intellectually, my emotional response to this chapter was not so easy to pinpoint. I was at once professionally reinvigorated and unsettled by the writing. I will try here to describe how these feelings co-exist in me.

More than anything else, I am revitalized by this chapter. The authors provide a larger cultural explanation for what I think is the most fundamental question regarding computer use in schools: Why have educators not more effectively embraced the power of this technology to improve education?

As a teacher consultant supporting schools in technology planning, I have become increasingly frustrated with institutional and human barriers to change. Repeatedly, I enter schools (usually after the teaching day has ended) to begin planning with committees of teachers who are in a hurry to pick up kids from the sitter or get to their coaching duties, administrators who have no money, and community members who want their children using computers immediately. The problems are readily voiced: lack of time, lack of funds, and lack of information. As a consultant, my mission has been to fill the information gap, hoping that with more knowledge, school planning groups would reprioritize their time and funding resources. But this rethinking isn't happening, and my vision of assisting schools to plan for and use technology as a bridge to change is fading. By using Mead's argument that we are trying to teach "postfiguratively" while living in a "prefigurative" society, the authors have given me a broader context for understanding the resistance I encounter in schools. What I now understand is that the problem may be rooted more deeply than the lack of time, funds, and knowledge.

In particular, the opportunity to look anew at *teacher* resistance to change has been satisfying. For me, the most troubling and potentially destructive consequence of my exposure to teachers' resistance to change has been my own growing criticism of teachers because of what I took to be a conscious unwillingness to break from established teaching routines. I was at first surprised, then disgruntled at what I had perceived as indifference to their important roles as educators, timidity toward risk taking, and fear of losing control.

This chapter, however, has made me more aware of how culturally embedded society's beliefs about teaching are (i.e., children are "empty vessels" to be filled by adult teachers). Understanding why we hold so tightly to traditional teacher behaviors (rewarding memorization, recitation, and obedience)—even when we should know better— is relieving.

Given the framework provided by the authors, it is unreasonable to expect teachers (even with twenty years of "prefigurative" cultural experience), in isolation from the larger society, to adopt readily to new models of teaching and learning. Awareness of this cultural framework softens my pessimism about teachers' willingness and ability to respond to the rapidly changing needs of their students. The traditional barriers to effective integration of computers into the curriculum (little time, money, or information) may be more symptomatic of society's attempt to hold on to a "postfigurative" model than it is causal. This knowledge rejuvenates my professional spirit.

Yet, even as I am invigorated by the authors' perspectives, I am also personally unsettled by a core issue raised in the text. What is lost in classrooms—to students and teachers—as change slowly happens? Given the systemic nature of the problem and the propensity of education to stand still, the rate of teacher change will inevitably be slower than I had envisioned. That slow pace is likely to clash increasingly with the rapidly changing demands of the broader society and with the new ways of teaching that students require.

In this context, the warning given in the last paragraph of Hawisher and Selfe's chapter resonates as an ominous reminder that recasts the text into an even more compelling call for change. I am especially struck because, for 24 years, I often taught in ways my students could not learn. We were both unrewarded, and I didn't know why. What could be more tragic for us as teachers than to have perhaps our most valorous virtue betrayed, our "devotion to teaching"?

If teachers continue to teach without knowing, will they inevitably find their work increasingly less rewarding? If so, in what ways will unrewarded teachers diminish the chances that schools will become transformed into the "prefigurative" and more democratic, cooperative, open places for learning advocated by the authors?

These questions are probably unanswerable. But the wrenching and tearing that may occur as education ponderously reforms itself within a rapidly changing society suggests a disconcerting possibility for me as an advocate of computer-supported education reform. Even if my hope for change is realized, the change may be chaotic and the results probably unrecognizable to me. I am not sure I am prepared to continue working for this change, knowing that I may never sense my own progress.

From the beginning, I needed the answer to one preeminent question: In the context of existing political and cultural constraints, is it realistic to expect fundamental positive change within the current education system—even with the support of computer technology? I read the answer in this chapter, given with the "natural optimism of teachers," as a qualified yes. Change in education will occur in any case. It will probably be slow and its shape undefined. But with the help of newer forms of technology, teachers can dramatically accelerate positive change if we have the will and the willingness to listen to our students as they inform us of how they learn best.

Afterword: Knowledge, Learning and Change

Phyllis Kahaney
University of Hawaii at Hilo

The inspiration for this volume of essays began at a Writing Across the Curriculum seminar I conducted several years ago. Among the 22 people signed up for the year-long seminar series were a senior professor who the Dean warned me would resist learning new methodologies, and a newly hired professor who made a point of telling me several times how much she needed and wanted to learn new ways of looking at her students and her teaching. She was longing, she said, for a vehicle that would enable her to change, and she was pretty certain that this seminar would be the turning point for her in her wish to teach more effectively.

What happened over the next six months was quite the opposite of what I expected. The "resistant" senior professor argued with everyone in the seminar room the first day, but went to his classroom and began to try out some of the interactive techniques. They worked for him, and pretty soon he was stopping me in the hallway for advice, for articles to read, or simply to discuss the ways in which his classes were changing. His colleague, the young woman who said she wanted to change, was sullen and resistant by the end of the first all-day workshop; at the second workshop she announced that she had only come for the stipend she would receive; by the third workshop she banged on the table and announced in a loud voice that she was a lecturer, would always be one, and anyway the students hated her attempts to change the way she taught. It was clear to all of us present that she was excruciatingly uncomfortable with the new ideas and methods.

What had happened? What could explain the fact that against all expectations one changed, while the other resisted change despite a firm resolve to do so? What are the factors that explain why, year after year, in any given workshop that I teach, about 20% of the participants are able to make important changes in the way they teach, while about 60% make moderate changes in their teaching, and about 20%, no matter what, resist changing at all? Even though the format remains the same, even though the site and numbers remain the same, even though gender and age factors are similar in all workshops, it becomes impossible for me to predict who will change and who will not. Those who at first appear most resistant often change the most; those who seem most open and most enthusiastic often change least. Why?

THE QUALITIES OF CHANGE

The aim of this book is to explore the apparent built-in reflex in humans, in this case in teachers, to resist change. Resisting change appears to be a tendency that can be as benign as sticking with the same brand of chalk for 25 years, or as deeply rooted as the inability to shift from lecturing to interactive teaching, even when there is a stated wish to make such a shift. For example, the woman cited above from the Writing Across the Curriculum seminar stated that her students complained that her classes were boring; this, she said, was one of the motivating factors that led her to want to try something new as an instructor. But during the course of the seminar, she in fact resisted change at every turn. She "forgot" to try out any new strategies in her classroom between the first two sessions, she remained the absolute authority in her classes while ostensibly trying to decenter her teaching, and she finally commented that any attempt at changing her teaching was so dangerous that she was certain it would affect her chances of getting tenure. Though her words apparently invoked the language of change, her actions showed that she resisted it. She made resolutions, but she could not keep them.

Over time, as I got to know her, I noticed an emerging pattern. Her tendency to say one thing and do another showed me that change involves much more than the wish to behave differently. Rather, it seems that real change involves a) the ability to articulate a problem, to make what is implicitly happening explicit; b) access to a benevolent authority (a text, a teacher) that reflects the shape of the resistance back to the changemaker; and c) a community in which change can take place and in which the new behavior can be practiced and reinforced. It seems that when one of these elements is missing (in this case, the inability to articulate the problem as it really was—that change is having to find out how one is in the world), then change can sometimes appear to take place, but it is never long-lasting. Three weeks or a year later, changemakers are back to their old habit patterns, patterns they thought they had permanently transformed.

This discovery that long-term change involves peoples' abilities to synthesize information for themselves, together with the teacher's directions and the mores of the community in which the individuals live, should create a strong admonishment to those who argue for making change by creating willy-nilly new patterns and rules. Even when a new way of teaching or learning seems to be better, the laying of new patterns onto old, pre-existing structures dooms many people to failure. This may help to explain why so much of what passes for reform is so rarely long-lasting.

In the same way, if change can be viewed as a component in an ongoing process called "learning," instead of as a product or a "thing," then it would be easier to have a different relationship to change itself. Instead of experiencing resistance to change as an obstacle, we as teachers could come to expect resistance to change as part of the learning process and thus plan for various kinds of and degrees of resistance. If one plans for resistance to change, it then becomes part of the learning and teaching process rather than something to be overcome.

If, for example, I had understood all this during that first seminar, I might have been more successful in helping this teacher to find a way to articulate her limitations to herself. I might have met with her individually and asked her questions or watched her at work in the classroom (Vaughan). I might have helped her discover the outline of her personal construct (Diamond) or worked with her to discover whether issues of gender were a factor for her in making the changes that she said she wanted to make (Perry). If I had been more sensitive to the signs of resistance before they took shape and became a new construct, then perhaps the young junior professor would not have had to resist so hard.

WHAT DOES IT MEAN TO CHANGE?

It becomes evident that when we speak about teacher change we need to define carefully what it is we mean by change, and discover how any proposed change fits with or deviates from accepted norms. For example, our instinct as teachers is to resolve questions so that, when teaching physics or literature, we are ready to quickly become reductionistic. Textbooks encourage, in fact often require, students to understand the ideas presented in any discipline as a compendium of terms that leads the learner to indisputable conclusions or "facts." Yet we know that there are perennial disagreements among physicists, literary scholars, historians, and social scientists—to name just a few—about which interpretation should be accepted. We may agree about the facts or equations or arguments leading up to a conclusion, but even when the "facts" are incontrovertible, how the facts are to be interpreted is not so certain.

I am saying that knowledge is interpretive and is constituted within a given community. If we understand the nature of knowledge as an activity that does not always lead to a conclusion (and thus is not always subject to the kinds of measurement we have been trained for within the scientific tradition), then perhaps resistance to change can be seen as the beginning of an existential loosening-up process.

Yet we who are educators have a tendency to regard "real" change as something permanent and measurable. As a teacher, what I do most often is work to get students to change in some capacity. I create lessons that allow them to practice new skills; I expose them to new methodologies; I create a social environment that will support the skills they are learning; I test them about their new knowledge. I then operate under the premise that if they do their lessons, are attentive, and try what I teach then they should be able to make important changes in the ways they think, operate, communicate, and interact with the world around them.

In my zeal to make their lives as learners better, I forget that change is relative (it exists in time and space); that change is in flux (the contexts in which change occurs are constructed, deconstructed, and reconstituted both socially and personally, ad infinitum); that it is easy to mistake an apparent or a temporary change for permanent change. In my wish to make students' lives better, I tend to forget that change is a kind of continuous adaptation—not an end in itself. In this way, change mirrors the existential shifts in both the changemaker and the social milieu in which the changemaker functions.

REDEFINING THE MEANING OF CHANGE

Perhaps the question of the day, then, is: How do we as teachers and educators allow ourselves to move away from what is familiar, obvious, and known so that we can move into a system where we live more with questions, multiplicity, and not knowing? Until recently, the map of the world included the USSR, two Germanys, and one country called Yugoslavia. Today the map of the world is radically changed and still changing. The final form is not fixed, though we must draw maps so that we know where to go on our travels. Just as the geography of the world changes, so does the way we look at other things.

If we look at the changes in the bodies of knowledge in nearly all disciplines over the course of the last 50 years, we notice tremendous shifts. Not only are statements of fact different, but the tools by which those "facts" are measured have changed, and continue to change. Because technology has accelerated the pace of change, it is sometimes difficult to know which measurements are applicable and, once the measurement is made, what counts or no longer counts as knowledge. When we note that the measuring devices we use change quickly and oftentimes radically, thus impacting the way we make judgments, must we not also reevaluate the nature of knowledge and wonder about the conclusions we draw at any point in time?

WHAT DO WE MEAN BY KNOWLEDGE?

Implied in this discussion is a definition of knowledge that is different from the one we generally accept. Most of us teaching in the West derive our understanding of knowledge from the epistemological tradition of Western philosophy: to know is to be. This epistemology was reinterpreted by Heidegger (1949) when he questioned whether it is possible for an individual to know apart from the communal knowledge in which a thing is known. This reshaping throws into question the possibility of objective knowledge. If knowledge is not objectifiable, then the scientific tradition, in which objective knowledge is not only possible but desirable, becomes a questionable way of looking at the world.

This argument has been debated by modern philosophers of science. Such debates about theories of observation (both the rationalists such as Popper and Putnam and the nonrationalists such as Kuhn and Feyerabend) have given rise to the generally held belief that all observation is theory-laden (Newton-Smith, 1981), that there is no privileged framework from which we can assess all knowledge claims, and that all knowledge claims are therefore context-bound. If we are further given to understand that all knowledge proceeds within a linguistically and historically constituted framework (Heidegger, 1949), we glimpse the important ways that twentieth-century philosophers of science have moved away from the nineteenth-century positivist tradition.

Because of these still tightly held positivist beliefs, all of us educated in the West have been taught to make certain assumptions about the nature of knowledge. In this way, knowledge for the modern person has been taught as though it were quantifiable—something that could be measured and transmitted "scientifically." This viewpoint is reinforced at every turn by administrators, politicians, teacher educators, grant-giving agencies, scholarly journals—in short, by most events and systems related to education. In the modern Western world, knowledge has become synonymous with scrutiny, replication, and measurement, so that the act of knowing is the reinforcement of that which is collectively "known." As Paolo Freire (1972) points out, knowledge has become a commodity, teachers have become packagers of that commodity, and students have become the commodity's consumers.

LANGUAGE AND THE WORLD OF CHANGE

The essays in this volume are exploratory in nature. Their focus is on discovery; their aim is to report on and chart the creation of new patterns. The writers of the chapters in this book have taken a given perspective—technology, moral development, etc.—and have focused on the skills needed to find out for oneself, to learn how to be a learner who fosters continual change rather than an adherent to a way or system. As we learn to welcome the difficulties inherent in change-making, we notice that we and those around us are always in a state of becoming, and that we never actually arrive. Our language begins to reflect the world of change.

The exploration of what it means to speak to self and other (Bakhtin, 1986; Buber, 1970; Kierkegaard, 1941; Malraux, 1968) has given rise to a philosophy where meaning is always in the process of being determined. The capability of understanding in any given community can no longer be assumed; all collective belief becomes negotiable, subject to close and frequent questioning. In coming to see that we must continually negotiate meaning, we have had to admit that we can assume very little. In the void left by such continual negotiation, the tendency of some has been to build new structures to replace the old ones. If the social climate for learning, for example, means that cultural pluralism must be taken into account, then cultural pluralism becomes its own end. Courses are devised that set out to erase the old and replace it with the new. The old didacticism—reading only classics in

English classes, for example—is replaced by an equally virulent didacticism: in some places, no classics are read in English classes.

The avoidance of creating new structures to quickly replace discarded structures is difficult. Such an avoidance forces us to list our covert goals along with our conscious ones. It forces us to acknowledge that we live in a multifarious world. The tendency to resist change mobilizes all barriers—intellectual, social, psychological—so that the resistance to reading classics becomes a yearning to cleave to a new structure, the reading of no classics.

Thus, the exchanging of one tightly held position for another becomes a new kind of didacticism. While certain problems are solved by not reading classics, others are created. Other groups come to feel left out. Teachers complain that it becomes increasingly difficult to assume common references. People in the out-of-favor group begin to resent those who are now part of the favored group. The permutations are endless, but the irony is indisputable: in attempting to change what seems unworkable and unjust, new structures are formed which are often as rigid and unworkable as the ones they replaced.

KNOWLEDGE AS CHANGE

What is being collectively proposed, implicitly and explicitly, in this volume of essays is a radical departure from the tendency to create permanent change by creating new structures as a bridge for change. What is radical is the belief that presents itself again and again in these essays that change is really about finding out what is going on at a given time in a given place. Change is about asking questions. It is about not making assumptions about one's relationship to the world of knowledge. It is about studying constructs, one's own constructs and those of others (Diamond). It is about finding out how science can be understood and used nonreductionistically (Sinnott). It is about attending to the ways rules operate (Vaughan) and continuing to adapt to the world as it is in motion. It is about interpreting meaning and the political and social agendas of meaningmakers (Janangelo). It is about using new structures and methods to explore a radically and quickly changing reality (Perry). It is about transposing from one context to another (Martin) and even exploring a new way of ordering the world as it is in the present (Hawisher and Selfe). It is about articulating the moral parameters in which we operate (Tappan). It is about defining ourselves as educators in broader ways—as people who share information on their way to possibly more than one destination where there may be more than one reality.

This understanding of knowledge as something that leads to and is composed of multiple realities is different from the view put forth by the poststructuralists. While those involved in the poststructural criticisms acknowledge the world in flux, and the relative inability of the meaningmaker to objectively know any object (Derrida, 1976; Fish, 1989; Lacan, 1977) the effect of such an understanding in the everyday world is largely intellectual and remains primarily in the world of ideas. The same can be said for the nihilists (Turgenev, 1966) and the existentialists (Camus, 1951; Sartre, 1958, 1961) who, even though they write about real people in real dilemmas, tend to reduce their characters or arguments to a paralysis of action. These views present people who can think, but cannot act. They are locked in the self, cut off from the larger community, and unable to connect with a teacher or mentor who could possibly pull them out of the quagmire of the mind.

If we understand knowledge as something that is constructed both socially and individually within a culture, and if we see resistance to change as an impediment to that kind of knowledge-making, in a strange way resistance to change becomes something positive. Unlike the existentialists or nihilists, a person in resistance is taking some kind of action. Unlike the poststructuralists, the person resisting change is not altogether in her head; her resistance contains a component of affect (feeling), self and other (one resists *something*) and so the very act of the resistance can be said to be the beginning of the change. When action—of the self, of self and other, of self, other and culture— is married to a kind of reflectivity (Vygotsky, 1978) it is nearly impossible to continue on as one has. In understanding the world differently, in acting in the world as if it is different, and in reflecting on that action, a new reality is created. If a community exists or springs up around the person who understands, acts, and reflects differently, then the change made may be long-lasting.

What I am calling for here is a philosophy of learning and knowing that acknowledges that people still *act* in the midst of indeterminacy. In a contradictory, complex universe, the interfacing of the knower and the known paradoxically does not lead to paralysis, but instead leads to a celebration of knowers working to emphasize that which they know. The struggle to reconcile the new technology with preexisting ways of knowing and the difficulty of the workplace to accommodate to the changes in the understanding of and resistances to gender issues are evidence of the struggle to expand the philosophy of education to meet the present-day needs of the community. In this careful exploration of the world around us, we begin to consider that the map of our own territory has shifted, continues to shift, and that, if we are honest, will continue to shift *ad infinitum*.

This recognition has immediate consequences in the everyday

world. If instead of quickly resolving questions or disposing of them in other ways the teacher keeps the questions alive by living with them, creating classwork around them, and asking students to do the same, the world of the classroom becomes revolutionary. Students begin to view learning as relevant to their real-life struggles and questions. When there are no pat answers, the community of the classroom must struggle together to find out what they believe is true. When the community works together to define issues, to seek resolutions, to discuss options, and to discover meaning, then the tendency of students to resist learning decreases markedly. Learning becomes the property of every seeker (learner); teaching becomes a quest for knowledge. The tendency of the teacher to create new structures is dispelled by the transformative process of living with the questions. Learning becomes inquiry; knowledge becomes a quest.

There is much familiar in all this for those involved in interactive education. There are many teachers who work this way, and their students reap the rewards of going out into the world after their formal schooling still curious, still interested in learning. The call here is to go beyond instinct, beyond methodologies—even those that seem to work—and to dare to maintain an open-ended dialogue with self and with community.

This is the true empowerment—understanding that though relativism, ambiguity, paradox, and unknowingness create chaos in the knower, in fact here lies the real movement toward agency: the ability to ask questions without laying out answers, the possibility of exploring fully and richly without coming to final conclusions.

REFERENCES

Bakhtin, M. M. (1981). *Speech genres & other late essays.* Austin, TX: University of Texas.

Buber, M. (1970). *I and thou.* (W. Kaufman, Trans.). New York: Scribners.

Camus, A. (1951). *The stranger.* (Stuart Gilbert, Trans.). New York: Vintage Books.

Derrida, J. (1976). *Of grammatology.* (G. Chakravorty Spivak, Trans.). Baltimore, MD: Johns Hopkins University.

Fish, S. (1989). *Doing what comes naturally.* Durham, NC: Duke University.

Freire, P. (1972). *Pedagogy of the oppressed.* Harmondsworth, UK: Penguin Books.

Heidegger, M. (1949). *Existence and being.* (D. Scott, R. F. C. Hull, & Alan Crick, Trans.). Chicago, IL: Henry Regnery.

Kierkegaard, S. (1946). *Repetition.* (W. Lowrie, Trans.). Princeton, NJ: Princeton University.

Lacan, J. (1977). *Écrits: a selection.* (Alan Sheridan, Trans.). New York: W. W. Norton.

Malraux, A. (1968). *Anti-Memoirs.* (Terence Kilmartin, Trans.). New York: Holt, Rinehart and Winston.

Newton-Smith, W. H. (1981). *The rationality of science.* Boston, MA: Routledge & Kegan Paul.

Sartre, J. P. (1958). *No exit.* (P. Bowles, Trans.). New York: French.

Sartre, J. P. (1961). *Nausea.* (L. Alexander, Trans.). New York: New Directions.

Turgenev, I. (1966). *Fathers and children.* (E. Simmons, Trans.). New York: Holt, Rinehart and Winston.

Vygotsky, L. (1978). *Mind in society.* Cambridge, MA: Harvard University Press.

Author Index

Subject Index